ENERGY KINGDOMS

CENTER ON GLOBAL ENERGY POLICY SERIES

CENTER ON GLOBAL ENERGY POLICY SERIES

Jason Bordoff, series editor

Making smart energy policy choices requires approaching energy as a complex and multifaceted system in which decision makers must balance economic, security, and environmental priorities. Too often, the public debate is dominated by platitudes and polarization. Columbia University's Center on Global Energy Policy at SIPA seeks to enrich the quality of energy dialogue and policy by providing an independent and nonpartisan platform for timely analysis and recommendations to address today's most pressing energy challenges. The Center on Global Energy Policy Series extends that mission by offering readers accessible, policy-relevant books that have as their foundation the academic rigor of one of the world's great research universities.

Robert McNally, *Crude Volatility: The History and the Future of Boom-Bust Oil Prices*

Daniel Raimi, *The Fracking Debate: The Risks, Benefits, and Uncertainties of the Shale Revolution*

Richard Nephew, *The Art of Sanctions: A View from the Field*

ENERGY
KINGDOMS

OIL AND POLITICAL
SURVIVAL IN THE
PERSIAN GULF

JIM KRANE

Columbia University Press
New York

Columbia University Press
Publishers Since 1893
New York   Chichester, West Sussex
cup.columbia.edu

Library of Congress Cataloging-in-Publication Data
Names: Krane, Jim, author.
Title: Energy kingdoms : oil and political survival in the Persian Gulf /
Jim Krane.
Other titles: Center on Global Energy Policy series.
Description: New York : Columbia University Press, 2019. | Series: Center on
Global Energy Policy series | Includes bibliographical references and index.
Identifiers: LCCN 2018027640 | ISBN 9780231179300 (cloth : alk. paper)
Subjects: LCSH: Petroleum industry and trade—Persian Gulf Region. |
Petroleum industry and trade—Political aspects—Persian Gulf Region. |
Energy consumption—Persian Gulf Region. | Energy policy—Persian
Gulf Region.
Classification: LCC HD9576.P52 K73 2019 | DDC 338.2/72809536—dc23
LC record available at https://lccn.loc.gov/2018027640

Columbia University Press books are printed on permanent
and durable acid-free paper.
Printed in the United States of America

FOR CONNIE

CONTENTS

ACKNOWLEDGMENTS

I spent four and a half years living in the Persian Gulf, from 2005 through 2009, and have had the good fortune to return many times since. I found in these six countries a disarming warmth and hospitality and a profound natural beauty. I was unprepared for the huge amount of personal interest that I would develop in the region.

The Gulf is beset by a number of urgent problems, just one of which is covered here. The importance of energy to daily life was driven home to me during a blackout in Dubai. There was no escaping the 110°F (40°C) heat, which was magnified by the design of buildings that quickly trapped heat and offered no means to vent it. The experience made tangible for me that energy policy in these producer states needs to be recalibrated for the longer term, rather than for a short era of conspicuous consumption. This book examines the drivers behind the Gulf's profligate treatment of its domestic energy resources, the damage that overconsumption has brought, and the pathways toward a more sustainable and enlightened understanding of the fossil fuels that have transformed the region.

None of the research in this book would have been possible without the assistance of dozens of people, who contributed in ways large and small. I made numerous friends in the region, many of whom helped in some way, whether offering places to sleep, shared meals, anecdotes over a beer, arguments (clarifications!), emailed links, or even copies of their electricity bills.

I also met my wonderful wife, Chloe, in nearby Baghdad, and the explorations of the Gulf that I describe in this book and my previous one were done as much through Chloe's eyes as mine. Saying I couldn't have done it without her is an understatement. Our adventures ranged from hikes among the mountain villages and canyons of Ras al-Khaimah to our secret campsites in Fujairah, the Musandam, Jebel Misht, and, most memorably, Jebel Rawdah; our breakfasts on the beach; and cocktails among the dunes and atop the Burj al-Arab. Best of all was the birth and first year of life of our son, Jay.

After leaving the Gulf, we spent our next four years together in Cambridge, where—on the first day of my doctoral studies—Chloe gave birth to our daughter, Connie, to whom this work is dedicated. While Cambridge was more work than fun, I came to enjoy its eccentricities, its medieval pubs, and cycling under vast East Anglian skies churning with clouds. Chloe's backing was crucial in allowing me to spend a year doing fieldwork in the Gulf, which I did in numerous three-week jaunts to all six countries.

At Cambridge I was lucky to work under the impressive faculties of David Reiner, whose knowledge of literature in political science, economics, and energy policy is matched by his affability and dedication. I am grateful for his diligence in providing comments and edits that helped shape this book. We held many of our discussions at ancient pubs in the medieval city as well as in attendance at two fabulous Cambridge Beer Festivals.

Since leaving Cambridge, I have been extremely lucky to find myself employed by the Baker Institute for Public Policy at Rice University, in Houston. Rice deftly combines intellectual power and Southern grace on a campus replete with live oaks, drenching humidity, and high-level policy discussions. At Baker, I owe a huge thank you to Ken Medlock, the director at the Center for Energy Studies, and Ambassador Edward Djerejian, the institute's founding director. Ken in particular has helped shape my thinking on energy, as have the regular debates and events at the center. For endowing my research fellowship at the institute I also owe a giant debt of gratitude to Wally Wilson, a supremely kind and generous Houstonian with whom I've swapped many a tale of Middle Eastern intrigue. Also at Rice, I am indebted to Elsie Hung for diligent research support, particularly with data gathered to illustrate this manuscript; Marwa Shalaby, who provided statistical assistance with one of my chapters; Mohammad Tabaar, who provided comments and insights on my Iran material; and my colleagues Nathan Citino and Yasser Faquih, who provided input or source material. Pedro Rodriguez of the IMF helped me convert his demand equation for use with my price-elasticity calculations in chapter 5, as did Rice's Mark Agerton and Sean Leong. Also helpful along the way were Kristian Coates-Ulrichsen, now a colleague at Rice, who provided comments on my nearly finished manuscript and often read and critiqued early work, as did Mary Ann Tétreault, Pete Moore, Jocelyn Sage Mitchell, and Matthew Gray. Mike Wood at the Kuwait Ministry of Electricity and Water provided useful details and encouragement, and Abdullah Baabood at Qatar University helped with the accuracy of my Oman anecdotes.

I must also offer profuse thanks to my ever-diligent editor, Bridget Flannery-McCoy, at Columbia University Press. Bridget has been exactly what I wanted in an editor: thorough, exacting, professional, kind, and enthusiastic.

Finally, my family. This book would have emerged much earlier if it weren't for Jay and Connie, whose infectious personalities lured me home by dinnertime most nights—even earlier during little-league baseball season. My wife, Chloe, deserves a Ghawar-sized reservoir of my love and gratitude for helping with the most important aspects of writing this book: allowing me the indulgence of going back to school, putting up with the resulting economic privations, and being the stabilizing cornerstone of our new life in Houston. Chloe did all this while keeping the home fires burning, raising our kids, helping Syrian and Iraqi refugees adjust to life in America, and being an outrageously lovable wife in general, all in good humor.

ENERGY KINGDOMS

INTRODUCTION

In one generation we went from riding camels to riding Cadillacs. The way we are wasting money, I fear the next generation will be riding camels again.

—KING FAISAL OF SAUDI ARABIA, AS QUOTED IN MAI YAMANI,
*CHANGED IDENTITIES: THE CHALLENGE OF THE NEW GENERATION
IN SAUDI ARABIA*

Substitute "oil" for "money" in this cynical prophecy, and you get an idea of the quandary facing the Persian Gulf monarchies: Saudi Arabia, the United Arab Emirates, Kuwait, Qatar, Oman, and Bahrain. These six small states developed at a breakneck pace thanks to the oil reserves discovered under their desert sands less than a century ago. But they are now in the throes of a mighty energy dilemma. This problem stems not from the depletion of this oil—the "peak oil" hypothesis of a decade ago—but from skyrocketing demand for the very fuel that drove their rapid ascent into the modern world.[1]

During King Faisal's reign, in the 1960s and 1970s, there was little to suggest that his own subjects might someday require so much energy that their needs would interfere with the kingdom's exports. The monarchies were flush with oil, which flowed from supergiant fields discovered from the 1930s through the 1970s—Ghawar in Saudi Arabia, Kuwait's Burgan field, the Murban structure in Abu Dhabi.

These repositories provided the petroleum that powered the postwar Free World. Gulf oil fueled the West German *Wirtschaftswunder*, Japan's economic miracle, and the suburban commuter belts of the American colossus. It was easy oil, pooled in boundless reservoirs that practically geysered into action with the prick of a drill bit. Almost all the oil produced could be sold abroad; Gulf populations were tiny, their economies undeveloped. Oil demand in the six monarchies was a mere rounding error on global consumption.

The Gulf became the strategic heartland of America's energy security. When the Soviets invaded Afghanistan in 1979, Washington saw a threat to the oil; US president Jimmy Carter declared that America would go to war, if necessary, to defend the monarchies. A decade later, President George H. W. Bush put the Carter Doctrine into action, rolling back Saddam Hussein's 1990 invasion of Kuwait. The doctrine remains in force today. Since the early 1970s, America has provided security for these weak, young states and made sure tankers brimming with oil could thread their way through the Strait of Hormuz and other chokepoints to keep the world supplied.

In each of the six Gulf monarchies, a traditional ruling sheikh divided up the riches. With oil's help, they lifted their subjects out of the poverty that had entrapped countless previous generations. Rulers lavished their countrymen with cheap gasoline, cheap electricity, and cheap water. Subsidies on energy were a key part of national development plans that also provided jobs, housing, medicine, and education. Oil allowed ruling sheikhs to make their subjects wealthy and complacent. In return, subjects threw their support behind the sheikhs. It was a virtuous cycle.

Those days are gone. Forty years of compounding annual growth have raised Gulf energy consumption to some of the highest levels in the world, measured on a per capita basis or—more importantly—in terms of oil consumed per unit of gross domestic product. As the rest of the world grows more energy efficient, the sheikhdoms of the Gulf are going the other way, using ever more energy to produce a dollar of economic growth. Saudi Arabia consumes ten times more oil than the global average per unit of GDP.[2] The situation in neighboring monarchies is no less startling. For economies based on oil exports, such inefficiency is bad news. If these trends continue, the Gulf monarchies could lose their long-held roles as the world's premier energy suppliers.

The prodigious burning of fossil fuels in the Gulf not only is undermining national economies but also is a major global source of the greenhouse gases warming the climate—including, disastrously, their own. The fiery summers of 2016 and 2017 have tormented inhabitants with record-setting temperatures above 120°F (50°C).

Carbon dioxide emissions from the Gulf have grown by an average of 5 percent per year since 1990 versus 2 percent for the world as a whole.[3] In 2015, the International Energy Agency joined the chorus of multilateral organizations calling for reductions in Middle East oil consumption and associated emissions. Global climate goals cannot be met without a major change in behavior in the Gulf. Nor can climate objectives be met without a reduction in oil demand globally.

For a century, oil has been the world's paramount fuel: it is energy dense, plentiful, and simple to transport and use. It has held a virtual monopoly over transportation since the early 1900s, when Henry Ford's gasoline-powered Model T proved superior to Edison's electric vehicles and the coal-powered Stanley Steamer. While natural gas and coal both compete with other fuels and technologies in power generation, oil has no ready substitutes. Before the ascendance of climate concerns, the only times humanity sought oil substitutes such as biofuels and electric vehicles were when oil prices spiked. Now, the battle against carbon dioxide has created an active market for oil substitutes, no matter how low the price of oil.

The Gulf countries are caught in the pincers of a climate dilemma. On the one hand, the region is one of the most climate stressed and dependent on greenhouse gas mitigation. Higher temperatures could render it uninhabitable *within the current century*. On the other hand, oil exports remain the region's economic livelihood and the source of its longstanding protection by the United States. Actions to address climate change—specifically, global efforts to reduce consumption of fossil fuels—pose both an economic and a security threat. It is a predicament that requires thoughtful long-term planning and sacrifice.

What forces are behind the Gulf's feverish demand for its chief export commodity? Many other countries have experienced fast-growing population and income but never reached the levels of energy inefficiency that characterize these six. What makes the Gulf different? Can the region's tribal elites tame demand without jeopardizing their control over the state? Can the ruling sheikhs cope with the global transition to cleaner energy?

These are the questions that drive this book. The early chapters examine the history of energy demand in the region and outline the events and practices that have pushed the Gulf from a negligible to a world-beating consumer of its own resources. Further chapters look at opportunities for reform not just to energy consumption but to the political structures that have contributed to inefficiency. The closing section provides a sobering preview of the challenges facing the world's premier petrostates and their top export.

The central argument is that the Gulf monarchies' political and economic systems contain contradictory properties. One of their key political institutions, subsidization of energy, undermines their chief economic institution, the export of oil and gas. Over the long term, these two crucial components of governance cannot remain in conflict. Either the political structures will bend or the economy will yield.

Academic wisdom is that the political structures cannot bend without grave consequences. Scholars theorizing about Gulf politics since the 1980s have nearly unanimously dismissed the possibility of reforming energy subsidies, arguing that subsidies are key parts of the all-important social contract between state and society. Citizens get cheap oil, water, and power and in return bestow fealty upon the families who rule them. Touch these offerings, and the whole bargain is liable to unravel.

In this book, I dispel this long-held idea. Political structures can and must bend. Subsidies are reformable because the distortions they have created are too big to ignore. Energy policy in the Gulf is the polar opposite of the policies in place in Europe, North America, and other energy importers of the developed world. In those places, rationalized pricing instills in consumers a clear understanding of energy's value. Buildings are fitted with insulation and other features that minimize energy demand. Fuel efficiency is a key variable in car and appliance purchases. When energy prices rise, consumers reduce energy use. They use less air conditioning, heating, lighting, or fuel, or they upgrade to more efficient technology. In some countries, electricity prices are high enough to encourage building owners to generate their own electricity with rooftop solar panels.

An altogether different incentive structure governs energy use in the Gulf. When international oil prices are high, exporting countries of the Gulf undergo an *increase* in demand and *reduced* efficiency. Why? Because high oil prices bring windfall profits, and policy makers come under pressure to share the wealth. They distribute the windfall in ways that exacerbate energy demand—by boosting government salaries and embarking on building programs that increase per capita energy consumption at the very moment the rest of the world struggles to limit it. Ruling sheikhs have even been known to respond to high international prices by *reducing* domestic energy prices, widening the gap between local and international prices. High oil prices incentivize wasteful energy consumption in the Gulf because residents receive different signals than those that moderate consumption elsewhere.

In 2008, while oil had spiked to an all-time high of more than $140 per barrel—and with natural gas prices at similar highs—people in the Gulf were partying like it was 1999. As I chronicled in my 2009 book on Dubai, gargantuan SUVs filled the superhighways of the Gulf even as they were being traded in for Toyota Priuses in the West. While Germans lusted for the zero-emission *Passivhaus*, the Gulf underwent a frenzied building boom that covered the landscape in energy-intensive sprawl. Building insulation, long a standard component elsewhere, remained a frivolity. On hot summer days, residents swam in artificially chilled pools or, in Dubai, flocked to the Emirates Mall to ski in full view of shoppers wearing shorts and tank tops. At the office tower where I worked, colleagues propped open lobby doors when they went outside to smoke, so that they could feel a steady blast of artificially chilled air.

I found this kind of energy waste jarring, but it is absolutely rational given government policy in the Gulf. Electricity, desalinated water, and transportation fuels are provided at a fraction of world prices and—in the case of electricity and water—at a fraction of the cost of production. These subsidized energy products are among the sheaf of welfare benefits extended by the Gulf regimes to society in exchange for public support. Energy is a tool of political control. Since it is provided so inexpensively, the public treats energy as if it has little value. This is true of citizens born and raised in the Gulf, but it is also true of expatriate residents: although they may have come to the Gulf from countries where energy is priced at or above market levels, they change their behavior when provided with subsidized energy.

This behavior is now backfiring. With the exception of gas-rich Qatar, these monarchies face the unintended consequences of using energy as a political tool: an increasingly acute conflict between sustaining exports and maintaining subsidies. As suggested by King Faisal's prediction, regimes face a choice between short-term political stability and longer-term economic sustainability. As populations rise and energy production reaches a plateau, domestic consumption will gradually displace exports, as has happened in other oil-exporting states. Reforms that moderate consumption will be difficult, no doubt; citizens have gotten used to subsidies and won't want to see them go. But while difficult, they are not impossible, and such reforms are the only hope these states have in extending the longevity of oil exports and, perhaps, the regimes themselves.

1

BEFORE OIL

The ruling sheikhs of the Gulf, with their perfumed headscarves and gold-trimmed cloaks, can seem like exotic anachronisms in this age of global standardization. But the enduring trappings of old Arabia go beyond dress; they also include a successful brand of tribal politics. Today's reigning sheikhs and their families arose from ruling lineages that extend back millennia.

Oil, of course, plays a big part in the politics of the Gulf. But oil's role is a recent one. Before oil, there was isolation. This isolation was protective and rewarded toughness and specialization. It incubated a unique society and a political culture that remains surprisingly relevant today. For most of its history, the Arabian Peninsula drifted in an eddy of time, close to but apart from the main historical currents that convulsed the neighboring lands of the Arab and Persian Middle East.

Nearby Mesopotamia was the site of the first highly advanced human society, which coalesced around the bountiful waters of the Tigris and Euphrates Rivers some five thousand years ago. The seas, isthmuses, and caravan routes of the Middle East lay at the center of the Old World, funneling travelers between Asia and Europe. From 3000 BC until the thirteenth century, the Middle East was the cultural, economic, and often political center of all humanity west of India and China.[1] But despite the grand sweep of Middle Eastern history—the Silk Road trade, the advent of Christianity, the great civilizations—the deserts of the Arabian Peninsula languished outside this current. Most of the action took place elsewhere, in Mesopotamia, the Levant, and Egypt, where plentiful fresh water enabled food surpluses and the construction of great cities.

For two distinct periods, however, the Arabian Peninsula played a central role in human history. The first dates to 622, when the Prophet Muhammad founded the Islamic faith. The formation of Islam launched the golden age of the Arabs, enshrining the Arabian Peninsula forever as the geographic and cultural heart of the Islamic world. By the thirteenth century, Arabs had conquered much of the known world and spread their faith from Spain to China. For four centuries, Arabs led the Western world in philosophy, science, medicine, and poetry, even preserving European knowledge during the medieval "dark age" that gripped that continent.

But as Islam spread into more temperate lands, its command centers followed. In a paradoxical turn of fate, the glories of the Arab Empire largely bypassed Arabia. The western Arabian cities where Muhammad began preaching, Mecca and Medina, remained holy shrines of pilgrimage, but after the prophet's death in 632, most of the Arabian Peninsula sank back into isolation. The caliphates were administered from faraway capitals: Damascus, Cordoba, Baghdad, and Cairo. Punishing geography mired Arabia in a thousand-year time warp. Human settlement was deterred by the endless dunes and jagged *wadis* (canyons), the searing climate, the dearth of fresh water, and the limits of sea navigation.

The second golden age of the Arabian Peninsula is the one this book focuses on: the age of oil, which unfolded on Arabia's Persian Gulf coast 1,300 years after the Prophet's death. The birth of this new era is the focus of chapter 2.

Between the two golden ages of Islam and oil was a long epoch of isolation. Elsewhere in the world, global empires rose and fell, and civilizations were transformed by conquest, colonization, and technology. The Arabian Peninsula's geographic quarantine allowed the sheikhdoms of the Gulf to develop traits that remain relevant to this day, including a robust tribal culture and distributional autocratic rule that has its basis in the earliest forms of Arabian societal organization. The Gulf's inaccessibility also secured a mineral-rich realm for a small number of distant ancestors of the early Arabs. The meager size of the population ensured that, once resources were discovered, the size of the bounty relative to the size of the populace would bring prosperity.

IMPERIAL INTRUSION AND THE FOUNDATION OF HEREDITARY RULE

Early breaches of the Gulf's historical sequestration came in the form of contacts with European and Ottoman military delegations in the early 1500s. The Portuguese arrived first, maintaining a nominal but brutal presence until fading away in the mid-1700s.[2] The British and Ottomans were the most influential of the interlopers. Although neither empire spent much blood or treasure defending interests on the Arabian Peninsula, their authority had two lasting effects. First, since the imperial powers were unwilling to send their own citizens to colonize these lands formally, they instead concentrated power in the hands of preexisting tribal ruling families. Second, they pushed the Arab tribal leaders to define the boundaries of the territories they controlled. Many of these boundaries later became international borders.

The Ottomans and British regarded their Arabian territories as buffer zones that could shield more important possessions from enemy inroads. From the early 1500s until their empire dissolved during World War I, the Ottomans held superficial control over the peninsula's Red Sea coast, including the trading and pilgrimage cities of Jeddah, Mecca, and Medina. The Ottomans also maintained a tenuous grip on parts of eastern Arabia: Kuwait, Qatar, and the al-Hasa Oasis in today's Eastern Province of Saudi Arabia. Istanbul used its Arabian presence to thwart European inroads into its strategic eastern trading cities of Baghdad and Basra, in today's Iraq.

The British were the strongest external power in the Persian Gulf for 350 years. They arrived tentatively in the early 1600s, rose to dominance during the height of the British Raj in India in the late 1800s, and finally sailed away amid the crumbling of the imperium in 1971. They were interested in Arabia for its strategic location on trade routes between Europe and India. The British imposed their dominance around a series of truces, starting in 1835, which granted protection and political backing for ruling sheikhs who relinquished control over foreign affairs and trade. The last of these was signed with Qatar in 1916.[3]

While the Ottomans and British were rival intruders, they presided over a crucial change in the system of tribal rule on the peninsula. Before their arrival, communities in Arabia were not organized under the current system of *hereditary* sheikhly rule. Instead, a more ad hoc system prevailed, where the head of a respected family agreed to mediate disputes and manage relations with neighbors and distant powers.[4]

British and Ottoman treaty relations amended the old system. The British had a particular problem with ill-defined tribal rule and nebulous concepts of territorial control. They wanted to deal with identifiable rulers who controlled sovereign territory with clear boundaries.[5] Since these institutions did not exist, the British created them. British authorities gave political and financial backing to sheikhs who followed the terms of the queen's treaties. Once imperial powers recognized a local sheikh, they had vested interests in ensuring that "their" ruler and his family remained in control to enforce the treaty. This practice had the effect of solidifying and, later, legitimizing hereditary rule.

Afterward, British surveyors laid out borders between sheikhdoms that have, in many cases, become accepted international boundaries. These practices allowed the Gulf sheikhs to extend control over their territories and encouraged the settlement and loyalty of nomadic tribes.

SIX INDEPENDENT MONARCHIES

By the time the British folded their flags and set sail from the region in 1971, six independent Persian Gulf monarchies had emerged. Over time, the six have developed strong governing institutions and, for the most part, remained politically stable through momentous social and economic change. The disparate sheikhdoms quickly integrated with counterparts in the region and within the global economy. By 1971, all six were members of the United Nations. Between 1960 and 1967, all but Bahrain and Oman joined the Organization of the Petroleum Exporting Countries (OPEC). In 1981, the six monarchies banded together to form the Gulf Cooperation Council, or GCC, a loose union based on monarchical rule, self-defense, free movement, and coordinated laws. The GCC states (shown in figure 1.1) comprise all the countries of the Arabian Peninsula except Yemen, left out of the union because of its major differences with the six monarchies. These start with Yemen's chronic instability and underdevelopment and extend to the country's large population and small natural resource base as well as its republican (nonmonarchical) government.

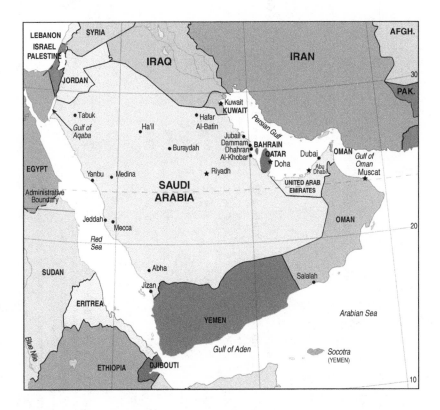

FIGURE 1.1 The Persian Gulf countries.

TABLE 1.1 Basic statistical indicators

Year of data	2015	2015	2010–2015	2015	2015	2014	2012	2012	2012
Country	Area (sq. mi.)[1]	Pop. (millions)[1]	Citizen %[2]	Foreign %[2]	GDP PPP (2011 US$bn)[1]	GDP per capita (current US$)[1]	Total oil output (kbbl/d)[3]	Hydrocarbon reserves per citizen (barrels of oil equivalent)[4]	Hydrocarbon revenue per citizen (2012 US$)[4]
Bahrain	268	1.4	48%	52%	60.85	$22,600	64	4,000	11,000
Kuwait	6,880	3.9	31%	69%	261.21	$29,301	2,767	92,000	73,000
Oman	82,030	4.5	56%	44%	161.58	$15,551	952	6,000	11,000
Qatar	4,427	2.2	14%	86%	302.49	$73,653	2,055	724,000	183,000
Saudi Arabia	830,000	31.5	67%	33%	1585.98	$20,482	11,624	16,000	11,000
UAE	30,000	9.2	12%	89%	605.3	$40,439	3,474	139,000	98,000

[1] World Data Bank, World Bank Group.
[2] GCC: Total population and percentage of nationals and non-nationals in GCC countries (latest national statistics, 2010–2015), Gulf Research Center, http://gulfmigration.eu/total-population-and-percentage-of-nationals-and-non-nationals-in-gcc-countries-latest-national-statistics-2010-2015/.
[3] International Energy Statistics, US EIA.
[4] BP, International Monetary Fund, and Qatar National Bank 2014.

The GCC countries are typically studied as a group, but the various monarchies bear widely different characteristics (some of the major statistics for each state are given in table 1.1).

SAUDI ARABIA

The Kingdom of Saudi Arabia is the world's only nation-state named for the family that rules it. The kingdom is dominant over other Gulf monarchies in terms of population, physical area, natural resources, and geopolitical influence (table 1.1). The organizing structures of Saudi society are among the world's purest—meaning that Saudi culture has undergone relatively little influence from outsiders, making it unique in many ways.

The al-Saud family's power flows from two sources: its origins in the central Arabian Desert, in the region known as the Nejd, and an eighteenth-century alliance with the Ikhwan, an army of nomadic Islamist followers of Muhammad ibn Abdul Wahhab.[6]

A Saudi kingdom emerged in the central Arabian Peninsula twice in previous eras and both times lasted less than a century. The first Saudi state, known as the Emirate of Diriyah after the ancestral hometown of the al-Saud, rose in the mid–eighteenth century and lasted until the Ottoman invaders crushed it in 1818. The Emirate of Diriyah sprawled between Oman and the Shia holy city of Karbala in southern Iraq, where Sunni jihadis destroyed Shia shrines and put thousands to the sword. The second Saudi state, the Emirate of the Nejd, held about half as much territory, concentrated in the eastern half of the peninsula. The Nejdi state lasted from 1824 to 1891, when Riyadh fell to the al-Saud's historic Nejdi rivals, the al-Rashid clan.

The modern kingdom is the al-Saud family's third attempt at statecraft. It has been in place about as long as the first. The kingdom's founding father, Abdulaziz al-Saud, or Ibn Saud, seized Riyadh and the Nejd from the al-Rashid in 1902. Over the next thirty years, Ibn Saud and his Ikhwan irregulars fought more than fifty battles in their quest to reassemble a vast kingdom covering most of the Arabian Peninsula. When the fighting was done, Ibn Saud melded four disparate territories into a country that he named for himself. Ibn Saud's Arabia was recognized as a sovereign and independent state in 1932.

The al-Saud rulers imposed the Nejdi's austere brand of Sunni Salafi Islam on all inhabitants, whether minority Shia in the east or the more liberal Hijazis in the west. Salafi, or Wahhabi, Islam remains a key pillar of the al-Saud's claims of religious legitimacy, stemming from state enforcement of conservative principles and its seizure and guardianship of holy places in Mecca and Medina. Like their counterparts in neighboring Gulf monarchies, Ibn Saud's sons continued to rule the Saudi kingdom based on indigenous institutions that evolved from long-held traditions.

For the Saudis, this singularity is a matter of pride. No outside power ever colonized the Nejd, the al-Saud heartland. Ottoman imperialists, also Muslim, made inroads, but considered the Nejd and much of Arabia a "hornets' nest." For non-Muslims, Arabia's holy cities have always been off-limits.[7] Chas Freeman, a former US ambassador to Saudi Arabia, maintains that Saudi Arabia's never-colonized status still shapes relations with its neighbors and the West.[8] "Saudi Arabia is the only society on the planet never to have experienced coercive intrusion by Western militaries, missionaries, or merchants. The kingdom has never compromised its independence. When the West finally came here, it came not as a conqueror, spiritual tutor, or mercantile exploiter, but as hired help."[9]

Saudi Arabia modernized more gradually than the other Gulf states. While its early independence and discovery of oil gave it a head start, the kingdom's larger area and its ultraconservative religious and social preferences slowed development. The rise of the modern Saudi state owes much to its oil-derived friendship with the United States.

The Americans capitalized on the strategic importance of a sparsely populated land endowed with so much oil. The 1945 meeting between President Franklin D. Roosevelt and Ibn Saud, aboard the USS *Quincy* in the Suez Canal, established the core principles of the relationship: US diplomatic and military backing in exchange for a commitment to oil exports and anticommunism. The American-led exploitation of the kingdom's oil and Saudi Arabia's geopolitical significance to the United States reinforced political control for the al-Saud, ensuring the ruling family received credit for oil-funded national development. US protection expanded to neighboring sheikhdoms when the British departed the Gulf in 1971. The Carter Doctrine of 1980 formalized the US role by declaring that America would use force, if necessary, to defend its interests in the Persian Gulf.

The key to America's strategic interest was the kingdom's willingness to invest in spare oil production capacity—"spare capacity"—and to deploy it to bolster US policy in the Middle East. Saudi Arabia became the world's "swing producer" because of its ability and willingness to balance the market by adjusting its production.

Holding spare capacity is no trivial matter. No other oil producer has been willing to invest billions of dollars in infrastructure that sits idle. Certainly no shareholder-owned company would do so. But Saudi Arabia, for decades, has deliberately maintained more capacity to produce oil than it uses. The kingdom does so because it reaps geopolitical power from its ability to protect the oil-importing world from volatile price spikes. This role enhances the kingdom's value as a US ally and as a contributor to global financial stability.

Spare capacity is the factor that still obliges Washington to work hand in hand with the Saudis in the region. The Saudis raised output to stabilize oil prices in response to Iraq's invasion of Kuwait in 1990, the US-led invasion of Iraq in 2003, the 2011 campaign in Libya, and antinuclear sanctions that blocked exports from Iran until 2016. Oftentimes, Saudi spare capacity protects the US motorist from US foreign policy.

The kingdom's sheer size and global importance signify the high stakes that rest on its successful stewardship of its natural resources. With the exception of two short periods in the 1980s, Saudi Arabia has been the world's number-one oil exporter for nearly half a century. Its well-being depends on Riyadh's ability to maintain its commanding role in oil markets, since oil exports form the basis for the strategic interest and protection of the West. This protection undergirds the hard security needs of all six Gulf monarchies.

KUWAIT

Kuwait is a triangular swatch of rippling sands wedged between Iraq and Saudi Arabia. The diminutive state is dominated by Kuwait City, a pearling and merchant trading haven that has thrived on that spot since the 1700s. The al-Sabah family has supplied each of the fifteen sheikhs who have ruled Kuwait since the 1750s, including Sheikh Mubarak the Great, who reigned from 1896 to 1915 and from whom all Kuwaiti rulers must be descended.[10]

Kuwait owes its autonomy as an independent sheikhdom to the al-Sabah family's prescience in allying with the Ottomans, the British, and, later, Washington, thus preventing neighboring powers from swallowing it up. Power flowed to the al-Sabah by virtue of the family's good relations with merchants brokering trade among India, Iraq, and the Levant. Trade opportunities attracted the British East India Company in the late 1700s, and the company, in turn, enhanced stability and prosperity. In 1899, Kuwait became a formal British "protected state," enshrining al-Sabah control.[11] The discovery of oil in 1938 left the ruling family in undisputed power.

Modernity came quickly. Social-welfare pacts established in the 1940s yielded generous citizen benefits that became the envy of the Gulf. Kuwait's success in boosting living standards—and the swagger of Kuwaiti citizens who received them—ignited expectations across the region. Kuwaiti sheikhly patronage became the model for the state-society social contracts in all the oil monarchies. Oil revenues also allowed Kuwait to wean itself from dependence on Britain. When the British departed in 1961, Kuwait declared formal independence.

What sets Kuwait apart from other GCC countries is politics. It remains the most politically liberal of the six monarchies, with a vibrant political life and a relatively free press. It is the only Gulf state with an active parliament that exercises significant power. The downside of these freedoms is that Kuwait's parliament has, especially in recent years, used its power to block foreign investment and development. The resulting economic stagnation has trimmed the Kuwaiti swagger, leaving the one-time frontrunner trailing its newly ascendant neighbors.

Some scholars argue that Kuwait's political freedoms arise from its long tradition of merchant power and autonomy.[12] More recent work argues that its pluralism is the result of Kuwait's unfortunate location next to Iraq, an aggressive neighbor that harbored claims to the entire national territory. The American political scientist Michael Herb maintains that the al-Sabah would never have invited citizens to participate in politics if the family had not needed to rally the populace against Iraqi intimidation.[13] Iraq first threatened to invade at the time of independence and, three decades later, made good on that threat. In 1990, Saddam Hussein's army overran Kuwait, triggering an international outcry. In 1991, a US-led international coalition of 700,000 troops pushed the Iraqis out and restored the al-Sabah and their parliamentary rivals to power, ensuring the political stalemate would continue.

THE UNITED ARAB EMIRATES

The United Arab Emirates is a federation of seven semiautonomous sheikhdoms: Abu Dhabi, Dubai, Sharjah, Ajman, Umm al-Quwain, Ras al-Khaimah, and Fujairah (figure 1.2). Before oil, these lands were the most desolate corner of a desolate region—among the most poor, secluded, and sparsely settled areas of the Gulf. The Maine-sized territory was so inhospitable that the population hovered at roughly 80,000 for more than a millennium, from the arrival of Islam in AD 630 until the 1930s.[14]

The disparate lands that became the UAE were dominated in the nineteenth century by the seafaring city-states of Sharjah and Ras al-Khaimah, governed by the al-Qassimi family, known collectively as the Qawasim. To the British, Qawasim naval prowess looked more like piracy. The British dubbed the lower Gulf region the Pirate Coast and launched a series of amphibious attacks that brought the gritty city-states

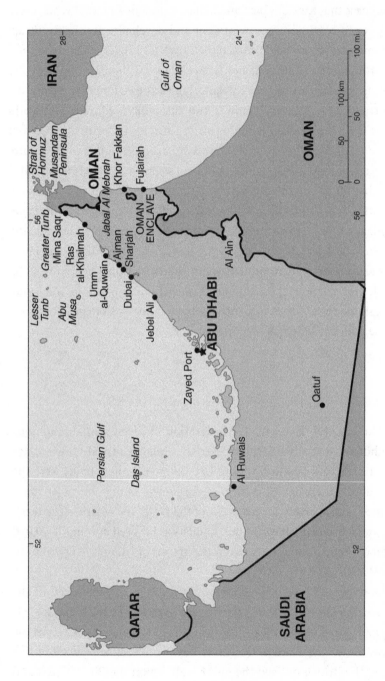

FIGURE 1.2 The United Arab Emirates.

under British domination.[15] The area became known afterward as the Trucial Coast, named for the series of truces signed with the British.

The al-Nahyan family of Abu Dhabi and the al-Maktoums of Dubai were pro-British, and their sheikdoms grew to dominate the Trucial Coast federation, overshadowing the more hostile Qawasim-ruled emirates. Abu Dhabi's discovery of oil in 1958 gave it the wherewithal to control the federation. In 1971, six of the seven sheikhdoms banded together as the UAE, an independent country governed from Abu Dhabi. Ras al-Khaimah joined reluctantly in 1972, lacking funds and diplomatic backing for independence.[16]

Oil abruptly reversed the desolation of the UAE. The federation is now second only to Saudi Arabia in terms of population and economy. Its nine million inhabitants are dominated by expatriates, who make up 85 percent of the population—perhaps the highest proportion of foreign residents in any major country. The historic entrepôt port of Dubai has maintained the role of commercial capital since 1959, when its port expansion enabled it to accept cargo ships. Dubai has since expanded into a global hub for trade, logistics, banking, and tourism. Abu Dhabi, with 81 percent of the UAE's land and 93 percent of its oil and gas, controls domestic politics, security, and foreign affairs. Abu Dhabi citizens enjoy the highest per capita GDP in the Gulf outside of Qatar, around $93,000 in 2014 versus $63,000 for the UAE as a whole.[17] Ras al-Khaimah and Fujairah have created their own industries in ceramics and bunkering, while the three others serve as bedroom communities for the expanding Dubai–Abu Dhabi metroplex.

The UAE and Kuwait possess nearly equal hydrocarbon resource bases but share few similarities in governance. Kuwaiti political openness and press freedom contrasts with the UAE's tighter controls on politics and opposition speech, which include long jail terms for political opponents. On the other hand, the emirate of Dubai is the most socially tolerant of any of the Gulf sheikhdoms and one of the world's freest economies. Dubai's openness to foreign culture, investment, and migration has allowed it to thrive after depletion of its small oil reserves, and it has built the region's first successful post-oil economy.

QATAR

A settlement known as Qatar—or Catara—has endured on the thumb-shaped peninsula jutting from the Arabian landmass as far back as the second century, as chronicled by Ptolemy in the first known map of the region. The al-Thani family, which follows the same Wahhabi interpretation of Sunni Islam as its counterparts in Saudi Arabia, has controlled the barren peninsula since the early 1800s, a period that extends through Ottoman fealty, the establishment of British dominance in 1916, and Qatari independence in 1971.

In 1939, drillers on Qatar's west coast struck oil, finding the modest (by Gulf standards) Dukhan oilfield. Prosperity came in fits and starts, with Doha modernizing into a second-tier Gulf trading port. Qatar looked destined for insignificance when its course was altered by two momentous events. The first took place in 1971, when a Royal Dutch Shell drilling crew discovered the world's largest natural gas field. The offshore find was a disappointment at the time, since there were no export markets nearby. Later, the gas proved transformational. Second, the 1995 palace coup launched by Hamad bin Khalifa al-Thani decisively altered the sheikhdom's trajectory. Sheikh Hamad overthrew Sheikh Khalifa, his father, a more cautious ruler who had allowed Riyadh to maintain a strong influence over Qatari affairs. Upon seizing power, Sheikh Hamad leveraged Qatari natural gas not only to maximize the country's prosperity but to forge a foreign policy and media venture outside Saudi influence.[18]

Qatar's foreign-policy stance has frequently contradicted those of Riyadh and Abu Dhabi. Qatar has maintained friendly ties with Iran while backing Islamist political opposition groups outlawed elsewhere in the Gulf (the Muslim Brotherhood in particular). Its state-owned Al-Jazeera TV network regularly airs provocative coverage that at times embarrasses or angers its Gulf neighbors. In recent years, these issues have embroiled Qatar in diplomatic and trade blockades led by three of its erstwhile brethren, Saudi Arabia, the UAE, and Bahrain.

Qatar stands out as an outlier for other reasons as well. Qatar's population is the smallest of all Gulf states but Bahrain. Its 278,000 citizens make up less than a fifth of the total population of 2.2 million, which is dominated by resident foreign workers. The tiny monarchy is the only major natural gas exporter in the Gulf and surrounding region. Over the past decade, Qataris have emerged as the wealthiest people on earth, with per capita GDP reaching $118,000 in 2015 (see figure 1.3).[19] Average household income for citizens was almost $300,000 in 2014, more than triple the $80,000 earned by the average expatriate.[20] The huge size of its resource base relative to its tiny population allows room for yet more growth and the preservation of an independent foreign policy. Whether Qatar can retain its individualism alongside its membership in the GCC bloc remains in question.

OMAN

The Sultanate of Oman is the Arab world's most remote state, cut off from the rest of the Middle East by sea and the vast sands of the Rub' al-Khali desert, known as the Empty Quarter. As a result, the capital, Muscat, has long been one of the most important regional seaports, bringing Oman more foreign contact than its neighbors. All but a few miles of Oman's coast lies not on the Persian Gulf but on the Indian Ocean, closer to global trade routes. Muscat's inhabitants and culture reflect this difference: Swahili and Baluchi languages are mixed with Arabic. Omani national dress and cuisine is closer to that of Pakistan than the Gulf. Religiously, as well, Oman is different. Its ruler and three-quarters of its citizens belong to the enduring Ibadi sect of Islam, which maintains numerous distinctions from the two main branches of Shiism and Sunnism. Oman is the world's only majority-Ibadi country.

Oman's history also diverges from that of its Gulf neighbors. The sultanate was the linchpin of a commercial empire based on trade in African slaves. The Omani sultan governed for a time from the slaving outpost of Zanzibar, an Indian Ocean island now part of Tanzania. At its height Oman even held colonies of its own, controlling territories on the East African coast[21] as well as parts of what are now Iran and Pakistan.

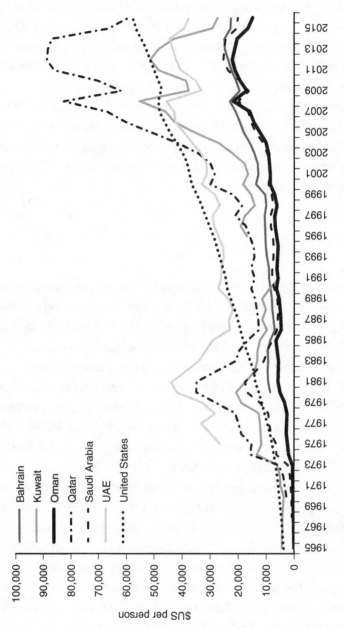

FIGURE 1.3 GDP per capita in the GCC vs. the United States.

Source: World Bank World Development Indicators database (2017).

Oman fell into decline toward the end of the 1800s as the British crack-down on the slave trade deprived it of revenue and surging British-Indian trade sapped Oman's fleet. Muscat lost Zanzibar and its African possessions to Britain and other European powers by 1900, amid a century of domination by the British.[22] Oman managed to hold onto one overseas colony, the Baluchi port of Gwadar, until 1958, when it sold the enclave to newly independent Pakistan.

Starting in the 1930s, Sultan Said bin Taimur—the father of the current ruler—colluded with the British to hold Omanis in stark isolation and severe underdevelopment. Said understood that his absolute rule was easier to defend if his subjects remained uneducated and impoverished. This state of affairs continued until 1970, when Said's only son, Qaboos, overthrew him and seized power. In 1971, Oman reemerged as an independent country and reopened itself to the world—becoming the last of the Gulf monarchies to modernize.

Oman remains the most absolute of the monarchies and one of the more potentially volatile. It persists as the poorest of the six (see figure 1.3) and is still governed by Qaboos, who—after more than four decades in power—has neither publicly named an heir nor institutionalized his family's role in governance. Oman's fast-growing and young population lacks the plentiful resource base that provides for its richer neighbors. Omani oil and gas fields are small, geologically complex, and scattered far from export terminals. Oman is not a member of OPEC, and, although it is a member of the GCC, it balances its somewhat cool relationship with Saudi Arabia with cordial ties to Iran.

BAHRAIN

The hulking stone fort on Bahrain's northern coast provides a taste of the island kingdom's long, multicultural history. Now known as the Qal'at al-Bahrain, the enormous pile of stones was erected by the Portuguese and added onto by the Persians. But the stronghold sits atop layers of previous buildings dating to 2300 BC that provide evidence of prior waves of migrants, including Greeks and Babylonians. Even earlier, Bahrain was the capital of one of the oldest civilizations in the Middle East, ancient Dilmun, which enjoyed trade links with Mesopotamia five thousand years ago.

In the 1500s, control of Bahrain shifted from Arabs to the Portuguese. In the 1600s, the island fell to the Persian Empire. Persia governed Bahrain until a Sunni Arab tribal clan seized control in 1783.[23] Since then the emirate has been governed by the al-Khalifa family, which fortified its power during the long period of British domination from 1880 until independence in 1971.

Unique among the Gulf monarchies, Bahrain's citizen population is 70 percent Shiite, a legacy of Persian control. Many Bahrainis speak Farsi as their first language. However, the al-Khalifa rulers, the country's elites, and the security forces are largely Sunni, which is a source of perennial discord between the regime and disenfranchised Bahraini Shia. Bahrain remains the second-poorest and least politically stable Gulf state.

Bahrain was also the first of the monarchies to discover oil, in 1932, which allowed the sheikhdom to modernize ahead of its neighbors. However, the island's small reserves were all but depleted long ago. Bahrain has for decades depended on the largesse of Saudi Arabia, at the cost of allowing Riyadh deep influence over Bahraini affairs. The Saudis provide Manama with half the revenues from the Abu Safah oilfield, equivalent to 75 percent of Bahrain's total oil production, despite the fact that the Abu Safah field lies under Saudi territorial waters. A Saudi pipeline to the island ferries a further supply of light crude for Bahrain to refine and export.[24]

FOUNDATIONS OF THE RENTIER STATE

In each of these domains, power accumulated in the hands of ruling families that remain in control today: the al-Saud in Saudi Arabia, al-Sabah in Kuwait, al-Nahyan in Abu Dhabi, al-Maktoum in Dubai, al-Thani in Qatar, al-Said in Oman, and the al-Khalifa in Bahrain. These once nominal tribal sheikhs evolved into dynastic "rulers" and, later, "heads of state" in the European fashion.

It is remarkable that the same handful of families has managed to control these monarchies for hundreds of years, across periods of all-encompassing change. A comparable counterfactual would have the Native American tribes retaining absolute power in North America despite widespread immigration and invasion. Tribal power in the Gulf might be more understandable if these countries had remained far-flung backwaters and continued to lie outside the main currents of globalization. But the Gulf ruling families found themselves in control of resources critical for global commerce and modern life. How did these isolated territories manage to transform into multicultural modern states with the same traditional ruling families at the helm?

As told by the scholars of political economy who chronicle the Gulf's rise, the sheikhs survived by buying the support of their people. When the Gulf monarchies discovered and then nationalized oil, the sheikhs seized the assets that would underwrite *both* modernization and their families' continued rule. Governance had always rested on patronage; before oil, patronage depended on sheikhs' ability to squeeze funds—more accurately described as *rents*—from the various parties who sought access into the region. Once oil arrived, export earnings became the chief source of rents.

Because of the importance of rents in governance, the Gulf states are described by political scientists as "rentier states." This description is based on the concept of "economic rent," which remains crucial to understanding the politics and development of the Gulf. What are economic rents and how are they different than, say, the monthly rent a tenant pays a landlord? To an economist, a landlord is an investor who earns—and is entitled to—a profit because he has risked financial capital. Economic rent is different. In this book, rent describes a financial reward for a "gift of nature" such as mineral deposits or a strategic location. Unlike the landlord, income from economic rent doesn't require the recipient to risk his own capital, work particularly hard, or even demonstrate any commercial expertise. Economic rents are unearned. It's money for nothing.

Rents in the modern Gulf take the form of *excess profit* that goes beyond a reasonable rate of return. In the case of petroleum, the rent portion is generally accepted as the surplus left over after oil is sold and deductions are made for the costs of exploration, production, processing, marketing, and transport. In low-cost oil-producing states like those in the GCC, rent might make up 90 percent of the revenues from international sales.

In the Gulf, political power was—and is—based around rents. In the 1800s, Gulf sheikhs signed treaties with foreign powers, the Ottomans and British in particular, because the foreign powers provided rents as part of the bargain. Rulers considered rents as personal income they could use for public benefit. They distributed some of the cash to build support among their subjects. In the 1930s, Sheikh Saeed al-Maktoum, the ruler of Dubai, received rents because the territory he controlled included the Dubai Creek, a sheltered saltwater inlet around which clustered Dubai's homes and souks. The creek was a useful landing and stopover site for British flying boats traveling between London and India. Britain's Imperial Airways paid Sheikh Saeed 440 Indian rupees a month (about $150, or £30), plus a landing fee of 5 or 10 rupees.[25] The stipend amounted to a small sum in British terms but provided the sheikh with a source of rents to maintain power and fend off his rivals.

Ibn Saud, who governed Saudi Arabia without entering into treaties with foreign powers, also secured rents to distribute among his subjects. Before oil, Ibn Saud's main revenue source flowed from hajj pilgrims paying fees to visit Mecca and Medina. But the king also convinced the British to provide him a yearly subsidy based on his recognition of Britain's dependencies on the Trucial Coast. These sources of rent allowed Ibn Saud to distribute patronage to Bedouin tribes in the form of cash, tea, sugar, and textiles. He provided subsidized food to residents of Jeddah, Riyadh, and other towns.[26] When oil was discovered, the ruling sheikhs captured those rents, too. Oil rents flowed into sheikhs' preexisting distribution channels, becoming the paramount financial resource for maintaining political control.

Over the centuries, Gulf ruling families built governing institutions that turned out to be surprisingly durable. The sheikhs' ability to capture and distribute rents is one part of the story. Credit for other stabilizing factors goes to the imperial powers, particularly the British. As mentioned, foreign powers persuaded the tribes to organize themselves into defined territories under the leadership of a single family. This produced six independent and largely stable states led by long-serving and capable family rulers. These sheikhs eventually led their nation-states to independence. The robust monarchies of the Gulf stand in stark contrast to the shaky governance institutions the colonial powers left behind in Africa and other parts of the Middle East, many of which have disintegrated into strife. Since independence, tribal rule in the Gulf has survived numerous destabilizing trends, including modernization, globalization, political Islam, pan-Arabism, and even violent extremism.

The notion that oil helped incubate durable ruling institutions and development is controversial. Many scholars believe that discovering oil triggers a "resource curse" that undermines development.[27] Later work has clarified the effects of this so-called resource curse. It is probably more accurate to say that rather than undermining development, oil cements existing ruling institutions in place.[28] If a country happened to be democratic when oil is discovered—Norway is a good example—it tended to remain that way. If a country happened to be a tribal autocracy, like the Gulf monarchies, pre-oil institutions are likely to persist. Oil had another notable effect. Its presence made Western powers, particularly America, eager to befriend and protect the Gulf's ruling families. Defending these regimes was necessary because of the weakness of their own militaries and the global importance of the region's petroleum supply.

In short, oil turbocharged the Gulf's homegrown political structures to such an extent that all the world soon learned of them. In the 1970s, after a 1,300-year hiatus, history's spotlight swung back over the Arabian Peninsula. A new Gulf personality type would soon sweep onto the global scene: the jet-setting oil sheikh.

2

THE OIL AGE ARRIVES

From the nostalgic perspective of the *khaleeji*—the Gulf Arab citizen—the pre-oil days were a kind of dreamtime. Countless generations had lived under the same daily rhythms. Human contacts were few, and they arrived upon plodding camel caravans or aboard wooden sailing dhows. The Bedouins' intricate social codes and gallant hospitality, perfected and nurtured over centuries, were the outcome of the sparseness of life and the dangers of the environment.

The Bedouin way of life was romanticized by Wilfred Thesiger, a wandering Briton who accompanied a group of nomads across the drifting wastes of the Empty Quarter in the 1950s. "To arrange three stones as a fireplace on which to set a pot was the only architecture that many of them required," Thesiger wrote.

> They lived in black tents in the desert, or in bare rooms devoid of furnishings in the villages and towns. They had no taste nor inclination for refinements. Most of them demanded only the bare necessities of life, enough food and drink to keep them alive, clothes to cover their nakedness, some form of shelter from the sun and wind, weapons, a few pots, rugs, water-skins, and their saddlery. It was a life that produced much that was noble, nothing that was gracious.[1]

Thesiger's idealized depiction notwithstanding, it is difficult to imagine the frightening crush of change that oil unleashed. Where foreign powers, sometimes in collusion with regional elites, had previously sought to fend off modernization, the oil age abruptly pried open these insular societies. Western technology and culture upended the social order, bringing wealth, rebellion, and loss.

THE SMOKY MOUNTAIN AND OTHER SALT DOMES

By the early 1900s, oil went from being a provider of illumination in kerosene lamps to a fuel for transportation in automobiles equipped with internal combustion engines. The automobile age gave oil a huge boost, kindling demand for gasoline, which had up until then been a waste product.

Then, in 1911, Winston Churchill converted Britain's Royal Navy from coal to oil, quickly conferring strategic importance upon the fuel—and the lands in which it could be found. Importing countries competed for access to oil-rich regions as a military necessity. The Dutch supply came from Indonesia. France's Rothschild and Sweden's Nobel families bought into oil in Azerbaijan and supplied it to Europe and Japan. The British government acquired a controlling share of the Anglo-Persian Oil Co.—today's BP—to ensure supply from new oilfields in Iran and Iraq.

As oil demand grew, the world's military powers turned their attention to the hermit sheikhdoms of the Arabian Peninsula. Arabia's 1,300-year sequestration would end when a crew of American wildcatters from Standard Oil of California docked their vessel at the island of Bahrain. Abdelrahman Munif's classic novel *Cities of Salt* captures the pre-oil period and the subsequent upheaval. Munif's rendering of the transformation of Saudi Arabia is a chronicle of cultural ruin. American prospectors arrive in a remote but lush *wadi*, a caravan stop favored for its bubbling springs and green date palms. Resident tribesmen look on in shock as the

Americans erect fences and bulldoze the landscape, working shirtless in the blazing heat:

> Within days everything in the wadi changed—men, animals and nature—for no sooner had the American, his friends and their companions been settled in than a large number of other people arrived. No one had ever dreamed such people existed: one was short and obese with red hair and another was tall enough to pick dates from the trees. Yet another was as black as night, and there were more—blond and red-headed. They had blue eyes and bodies as fat as slaughtered sheep, and their faces inspired curiosity and fear.[2]

Worried residents brought their complaints to the emir, who tells them to embrace the new age:

> "You have been patient and endured much. God is your witness but you will be living as if in a dream. . . . You will be among the richest and happiest of all mankind, as if God saw none but you. . . . Under our feet . . . there are oceans of oil, oceans of gold. Our friends have come to extract the oil and the gold," the emir says. "By the end of the new year, God willing, you'll have money up to your ears."[3]

Munif's fictionalized wildcatters were based on prospectors from Standard Oil of California, known as Socal, now Chevron. Socal was a splinter company of John D. Rockefeller's Standard Oil monopoly, broken up by the US Supreme Court in 1911. Rockefeller's unsavory business practices turned American public opinion against him. The breakup of Standard Oil was initially a setback for American competition for global supply. But, as the court intended, the surviving splinter companies soon asserted themselves.

In 1932, the San Francisco–based Socal began drilling its first well in Bahrain. The aptly named Oil Well Number 1 sat at the foot of Bahrain's highest point, a rocky salt dome known as Jebel Dukhan—the Smoky Mountain. After 220 days grinding downward, Socal's drill broke through a layer of blue shale 1,250 feet below the surface. The crew heard a whooshing sound and soon got the first whiff of the oil that would transform Bahrain and the other desolate lands surrounding it.

Crews erected derricks, pipelines, tanks, roads, and piers. The toffee-colored crude oil that flowed from under the desert was piped to the coast and shipped to industrializing Europe and Asia. Over the coming months, years, and decades, Westerners would flock to the region in search of characteristic salt domes like Jebel Dukhan, formations that often signal the presence of oil and gas trapped in geological fissures deep underground.

Socal's big prize was next door, in Saudi Arabia. In 1933 it signed a concession agreement with the new king, Ibn Saud, who had just achieved formal recognition as the absolute ruler of a consolidated kingdom. Socal shipped Ibn Saud what must have seemed at the time like a rent mother-lode: $775,000 in gold bullion. In return, Socal received a sixty-year concession over 360,000 square miles of eastern Saudi desert.

The concession gave Socal exclusive rights to extract and market any petroleum it found while leaving the company to assume all the risks of exploration and costs of development. The company received nothing if it found nothing. If it struck oil, Socal held the rights to produce and export it far into the future, long after Ibn Saud would be gone, right up until the year 1993. The fledgling Saudi state simply had no means to find or produce oil, and it did not understand the magnitude of the wealth it had consigned to foreign control for multiple generations.

Socal didn't yet know what a huge prize it had won, either. The firm sent just two geologists to explore the vast concession, a region a third larger than Texas. Later, it expanded the crew to ten. By 1934, the wild-catters had zeroed in on an intriguing geological structure in the al-Hasa region near the Persian Gulf coast, another rocky hill that bore the characteristics of a salt dome. They named it the Dammam Dome, after a nearby village. On April 30, 1935, Dammam No. 1, the first oil well drilled in the kingdom, was spudded in.[4]

Drilling on the Dammam Dome proceeded slowly. Drillers' logs chronicle hard limestone at 260 feet, water at 312 feet, tar at 385. At 1,774 feet, there were initial signs of oil and gas. By the end of August, when the well reached a depth of 1,886 feet, Socal's drillers produced the first crude oil from a drilled well anywhere in the kingdom. Well No. 1 began coughing out crude oil, but at the paltry rate of 50 barrels per day (b/d). By September, the flow remained under 100 b/d. These sorts of flows would have delighted an oilman in Texas but looked dire to prospectors who had invested so much so far from home. In early 1936, crews brought in a speedier rotary rig from Bahrain and pushed ahead with Dammam No. 2. Within six months, they again struck oil. Dammam No. 2 was flowing—at a very profitable rate of nearly 4,000 b/d. But soon the flow tailed off to a few hundred.

Evidence of oil was encouraging, but Socal lacked the capital to exploit the Saudi concession fully. In 1936, Socal sold half its interest to Texaco, a larger US oil company that arose from the East Texas oil patch. The two formed a joint venture called Caltex. More men came to the oilfields of al-Hasa and built a permanent camp on a 70,000-acre plot handed over by Ibn Saud.

On December 7, 1936, Caltex spudded in Dammam No. 7, a test well meant to probe new depths.[5] Through 1937, drilling surpassed the lowest points of previous wells, reaching 3,300 feet by October but still releasing no oil. Socal executives in San Francisco began reassessing the viability of the Saudi concession, which was starting to look like a white elephant. Socal's chief geologist, Max Steinecke, told his men to drill No. 7 a little deeper. It was a command that would change the world. The men drove the bit down to 4,727 feet, nearly a mile below the surface. At these depths, the Cretaceous zones that were so fruitful in Bahrain gave way to an earlier geological stratum, the late Upper Jurassic.[6] On March 4, 1938, Dammam No. 7 began to flow. A heavy crude oil emerged at the cautiously optimistic rate of 1,585 b/d. A few days later the flow improved to a respectable 4,000 b/d. This time the oil poured forth without letup.

Caltex drilled its other wells deeper into the Upper Jurassic pay zone, and they, too, began to produce prodigious amounts of crude oil.[7] By the measures of the day, flows of 3,000 to 4,000 barrels per day were immensely profitable, sufficient to please executives in San Francisco and Houston. But later discoveries in the kingdom would be much larger, with flow rates that beggared belief.

Socal's concession would turn out to be worth upward of $1 trillion. It was becoming clear that Saudi Arabia stood at the absolute apex of the oil-producing world, a crucial cog in the global economy.

THE PERFECT SETTING

In governance, geology, and geography, Saudi Arabia and the other Gulf monarchies were ideal hosts for the oil business. In each of these sheikhdoms, just one man called the shots. Autocratic governance was a huge advantage. It allowed oilmen to deal directly with rulers or designated subordinates. There were no legislatures to slow things down and no other veto wielders in these highly centralized states.[8] The ruler's *diwan* was the only stop.

Neither were there any private claims on the oil, nor on the land above it, which had been considered open grazing land until companies fenced it off. Mineral ownership and surface rights were in the hands of the state, personified by the ruling family. The ease of access allowed for economies of scale. Companies amassed enormous concessions and exploited them as they saw fit. Further, the geology was unbeatable. Middle Eastern oil lies comparatively close to the surface, just over a mile below ground, on average.[9] Most of the big Gulf fields lie near the coast, making field-to-terminal transport distances short. No long pipelines were needed to bring the oil to port. Reservoirs also benefited from high levels of underground pressure, which was sufficient to drive the oil to the surface and out the borehole at prolific rates. In the 1930s, the average Gulf well flowed at 6,000 b/d, while the average US well managed just nineteen barrels daily.[10] Most important, reserves were—and are—enormous. The majority of the world's "elephants"—its biggest oil and gas fields—sit within a five-hundred-mile radius of Kuwait City. The largest, Saudi Arabia's Ghawar, produces 5.8 million barrels per day, more than all but three entire countries.[11] Finally, Gulf geography couldn't be more convenient. The region lies at the center of the world, between the big markets of eastern North America, Europe, and Asia.

So when on October 16, 1938, Caltex brought news of the Dammam find to Ibn Saud, the Saudi king knew that the promised golden age had arrived. After centuries of slumber, Saudi Arabia was in business. The camp at Dammam expanded with family cottages and shops. Wives came from America. The camp took on a new name: Dhahran.[12]

It took little more than a year before the first export cargo was ready to sail. On May 1, 1939, the initial 80,000 barrels of virgin Saudi crude were pumped aboard the tanker *D. G. Schofield*. During the loading, Ibn Saud and his court hosted a three-day celebration on the dock at Ras Tanura, with thousands in attendance. The Dammam field would eventually produce 32 million barrels.[13]

The crude oil that flowed so profusely from Dammam No. 7 would be found again and again under the barren east Arabian landscape, in reservoirs of unprecedented size. All those in Saudi Arabia would be overseen from the Dhahran camp, which, it turned out, sat at the center of the richest prospecting ground in the world. Drillers also struck crude in surrounding sheikhdoms. Oil was found in Kuwait in 1938, Qatar in 1939, Abu Dhabi in 1958, and Oman in 1962.

For most observers, oil was an unalloyed blessing. At last, one of the world's most deprived regions would have resources for development. And indeed, changes began to penetrate all aspects of the Gulf, from the built environment, to the size and makeup of society, to public health and education, to cultural habits—even the language. Still, some sensed that dark days were ahead. Echoing Munif, Thesiger felt that the desert Arabs were better off without oil, since the "evil that comes with sudden change far outweighs the good."[14] "All that is best in the Arabs has come to them from the desert. Their deep religious instinct . . . their pride of race, their generosity and sense of hospitality, their dignity . . . their humor, their courage and patience," he wrote. Thesiger preached that "the Arabs are a race which produces its best only under conditions of extreme hardship and deteriorates progressively as living conditions become easier." But despite such misgivings, the low-cost Arabian producers—advantageously governed, uniquely endowed, and favorably positioned—would soon dominate the oil business.

The oil produced from the Dammam Dome, at Jebel Dukhan in Bahrain, at Burgan in Kuwait, and at the offshore Zakum field in Abu Dhabi did not stay in those countries. Arab oil flowed out of the ground and was pumped onto tankers and cooked in refineries in industrial Europe and Asia. Cheap Middle Eastern oil provided the discount gasoline and diesel that fueled the Free World's mammoth post–World War II expansion, allowing the spread of an energy-intensive Americanized lifestyle.

The Gulf monarchies became the fueling station to the world. The peninsula's scant population and underdevelopment were now competitive advantages. Its few inhabitants were too poor to consume oil. Even if their poverty was temporary, oil reserves were so vast relative to the population that no one could foresee a day when domestic demand might impinge on exports.

At the time of first oil, most of the energy consumed in the Gulf still came in preindustrial form: human and animal labor, fueled by food. For cooking and heat, people burned biomass, mostly in the form of dung. Transportation was powered by animals or the wind. People rode beasts or bicycles, sculled boats or walked, or they sailed aboard the ubiquitous dhow, lateen sails billowing. Wind power also drove water pumps and provided cooling, via the wind towers, or *barjeel*, that still rise above preelectricity buildings in the region.

In those days, oil was of little use on the Arabian Peninsula. People burned it for illumination and daubed it on the hulls of their boats as waterproofing. Until the region's first major refinery was built at the Saudi export hub of Ras Tanura in 1945,[15] most oil products had to be imported—hardly a problem, since there was so little demand. Even when the Ras Tanura refinery opened, less than 5 percent of its output was consumed inside Saudi Arabia. The rest was exported.[16] The Gulf countries had few roads, cars, or anything else that ran on petroleum. There was no electricity, no refrigeration, and no air conditioning right up into the 1950s in Bahrain, Kuwait, Qatar, and Saudi Arabia and until the 1960s in the UAE and the 1970s in Oman.

The state of development in the Gulf would change, of course. When it did, few were prepared for the speed at which it would unfold.

THE AGE OF THE SEVEN SISTERS

Oil production in the Gulf and in much of the world was managed by a group of big Western oil companies known as the Seven Sisters. In Saudi Arabia, four of the American sisters combined in 1947 to form the Arabian-American Oil Co., or Aramco.[17] They were Socal and Texaco, joined by Standard Oil of New Jersey (later Exxon) and Standard Oil of New York (Mobil). The three remaining "sisters" were Shell (of Dutch-British origin), Gulf Oil (a Pittsburgh firm that later merged with Chevron), and the Anglo-Persian companies that became BP.

For oil consumers, the postwar era of the Seven Sisters was practically utopian. Energy was secure, plentiful, and cheap. Western companies ran the show. Prices, by today's standards, were rock steady. These seven operating companies colluded to keep oil under $2 per barrel from the 1950s until 1970.[18] For oil-producing countries, the Seven Sisters were far more than just extractive enterprises. In states with minimal institutional capacity, it fell to Western oilmen to provide essential services. The oil business was a legitimacy resource right from the start, beyond the simple provision of rents and cheap energy.

The US oil companies that joined to form Aramco sought to bolster the power of the friendly al-Saud family as a way to counter threats to the company's monopoly access to Saudi reserves.[19] Western expertise and technology delivered by international oil companies (IOCs) reinforced the ruling families' grip on power, by making the sheikhs appear competent. Rulers understood their dependence on the oil companies and, for a few decades at least, treated the firms with deference.

There were those, like Abdullah Tariki, the very first Saudi oil minister (and future OPEC cofounder), who demanded that the government nationalize the Westerners' holdings, but they were forced out. For the oil companies, friendly autocrats were preferable to unpredictable democrats who might succumb to populist demands and seek "resource nationalism." Propping up royals was an act of self-preservation.

A 1958 memo from Aramco vice president James Terry Duce to the US State Department reveals the depth of Aramco's involvement in developing Saudi Arabia. The administration, research, and engineering roles that Aramco pursued on behalf of the king went far beyond the usual profit-maximizing roles of a shareholder-owned company. Many of Aramco's pursuits were, in fact, governance duties normally overseen by a state. Duce argued that the company's work could even help stabilize the Middle East, as long as it was protected from expropriation:

> The industry provides and will continue to provide housing, schools, training, pays good wages, maintains hospitals, does research on health problems and particularly on endemic diseases, such as trachoma, and does many other things which are so necessary to build up the standard of living in the area. . . . All these will add to the prosperity of the area and form a base upon which a flourishing economy can be built providing, of course, the resultant funds can be efficiently used. The industry should, therefore, be protected from raids on its financial position so that it can continue to make its full contribution to the wealth and stability of the Middle East.[20]

Aramco's projects helped create the foundations of the modern Saudi state. These included eradicating malaria and smallpox; undertaking port, road, rail, and other infrastructure projects; building waterworks and desalination plants; and training a Saudi workforce, which created a commercial class.[21] Aramco's presence shaped governance and institutional design, particularly in the kingdom's newly founded Eastern Province, formerly al-Hasa, which had been annexed by the al-Saud in 1913, just two decades before the American wildcatters arrived.

Saudi Arabia and its oil were so strategically important to the West and its allies—then referred to as the "Free World"—that control over these vital realms could not be entrusted to a private company alone. The US government, as Duce's correspondence shows, stayed deeply involved. There were a host of reasons for close US engagement. As early as 1960, Saudi Arabia was understood to hold about a fifth of global crude oil reserves, at a time when its population was just 4 million—pointing to a major long-term source of supply. A decade later, Saudi proven reserves accounted for more than a quarter of the global total.[22] Washington wanted to ensure Saudi oil was Free World oil, sustaining America's ideological and economic battle against communism. The fear was that the Soviet Union, steward of huge oil reserves of its own, would continue expanding relentlessly southward and take control of or even subsume these politically weak but oil-rich lands. Saudi Arabia was also far more accommodating than other producer states. US relations with Iran, Venezuela, Mexico, and Indonesia were prickly. Certainly these more developed countries would not brook similar levels of US involvement in their national affairs.

Aramco, meanwhile, was so tied into the US government that it had an office in Washington where it could receive guidance from senior executives who also worked for the CIA. Aramco's Department of Government Relations was modeled after the State Department, and the company's Arabian Affairs Division replicated the State Department's intelligence arm, the Bureau of Intelligence and Research. The US government depended on Aramco for intelligence on the kingdom.[23] The political scientist Robert Vitalis portrays Aramco's Government Relations Organization as a CIA front and Duce as the oil company's main CIA liaison.[24] Col. William Eddy, a longtime US intelligence operative, interpreted for Ibn Saud during his 1945 meeting with President Franklin D. Roosevelt aboard the USS *Quincy*. During the 1950s, Eddy worked for Aramco in the kingdom, acting as a key liaison between the Western oilmen, the US government, and Ibn Saud.[25]

In this way, the strategic necessity of maintaining US access to Saudi oil—and profits for US oil firms—dictated American preference for a pliable authoritarian regime. With so much American input, the old-world desert kingdom even began to look like America. Aramco's 1952 Riyadh–Dammam passenger railway stands out as a classic American throwback. Designed and built by San Francisco's Bechtel, the railroad features four comfortable and spacious train stations built in the WPA style, embellished with Arab crenellations and archways that resemble openings on a Bedouin tent.[26]

THE OBSOLESCING BARGAIN

In the long run, the Arabian oil concessions were too generous to survive. The initial agreements gave single firms or small consortia exclusive rights to a significant portion of the planet's oil reserves for most of a century. The problem lay in the inflexible contractual terms. Host governments had an incentive to grant favorable conditions to IOCs when their primary goal was to *attract* foreign investors. Host governments wanted to lure Western firms to bet on oil exploration on their territory, rather than on someone else's. But once production had started—and the risk of alternate offers and dry holes was overcome—the initial concession terms looked extremely favorable for investing companies.

Prior to the mid-1940s, oil companies typically paid host governments yearly royalties of less than 15 percent of gross revenues. Early concession agreements put royalties under 3 percent.[27] For the heads of state, these stingy terms acted as a tourniquet that constrained the flow of rents, the lifeblood of patronage-based politics. Worse, with terms locked in for multiple decades, there was no improvement in sight.

There was Socal's original concession, which gave it sixty years of control over Saudi reserves worth $1 trillion or more, in return for about $775,000 in advance and initial annual payments.[28] Kuwait's 1934 concession with Gulf Oil and Anglo-Persian (later BP) was a similar giveaway. The Kuwaiti emir handed the companies a seventy-five-year lock on Kuwait's vast reserves—about a third as large as the Saudi reserves—for an advance of $180,000 and yearly payments of $100,000.[29]

These lopsided bargains were untenable. As host governments came to understand the scale of the national wealth they had consigned to foreign control, the concession terms became an embarrassment. Over time, producer states began to exploit their trump card—the threat of nationalization—to improve the arrangements. The prodigious diplomatic talents of men like Col. Eddy would only delay expropriation.

Rulers of oil states harbored further grievances. They often urged IOC executives to find and produce more oil, in order to increase the flow of rents to the state. The IOCs typically demurred. The Seven Sisters remained beholden to the terms of the then-secret 1928 Achnacarry Agreement, which required companies to maintain tight control over the amount of oil reaching global markets in order to avoid overproduction, which would bring down prices and damage profits. To comply with the conflicting demands of host governments and the oil market, IOCs went as far as drilling in areas they knew would yield no oil.[30]

Western oil companies used other techniques to maintain control, such as deploying pipelines to extend the crude oil value chain across international borders. This diluted the bargaining power of host governments because their fates were linked with those of neighboring countries, which dealt separately with the IOCs. Decentralization also thinned concentrations of workers who might be tempted to strike.[31]

Despite these efforts, the companies' leverage began to slip. Over time, the advantage shifted to host governments. The irrefutable fact was that IOCs had constructed fixed assets worth billions of dollars on the sovereign territory of their concession partners. These "facts on the ground" could not be picked up and moved. Built infrastructure provided the initial leverage for host governments to demand changes in the terms of their concessions. Host governments also held legal jurisdiction over their territories and their subsurface resources. They held the power to reassert control in the national interest. The shift in advantage from foreign investor to host government became known as the "obsolescing bargain."[32]

ULTIMATUMS AND THE CREEP OF NATIONALIZATION

In 1938, Mexico provided a dramatic example of the power of a politician willing to shred a concession—and the inability of Western IOCs to do a thing about it. Mexican President Lazaro Cardenas, fed up with insulting treatment at the hands of British and American concessionaires, ordered the overnight expropriation of all foreign oil assets.

Mexico ejected the foreigners and handed their businesses to a newly created government-owned firm, Pemex. It was the first major nationalization of foreign oil assets. The seizure made Cardenas an instant hero; he is still celebrated each year on Oil Expropriation Day, a Mexican holiday. In 1951, Iran did the same with British assets, but a US-backed coup in 1953 restored a large share of foreign control.

Creeping threats of nationalization made IOC chiefs willing to cut deals. To avoid full expropriation, they agreed to changes in the original concessions. The first of these came in 1943, when Venezuela succeeded in pushing Standard Oil of New Jersey and Shell to grant it 50 percent of revenues, a huge increase on the previous rate of 15 percent.[33] Improved terms for Venezuela triggered a cascade of similar settlements of 50 percent. In 1950, Aramco granted these terms to Saudi Arabia.[34] Kuwait and Iraq won 50 percent by 1952.[35]

The 50/50 principle lasted for two decades. By the late 1960s, producer governments began another round of demands. The 1969 coup in Libya, where young Col. Muammar Qaddafi overthrew the inept King Idris, proved the catalyst. Qaddafi demanded a 55 percent share from the US-based Occidental Petroleum. Upping the ante, Qaddafi also insisted on an increase in the posted price of oil, then stuck at $1.80 per barrel. At the time, IOCs' "posted prices" determined only royalty payments to host governments, not the actual selling price. True contractual terms of crude oil sales, typically within the Seven Sisters cartel, were secret. Qaddafi was not alone in understanding posted prices as an IOC scheme for grabbing a disproportionate share of the rents. Libya's demands prompted an identical ultimatum from Iran. The Western IOCs began making the rounds, giving the same deal to all the producer countries, lest the profit-sharing calls continue to escalate.

By this time, decades of cheap oil had the industrialized world hooked. Development based on assumptions of inexpensive energy triggered a dangerous path dependence, encouraging ever more oil-intensive development and locking in high levels of oil demand. Meanwhile, Western IOC control over the oil trade was being weakened by declining oil production in the Western Hemisphere. The United States, once self-sufficient, had quietly become a net oil importer, growing increasingly dependent by the 1960s on barrels from the Middle East. Oil had become too vital to be cheap.

By the early 1970s, IOC dominance began to slip away. Appeasement became the last-ditch strategy. Executives did their best to hang on to their prizes as long as possible and get the best terms. If ties remained cordial, nationalization, when it came, might at least allow companies to retain their roles in refining and marketing oil, rather than producing it.

In the Middle East, the looming confrontation was hastened by a sharpening geopolitical divide. American backing for the 1948 founding of Israel had become a serious irritant in US-Arab relations. American oil executives repeatedly urged Washington to tone down support for the Jewish nationalist project, which they feared would bring their lucrative enterprise to a premature end. The pleas of the oilmen failed.

Within a few years, there would be an enormous shift in the terms of the crude oil trade. The Seven Sisters would stand aside and watch their foreign assets and concessions swept away in a tidal wave of nationalization. The rupture in relations between formerly pliant Arab rulers and their Western concessionaires would usher in one of the most spectacular transfers of wealth and power in human history.[36] The once poor and isolated Arab sheikhdoms would take center stage, emerging in control of one of the most crucial levers of the global economy.

3

THE BIG PAYBACK

By the 1970s, oil-producing countries had grown tired of being yoked to industrial powers in lopsided trade relations. Academic thinking of the era accentuated the humiliation. The popular "dependency theory" declared that producer countries had "surrendered" their primary resources to the rich North, which had captured most of the value by converting raw inputs into finished goods. Rich countries resold these goods back to the global South at inflated prices. This cycle constituted a "dependency trap," and the only way out was to seize national resources and industrialize.

Few oil producers had the nerve to step up alone and launch an outright expropriation of American or British corporate assets, as Mexico had done in 1938. Iran's 1951 nationalization of the Anglo-Iranian Oil Co.'s holdings offered a stark demonstration of the risks. Tehran's takeover resulted in a brutal UK-led clampdown that halted Iran's oil exports, undermined its economy, and led to events that brought down the country's budding democracy. Within two years, the resulting disarray brought a CIA-backed coup that handed the shah, a Western-friendly monarch, absolute power. After the 1953 coup, the new National Iranian Oil Co. (NIOC) still technically owned the country's oil sector. But NIOC operated under a consortium of western IOCs that controlled the terms—and the marketing—of Iranian oil.

Western oil companies had proven adept at dealing one on one with troublesome regimes. For producers, the key to restoring national control lay in collective action. In 1960, five oil-producing countries—Iran, Iraq, Kuwait, Saudi Arabia, and Venezuela—had laid the groundwork for such collective action when they founded the Organization of the Petroleum Exporting Countries (OPEC). At the time, few noticed. Ministers from OPEC's member states periodically sought to improve their negotiating power with the Seven Sisters, but for its first ten years, OPEC operated in a deferential manner.

By 1971, OPEC members understood that intimidation worked better than servility. First came veiled threats of nationalization, aimed at improving producer states' share of the rents. As IOC executives found their influence crumbling, they capitulated. Recognizing a shift in the balance of power, producer countries began methodically imposing sovereignty over national resources through a series of escalating demands, most of which were met by the oil companies' climbdowns. Over the next two years, OPEC countries issued ultimatums for increased revenue and higher prices, demanding "participation." Once again, the oil companies relented. Participation meant that, for pennies on the dollar, producer governments could reclaim formal ownership of a portion of the crude oil produced. They then sold the crude back to IOC concession holders at higher prices.[1]

Host countries did not just want better financial terms; they wanted more control over production practices. One major grievance revolved around the IOCs' wholesale waste of natural gas, which came to the surface as a byproduct of oil production. Gas was often simply "vented" into the atmosphere or "flared off"—literally burned up—at the wellhead. Western IOCs had no interest in gas, viewing it as a "stranded resource," a nuisance byproduct without a viable regional market or strategy for transport.

Heads of state, on the other hand, saw gas as a valuable tool for national development. In Kuwait, the government wanted to capture gas for domestic uses (such as electricity generation), but BP and Gulf Oil refused to invest in the necessary gas-recovery infrastructure.[2] Aramco's prenationalization venting of natural gas in Saudi Arabia was so profuse that Saudi greenhouse-gas emissions were actually higher in the 1970s than they were as recently as 2010.[3] In 1971, when Shell discovered Qatar's massive offshore North Field, the largest single gas reservoir known to man, the company viewed it as a disappointment because there were no export markets within pipeline reach. Shell capped and abandoned the well.[4] Diverging interests only made ruling sheikhs more determined. They accelerated the push for nationalization.

The gathering nationalization wave finally hit in 1972, crashing over the global oil patch like a tsunami. That year alone, Venezuela, Algeria, and Libya grabbed controlling shares of their oil sectors, sending long-time concession holders packing. In 1973, Iran took over all remaining assets of the old 1953 consortium. Saudi Arabia, Kuwait, and Qatar began revoking their concessions at the same time. Nationalizing states joined OPEC, if they weren't already members. The burgeoning cartel welcomed the UAE, Indonesia, and Nigeria.

By 1973, OPEC controlled 51 percent of global oil output. The decades of IOC control over oil supply and prices were over. Nationalization didn't just give OPEC members bargaining power. It also gave them strategic power: the capability to disrupt the global economy.

THE FIRST OIL SHOCK

And disrupt the global economy they did. In 1973, the six Gulf OPEC members embarked on two tests of their newfound market power. The six unilaterally raised oil prices by 6 percent in April and then by another 12 percent in June. But these uncontested increases were just the precursors to a much bigger collective action: the 1973 oil embargo.

The impetus for the embargo was Israel's 1967 seizures of Arab land, including the Al-Aqsa Mosque in Jerusalem, Islam's second-holiest site. The Arab OPEC countries had perceived this as an egregious imposition upon their sovereignty, and the sweeping nationalizations of oil sectors—and the feeling of collective power these seizures produced—may have emboldened the Arab leaders to take a stand against this affront. Their sights were set not just on Israel but on the countries that were offering support—most notably the United States, whose stubborn backing of Israel's occupations was the driving force for the embargo.

Pressure had been building for years. Diplomatic cables from the US embassy in Jeddah and the US consulate in Dhahran chronicle the outrage in Saudi Arabia and across the Arab world at US arms sales to Israel (which tilted the regional balance of power toward the Israelis) and the seeming inability of Saudis and other Arabs to get their concerns taken seriously in Washington. One diplomat described Saudi King Faisal as "frustrated and bitter" over Washington's "pro-Israel posture" in a 1972 telegram.[5]

Aramco's executives were particularly worried. In 1969, Aramco vice president Frank Jungers told the US consul-general in Dhahran that the Saudi oil minister had threatened to revoke Aramco's concession if the dispute continued.[6] The messages coming from the embassy conveyed the same concern. "We hope [the US government] will not agree to sell additional arms to Israel. Damage to our interests in Arab world, including S.A., could be irreparable," a 1970 US embassy cable declared. Threatened retaliation included breaks in diplomatic ties, boycotts of US firms and goods, denial of US access to Arab bases and ports, and conversion of dollar-based cash reserves to European currencies. More support for Israel, US diplomats in the Dhahran consulate wrote, "could trigger a mass exodus of bulk of American community and could seriously harm our interests. . . . We fully share ARAMCO's concern re possibility that additional arms sales to Israel could loosen spate of violence against Americans in S.A."[7]

Over the years, King Faisal sought to convince Washington to take a "more balanced" approach. Following his father's lead, Faisal asked a succession of US presidents to acknowledge the Palestinian cause and press Israel to return Arab lands. The king told President Richard Nixon that the restoration of "old Jerusalem" to Arab control was his top priority. Faisal's continued failure in these entreaties was a particular frustration.[8]

By August 1973, Faisal had seen enough. Washington would not budge. The king assented to a private request by Egypt's Anwar Sadat and Syria's Hafez al-Assad to back their attempts to reclaim territory Israel had seized six years earlier.[9] The Egyptian and Syrian plan included a clever twist: it sought to impose an economic cost for the continued US backing of Israel, in the hopes that America might reconsider. Oil, these heads of state realized, was the best source of leverage the Arab world possessed. The decision to unsheathe the "oil weapon" was kept secret. If America intervened on Israel's behalf, Faisal agreed, Saudi Arabia would cut oil production and halt exports to America and any others who backed the Israelis.

On October 6, 1973—Yom Kippur—Egypt and Syria simultaneously launched surprise attacks, punching into the Israeli-occupied Golan Heights of Syria and Egypt's Sinai Peninsula.[10] The Arab armies' territorial gains were short-lived. As Faisal had feared, America intervened on Israel's behalf, flying in $2.2 billion in emergency US munitions on American planes, which were filmed landing in Israel in broad daylight. Rearmed, Israel proceeded to rout the two Arab armies and reoccupy the Syrian and Egyptian land.

As promised, King Faisal channeled Arab outrage and implemented the embargo. OPEC unilaterally raised prices by 70 percent, and the seven Arab OPEC states imposed 5 percent monthly production cuts. Saudi Arabia halted all shipments of oil to the United States. Altogether, 5 million barrels per day were taken off of world markets, which then were consuming around 45m b/d.[11]

The effectiveness of the embargo in driving up prices and wreaking political and economic havoc is legendary. Nearly two decades of postwar economic expansion had pushed Free World oil demand to new heights. At the same time, US oil production was in decline. America depended on imports for more than a third of its needs.[12] Consumers in the United States and around the world paid dearly for America's support for Israel. The production cuts triggered a huge spike in oil prices that went far beyond the 70 percent demanded by OPEC. By 1974, market forces and panic buying led to a *quadrupling* of oil prices from around $3 per barrel in 1973 to $12 in 1974. Prices for oil imported to the United States stayed above $12 even after the embargo was called off in March 1974 and held roughly constant for the next five years.[13]

The nationalizations had been timed perfectly. It was the producer countries, rather than the Western IOCs, that reaped most of the fruits of the spike in oil prices. In the wake of the embargo, Gulf regimes finished the business of kicking out their long-term foreign partners. Kuwait took 60 percent of the BP-Gulf concession in 1974. Qatar did the same to Shell and BP. A year later, Kuwait took the remaining 40 percent and handed BP and Gulf Oil a paltry $50 million in compensation.[14]

Saudi Arabia, despite leading the embargo, pursued a more cautious strategy of nationalization. The Saudi government had already purchased 25 percent of Aramco's assets in 1973. A year later it raised that to a controlling stake of 60 percent. But the Saudis wanted to maintain close ties with American IOCs and with Washington, by then a big importer and strategic Cold War partner. The Saudi objection to US backing for Israel was tempered by bigger concerns. The kingdom needed American experts to keep Aramco's operations running, and it needed American IOCs to continue marketing Saudi oil around the world. "You are the evil we cannot live without," a prominent Saudi official told the US embassy.[15] Saudi nationalization remained quiet and disciplined, and the Saudi government did not take full ownership until 1980, when it paid a mutually agreeable price.[16]

Overall, the combined effects of embargo and nationalization caused a sea change in global energy. The transformation comprised five major effects:

- *Control of global oil* passed from Western IOCs to national oil companies (NOCs) in the developing world. In 1970, IOCs controlled access to 85 percent of global oil and gas reserves. By 1980, that share had plummeted to just 12 percent, with states taking control of 88 percent.[17]
- Nationalization resulted in a similar revolution in the *share of oil revenues* flowing to oil-exporting states relative to those controlled by IOCs. Where Middle Eastern governments' combined tax and royalty rates stood at around 2 percent in the 1940s and 50 percent in the early 1970s, by 1975 they reached an average of 85 percent.[18]
- OPEC control over pricing and output also allowed exporting countries to increase the *amount of revenues* flowing to their treasuries.

The change was breathtaking. Saudi revenues jumped *forty-fold* between 1965 and 1975, from $655 million to $26.7 billion. For the entire Gulf region (including Iran and Iraq), the $71.6 billion in government revenues reaped in 1975 were thirty times the $2.3 billion earned in 1965.[19]

- Oil-exporting countries also acquired *geopolitical power* commensurate with their influence over the global economy. Such power had heretofore eluded suppliers of primary products. Not long after the embargo, Saudi Arabia emerged as the world's energy broker of last resort, a role around which the kingdom built a long-term strategic alliance with the United States.

- High oil prices also incentivized importing countries to *reduce exposure to oil*, particularly from the Middle East. Big investments in exploration, diversification, and conservation grew out of the embargo.

By 1975, Saudi Arabia had emerged as the world's most important player in oil markets and was on its way to claiming the role of swing producer, building up its oil-production capacity to the point of being able to produce more oil than required to meet its export contracts. The kingdom's policy makers learned to use that spare production capacity to augment Riyadh's new geopolitical power. The kingdom could quickly move to increase production, which helped smooth markets and offset outages in times of crisis, and it could also slash production and send importers into a panic.

The Arab oil embargo of October 1973 had its origins in geopolitics, but its main effects were economic. For the conspirators, the events brought a paroxysm of instant wealth, followed by a much larger role in the global economy and in geostrategic affairs. Today, state-owned NOCs control some 90 percent of global oil and gas reserves and 75 percent of global production. IOCs have since been relegated to subordinate roles in less attractive locations. The masterful timing of the nationalizations allowed producer countries to capture the rents generated by the first modern spike in oil prices, as well as those that would follow. The oil shock marked a crucial turning point for the region. The events of that momentous period laid the groundwork for the era of extreme rentierism that would unfold in the newly independent Middle East petrostates.

The postnationalization era wound up modernizing the Gulf's economies while keeping intact the region's peculiar form of sheikhly governance.

The unusual combination brought about an unforeseen regime type, one that would confound the world's brightest political scholars for the next fifteen years.

THE OPEC STRANGLEHOLD

The Arabs' second golden age was the age of oil, and it had fully vested once they took full control of that resource. The seizures in power brought about a complete reversal of the terms of trade. Now, the industrialized North found itself yoked in a dependent relationship with the primary-product-exporting South.

If OPEC could control the prices of such a vital commodity, it could influence the economic performance of importing countries. This revelation came as another shock to the industrialized world. Political threats to oil flows suddenly became a huge concern. "Energy security" and Middle East "dependence" were buzzwords coined in that era that remain with us today. Oil-importing countries from Japan to France to the United States made frantic efforts to reduce their dependence on imported energy, particularly from the Middle East. To Westerners who had come of age amid the market stability of the Seven Sisters' collusion, the new state of affairs in oil was appalling—and dangerous.

"Never in recent history has there been a transfer of wealth and power on the scale and at the velocity that is now being witnessed," lamented Arthur Ross in *Washington Quarterly* in 1980. "Millennia of cultural, social and material developments supported by Western economic systems are threatened by this extraordinary development. Yet with few exceptions, the recipients of this transfer of wealth and power are political systems with little or no accountability to their own citizens, let alone to the world community."[20]

Ross reckoned the Gulf countries, including Iran and Iraq, had presided over a price increase of nearly 500 percent between 1973 and 1980.

They were earning *daily* rents of $400 million on costs of $8 million. And this despite the fact that the crude oil supplied was "unusable in its original form." Western buyers still had to transport it, refine it into products, distribute it, and market it. Primary-product exporters were now in the driver's seat. "It would be hard to recall when a worse bargain has been struck, and on such a scale," Ross griped.[21]

Among the ministers who founded OPEC—men who had prevailed against wildly unfair terms of the original concession agreements—these grievances must have sounded familiar. Importing countries sought recourse to the "OPEC stranglehold" through a host of emergency measures: conservation, technology switching, reinvigorated oil exploration outside OPEC's borders, and the stockpiling of crude in strategic petroleum reserves.

While most of the attention was focused on the importing world, transformative change was also taking place inside the exporting countries. Political scientists such as Seymour Lipset, Karl Deutsch, and Samuel Huntington had developed a theory that would be put to the test by the enrichment of Middle Eastern oil exporters. Termed "modernization theory," it predicted that, as the once-poor citizens of autocratic states gained wealth and stopped worrying about daily needs, their attention would turn to how they were being governed. Prosperity was a disruptive political force because it would trigger demands for political participation.

In other words, the $400-million-a-day windfall from the embargo would wreak havoc on autocratic petroregimes. According to the modernization thesis, it was only a matter of time before the sheikhs and sultans were toppled by citizens demanding a say in their own governance. The Arabs' rash embargo would backfire on its very authors, who would be dethroned before they could enjoy the new golden age. Huntington described a "king's dilemma." Absolute monarchs could bow out voluntarily, keeping scraps of their privilege as constitutional monarchs, or they could try to block modernization, using repression to hold onto power.[22]

Either way, predicted modernization theory, they were doomed.

4

FROM ENERGY POVERTY
TO ENERGY EXTREMISM

I n 1970, the American space program completed its seventh manned mission, and the Soviets landed a robot on the Moon. The ARPANET—the precursor to the internet—connected computers across North America. Doctors began using chemotherapy to stifle cancer. US life expectancy had grown from under sixty in 1930 to seventy-one by 1970, buoyed by improvements in public health and per capita income, which reached $5,000 per year in 1970, equivalent to $30,000 in 2016. America's middle class spent its weekends bowling, sipping Harvey Wallbangers at tiki bars, and guffawing over the antics on TV's *Laugh-In*.

In Oman, the advancements of the developed world sounded like science fiction. The capital city, Muscat, ringed by thick stone walls, had its gates locked after sundown.[1] Anyone wandering the city after dark was required to carry a kerosene lantern at eye level, for purposes of police identification.[2] The creeping poverty and isolation that afflicted Oman in the 1870s had ossified by 1970. Subsistence farmers still hacked out their timeless existence on narrow mountain terraces or on the coastal plains, using five-thousand-year-old *falaj* irrigation channels to sustain crops. Yearly per capita income was $350.[3] Even among urban Omanis, education beyond the Quran was nonexistent.[4] The country of 700,000 counted just three schools, supporting nine hundred children.

Life expectancy was an appalling forty-nine years. Oman only had two hospitals and fourteen doctors.[5]

Not only was there no TV or cocktails, there was no way to turn water into ice. The sultanate remained unelectrified well into the 1970s. Most Omanis got their energy from dung and firewood. In 1971, primary energy consumption for the country, including all commercial, industrial, and transport needs, amounted to the equivalent of 220 pounds of oil per person per year. In the United States that year, the equivalent figure was sixty-three times higher: more than 14,000 pounds.[6]

Oman was the most extreme and persistent case of pre-oil underdevelopment in the Gulf. It was the last of the Gulf monarchies to discover oil, finding it only in 1962. And because its oilfields were small and located far from the coast, exports got off to a slow start.[7] Oman's enigmatic ruler, Sultan Said bin Taimur, was a fundamental factor in Oman's underdevelopment. Outwardly, Sultan Said was polished and impressive. He could quote Shakespeare. He had traveled to Washington and met President Roosevelt. But at home, he purposefully kept his countrymen in the dark, preventing them from leaving the country or getting treatment for curable illnesses like trachoma and venereal disease.[8]

Said's prohibitions verged on the absurd. He forbade his subjects from installing bathrooms or gas stoves in their homes. Also banned were smoking, wearing glasses, watching movies, or playing drums or soccer. Carrying an umbrella or transistor radio warranted especially severe punishment. Ensconced in the ruler's palace since 1932, Said's survival instincts told him that if Omanis grew healthy, educated, and prosperous, they would throw him out. This was exactly what the era's modernization theorists—Lipset, Deutsch, and Huntington—had predicted. The sultan's British advisers agreed.[9]

The sultan had reason to fear unrest. A rising number of Omani citizens were indeed trying to vanquish him. A communist-inspired rebellion was underway in the southwestern Dhofar province, where an organized rebel army captured and governed territory. A British scholar who toured rebel territory described open-air schools teaching Mao's writings as a big improvement over opportunities in the rest of Oman.[10]

Omanis would be yanked into the modern age perhaps more quickly than any population on earth, but development wouldn't come as the result of a popular uprising that overthrew the monarchy. The driving force was oil wealth, combined with the impressive leadership feats of Sultan Said's only son, Qaboos.

Qaboos graduated from Britain's Sandhurst military academy in the early 1960s, served a year in the British infantry, and returned to Oman in 1964. Sultan Said welcomed his son home by clapping him under house arrest. Qaboos spent the next six years locked away in Sultan Said's palace with only his books and record collection for company. It gradually dawned on Said's British minders that young Qaboos would make a much better sultan. British officers helped the illustrious captive foment the coup in July 1970 that finally deposed Sultan Said.[11] The old sultan, wounded in the chaos of his own downfall, had to be airlifted out of the country by the British. Humiliated, he lived out his final two years in London's Dorchester Hotel.

The daunting task of modernizing Oman got a big push in 1973, when the Arab oil embargo tripled oil prices. Oman was producing 300,000 barrels per day, nearly all of it exported. The dynamic Sultan Qaboos wielded the windfall to push his country through one of the most concentrated transformations in world history. Qaboos managed to defeat or win over the communist rebels, educate and enrich his citizens, and build a national infrastructure that transformed and extended lives to developed-world levels in an astonishingly short period (see figure 4.1). Today's Oman is the most beautiful of the Gulf states, a Middle Eastern Switzerland of aesthetic modern settlements harmonized to their surroundings of date palm groves and ancient mountaintop fortresses.

How did Omanis respond to their newfound prosperity? According to modernization theory, they should have risen up and disrupted the political order. In fact, the opposite occurred. Prosperity in Oman reinvigorated the legitimacy of the Al Bu Said dynasty after the disastrous reign of Sultan Said. Sultan Qaboos's highly successful modernization had *reinforced* autocratic institutions, not undermined them.

In Abu Dhabi, a similar story was unfolding. Sheikh Shakhbut bin Sultan al-Nahyan maintained a comparable rule to Sultan Said, minus the absurdities. After discovering oil in 1958, Shakhbut strove to block

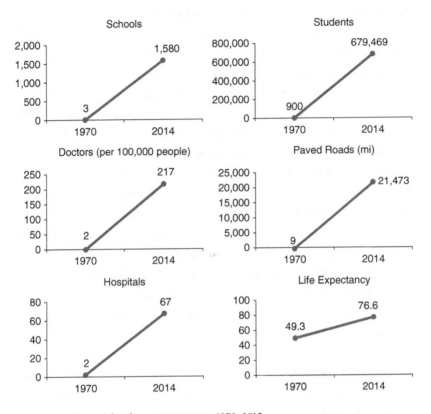

FIGURE 4.1 Omani development progress, 1970–2015.

Source: *Times of Oman*, November 17, 2015, http://timesofoman.com
/article/71936/Oman/45th-National-Day:-Oman-strides-forward.

modernization and maintain traditional rule. He was infamous for his distrust of banks and was widely rumored to use his mattress as the national treasury. Shakhbut's commitment to isolation was more than symbolic. Despite Abu Dhabi's location on an island, he refused to build a bridge to the mainland or road connections to neighboring emirates. Motorists from comparatively modern Dubai had to drive most of the hundred miles to Abu Dhabi along the beach. They could only ford the channel to the island at low tide.[12]

Shakhbut, too, was overthrown. His downfall came in 1966, at the hands of his younger brother, Zayed, also with British backing. Like

Sultan Qaboos, Sheikh Zayed quickly embarked upon building a modern state, shifting development into high gear and cementing his family in power. Abu Dhabi was finally connected to the mainland in 1967 and electrified in 1968, a few years before Oman but seven years after Dubai.[13]

While Abu Dhabi and Oman were extreme examples, development came extraordinarily quickly in each of the Gulf monarchies. Oil wealth, especially after 1973, provided traditional sheikhdoms with the capital to modernize into independent nation-states that could survive in a conflict-ridden part of the world. But what about traditional rule? Modernization theorists had predicted that wealth and development would drive the sheikhs out. Iran seemed to conform to the theory when it succumbed to revolution in 1979. But events didn't quite match the political scientists' playbook. As predicted, the absolute monarch—Shah Reza Pahlavi—was overthrown, and his former subjects did achieve a greater role in governance. But the shah wasn't replaced by a modernizing government. The new regime, led by a Shiite cleric, was a conservative theocracy that actually reversed aspects of the "Westernized" development pursued by the shah.

The predictive power of modernization theory was even less impressive in the case of Oman, Saudi Arabia, and the other Gulf monarchies. Rather than collapse, the Gulf ruling families used their expropriation of the global oil business to fortify control. With the possible exception of Kuwait, these countries became *more* autocratic as they developed, not less.

The crucial factor that modernization theory seemed to miss was that states had an alternative path for mainlining (and maintaining) power. With so much money coming in, sheikhs could simply *buy* citizens' support. And this, in the Gulf, was exactly what happened. Tribal sheikhs reinvigorated their tried-and-true patronage institutions with the proceeds of their oil revolutions. They held onto power not through repression or by blocking modernization—as theory predicted—but by spending oil rents to transform thoroughly and improve the lives of their subjects.

TAXES, RENTS, AND THE ROOTS OF SUBSIDIES

Throughout the Gulf monarchies, the 1973 oil windfall marked the beginning of a new approach to rule, one characterized by bountiful social welfare benefits. The sheikhs began to provide their subjects with land and homes. They distributed high-paying jobs in the bureaucracy, and they tilted foreign-investment laws to force foreign investors to give ownership shares to citizens. Prominent families—particularly those viewed as political opponents—were richly rewarded. Many of these received exclusive licenses to import and sell foreign goods—Toyota cars and trucks, Frigidaire refrigerators, Westinghouse air conditioners.[14]

The huge jump in oil rents in 1973 allowed Saudi Arabia to dismantle its tax bureaucracy. The kingdom liquidated much of its Department of Zakat and Income Tax and abolished the few taxes previously imposed on Saudi citizens, including cigarette taxes. The government even stopped collecting social insurance contributions. For good measure, the state abolished foreign residents' income taxes and gave foreign businesses a five-year tax holiday.[15] The bounteous oil wealth arriving from overseas meant that the state no longer needed to raise *any* income from society. Abolishing taxes allowed the Saudi government to preempt future "no taxation without representation" demands by Saudis interested in voting or otherwise getting involved in governance.

And, crucial for our story, kingdoms began to subsidize energy services such as water, electricity, and transportation fuel. What constitutes a subsidy? The IEA and OECD definitions say that subsidies are "any measure that keeps prices for consumers below market levels" and "any government action that concerns primarily the energy sector that lowers the cost of energy production, raises the price received by energy producers or lowers the price paid by energy consumers."[16] Perhaps the most applicable subsidy definition for this book is the "price gap," the difference between a commodity's local selling price and the price it would have fetched across the border—that is, its opportunity cost.[17] Table 4.1 shows overall outlays for the world's top-ten subsidy providers; all six Gulf countries make the list.[18]

TABLE 4.1 Energy subsidies in major energy exporters in 2015, ranked on per capita basis

	Oil (US$bn)	Gas (US$bn)	Coal (US$bn)	Electricity (US$bn)	Total subsidy 2015 (US$bn)	Total subsidy as share of GDP	Subsidy per capita (US$)
Kuwait	1.4	0.9	0.0	3.7	6.0	5%	1,547
Saudi Arabia	29.5	6.7	0.0	12.5	48.6	7%	1,542
Qatar	0.9	1.0	0.0	1.5	3.4	2%	1,508
Bahrain	0.4	0.0	0.0	1.2	1.7	6%	1,212
UAE	1.2	6.8	0.0	2.0	9.9	3%	1,082
Turkmenistan	2.2	2.4	0.0	0.9	5.5	15%	1,022
Libya	3.7	0.0	0.0	0.5	4.2	11%	668
Iran	20.9	17.9	0.0	13.6	52.4	14%	662
Venezuela	14.6	2.2	0.0	3.1	19.9	8%	641
Oman*	1.2	0.0	1.0	2.3	3%	$543	

*Oman's energy subsidy data was not differentiated by type of fuel.
Note: Subsidies are calculated using the price-gap method [international price − local price = opportunity cost/subsidy].

Source: IEA fossil-fuel subsidies database (2017), http://www.iea.org/statistics/resources/energysubsidies; Oman totals compiled from Central Bank of Oman 2015 Annual Report, http://www.cbo-oman.org/pub_annual.htm.

Subsidies for energy were partly spurred by the economic transformation that was underway. The regimes' energy munificence was also driven by their newfound control over new energy sources that became available after nationalization. For decades, natural gas had either been flared or vented as waste. Meanwhile, governments were building power grids and beginning to provide electricity to homes and businesses, mostly by burning diesel fuel. In some cases, that diesel fuel was imported at world prices because domestic refining capacity was insufficient or nonexistent.[19] Burning diesel made little sense when natural gas—a cleaner, cheaper, and more efficient power generation feedstock—was being wasted.

After nationalization, with NOCs in control, governments set about exploiting their gas bounty. They contracted for gas capture and distribution networks. Gas that had been flared or vented was instead burned as feedstock in power plants. The inefficient diesel-fired plants were relegated to use during periods of peak summer demand. The newly nationalized Saudi Aramco built its Master Gas System based on this principle.[20] With Saudi Aramco in control of the kingdom's natural gas, the venting of methane—a powerful greenhouse gas—plummeted. By capturing and burning fugitive methane, nationalization actually improved the kingdom's GHG footprint.[21]

Prices reflected the same logic. Since the surplus gas feedstock was essentially free—and otherwise too difficult to market overseas—consumers should not have to pay. Electricity prices needed only to cover costs of infrastructure, operations, and maintenance.[22] Stranded gas that had once gone to waste was thus used to develop these lightly populated states, providing improvements in lifestyle while shoring up political support for the ruling sheikhs.[23]

In 1979, oil prices rocketed upward once again, when the Iranian revolution reignited global alarm over oil supply. The Persian monarchy, convulsed by strikes and demonstrations, collapsed. Amid the chaos, Iranian oil exports of 3.7m b/d suddenly dropped to zero. The outage—a complete surprise—sent oil prices soaring for the second time in less than a decade. From $13 in 1979, oil reached $31 per barrel by the end of 1980.

Once again, importing countries scrambled to unwind their oil dependence, and unprecedented sums flooded the treasuries of oil-producing countries. These rents were the crucial factor that ensured the survival of the Gulf's tribal forms of governance.[24] Rents bankrolled the creation of the welfare state and the bureaucracy, paying for government jobs and welfare benefits that kept citizens loyal to their ruling sheikhs. In the most basic sense, rents turned public support into political stability. Crucially, oil rents colored policy makers' understanding of domestic energy. With a few strategic investments, ruling elites saw they could convert surplus energy into a tool for political control. So when international oil prices reached historic highs in 1979, prices in the Gulf did not budge. Paying through the nose for energy was considered a burden for importing countries, not for producers.

Besides placating the population, cheap energy was useful in attracting foreign investment and ramping up national development.[25] In the Gulf, ruling sheikhs used cheap energy to incubate domestic industry, to convince foreign businesses to open local franchises, and to lure in skilled expatriates who could operate new commercial sectors. All would receive cheap or free electricity and fuel.

RENTIER THEORY

As it became clear that *khaleejis* were not agitating for elections, scholars recognized that modernization theory would not help explain the region's stubborn lack of democracy and started looking for alternative theories to understand and explain the region's curious form of development.

One popular explanation at the time for why the Middle East remained a bastion of autocracy was that "political culture" was to blame. Political culture theories held that Arab states were hopelessly prone to autocracy because of patrimonial or "morally obtuse" tendencies of tribalism or Islam. Many Western scholars concluded that "immature" Arab societies simply weren't ready for democracy.[26]

Another theory, the one many still use to understand the region today, focused on the unique style of development provided by oil riches. In a 1987 edited volume titled *The Rentier State*, the economists Hazem Beblawi and Giacomo Luciani boldly declared that the massive transfer of wealth to oil states had brought about a new form of state-society relations. These were not typical "productive" economies that collected taxes from citizens and redistributed the proceeds in the form of services. The Gulf monarchies were "allocative" economies—rentier states—where the national treasury was funded by oil rents from overseas. Services were provided, but there was no need to extract taxes to pay for them. The gush of oil rents, particularly after the 1973 embargo and nationalization, left the state in command of nearly all national wealth—wealth it used to buy political support.

According to this new rentier theory, the exchange of welfare benefits for political support was enshrined in an unwritten social contract between state and society. As long as the populace received a generous share of the oil proceeds, ruling would be left to the rulers. Avoiding taxation was key. Taxes were well understood as a bedrock element of democracy. Societies that paid taxes tended to maintain an interest in how their contributions are spent. Taxes thus created an *accountability link* between governments and taxpayers, constraining the autonomy of governing authorities.[27]

Democracy failed to gain traction in rentier states because autocrats wielded rent streams to block it. Governance grew more centralized and autocratic.[28] Groups that held political power in the pre-oil past, such as merchants and rival tribes, saw their political functions relinquished in return for a share of the wealth.[29] Oil rents quashed the few tenuous advances toward democracy and funded the complex distributive welfare states of today.[30]

Compared with the ethical contortions of political culture, rentierism offered refreshing simplicity. Support for autocracy was based on citizens' economic self-interest. The welfare states of the Gulf became the envy of the developing world. People whose ancestors had scraped by through the millennia found their lifespans extended by decades. They were showered with modern comforts: air-conditioned homes, paved roads, and modern medicine. They were better educated, healthier, and wealthier. Who wouldn't support rulers who brought such positive change?

In the Gulf, cheap energy became part of the rentier playbook for fending off democratic pressure. Subsidies also came about for another reason. They are easy. Rentier states like those in the Gulf do not have strong administrative tools to operate complex social policies. Countries that do not tax their citizens lack the means to collect income data. They cannot easily divide society into those who need government help and those who don't. Taxation creates institutional depth, that is, a knowledge of society that allows for equitable redistribution. Rentier states forfeit this capacity. In these countries, subsidies are pervasive because there are few other mechanisms for governments to spread the largesse.[31]

Early rentierism turned out to be enormously successful. For the most part, ruling families enjoyed genuine legitimacy. But once the governing institutions of the rentier state were established, they proved hard to change. Where one generation was grateful for the state's antipoverty benefits, the next claimed them as entitlements. As people grew wealthy, they no longer needed subsidized gasoline or electricity. But the state kept providing energy benefits and much more besides. Once the precedent was established, the governance bargain seemed to dictate that these benefits were sacrosanct. Subsidies, ruling families learned, are sticky: easy to hand out, much tougher to retract.

Something similar took place in the academic realm. Rentier theory's explanatory power obscured a fundamental flaw. Subsidizing energy would ignite demand to such an extent that rent-based politics would compete with the rent-based economy for the same resources.

5

UNNATURALLY COOL

The story until now has been inspirational: a Horatio Alger tale of rags to riches on a regional scale and at breakneck pace. But this book's central argument is not that oil brought prosperity to a destitute people but that those once-deprived societies have become exceptionally wasteful, particularly with the one commodity their livelihoods depend on.

The Gulf monarchies did not just mutate from minor consumers into *average* consumers of oil and gas. The six Gulf ruling families unwittingly engaged in political practices that would lead their societies to become some of the most energy intensive on earth. As the oil they exported became more important as an input in their domestic economies, the political structures that kept the old families in control would become unwieldy.

As we will explore in chapter 6, what was not apparent at the time—to policy makers or regional scholars—was the crucial distinction between the distribution of *rents* and the giving away of in-kind *resources*. Over the next four decades, growth in domestic energy demand would begin to threaten Gulf monarchies' ability to export oil—and exportation was and is the backbone of both the economy and the political system.

The drastic changes in demand took place not over many generations but within the lifetimes of citizens who still inhabit these countries today.

In Dubai, I met with Mohammed Alabbar, one of twelve children raised by illiterate parents in a palm-thatch *barasti* hut. His mother cooked the family's meals over a fire. Alabbar grew up poor, and his upbringing in the 1950s and 1960s was far from unique.

Since there were few roads or vehicles in Dubai and no electricity or running water, there was no demand for modern energy services. Petroleum was imported and used sparingly. Kerosene was reserved for lamps that illuminated homes. Precious fresh water was stored in earthen jars, which kept it chilled through evaporative cooling. Toilets—even those in the ruler's compound—were pits dug into the sandy earth. Clean water was in such short supply that people bathed in the sea.

Homes of wealthier residents of Dubai and other coastal towns featured the natural cooling of the *barjeel*, the ubiquitous wind towers that captured passing breezes and funneled them indoors. Alabbar's family *barasti* had no such luxury. The loose weave of the palm thatch allowed breezes to penetrate.

But as he grew up, oil wealth flowed in. Alabbar became a successful property developer, paving the desert around him with cookie-cutter townhomes and shopping centers. In 2004, he started work on the Burj Khalifa, which would become the tallest building in the world—so tall that visitors to its observation deck can see all the way to Iran. Next door to the Burj Khalifa is another of his projects, the Dubai Mall, one of the world's largest. Alabbar upgraded his own accommodations too, trading the shack of his boyhood for a vast mansion with a six-hole golf course on its grounds. By the time I met him, he was a billionaire.

The growth in Alabbar's personal energy use over the course of a single lifetime was a microcosm of the city around him. His energy demand grew from tiny scraps of biomass and small amounts of water from an underground aquifer to enormous amounts of natural gas–generated electricity and fresh water produced via the energy-intensive process of desalinating seawater. The Burj Khalifa was probably the biggest single addition to the Dubai power grid, with an electricity load so massive it required a dedicated substation, the world's highest, on the 155th floor.[1] Every time someone flushes a toilet on the Burj's upper floors, electric pumps must push desalinated water nearly a kilometer into the sky to refill the tank.

The story of energy demand in the Gulf monarchies was Alabbar's story, writ large. A hydrocarbon society spread across the Arabian Desert, enabled by huge rent windfalls and a government that incorporated the distribution of fossil fuels into its social welfare practices. The subsidies for water, electricity, and fuel that helped jumpstart modernization also encouraged the kind of growth that used these resources intensively and with no concern for efficiency.

As development proceeded, the old ways became distant memories. No one planned the location of a home to maximize the cooling effects of shade or sea breezes anymore. Every structure was air conditioned, right down to curbside bus shelters.[2] Air conditioning became a crucial component in luring in expatriate managers with technical skills as well as foreign investors, tourists, and conventioneers. As the Gulf grew wealthy, citizens once able to cope with withering heat grew accustomed to over-chilled homes and offices.

Water, too, was suddenly in abundance. Indoor plumbing was installed in homes, but that was just the beginning. Houses had gotten much larger, and many had lawns, leafy gardens, and swimming pools. The desert cities of Doha, Muscat, Dubai, Kuwait City, and Abu Dhabi turned green, studded with golf courses, horse paddocks, and boulevards shaded by date palms and lined with flower gardens. This water was procured through intensive energy use; the Gulf produced most of it by burning oil and gas to distill fresh water from the salty sea.

For those in energy-importing countries, good times in the Gulf contrasted deeply with the realities they now faced.

THIRST FOR OIL

In February 1977, a somber President Jimmy Carter addressed the American public on television. Sitting in an armchair, with a roaring fire in the hearth next to him, Carter wore a beige cardigan instead of his usual buttoned-up suit. The president's choice of haberdashery was no accident. He had a message for Americans coping with the twin challenges of an extremely cold winter and high, postembargo energy prices: change your behavior. The president urged his countrymen to cut their use of energy by turning down the thermostat and donning a sweater.

"The amount of energy being wasted which could be saved is greater than the total energy that we are importing from foreign countries," Carter admonished, leaning forward in his armchair. He asked utilities to "promote conservation and not consumption" and told companies to shoulder the burden alongside citizens. Thrift and efficiency were his buzzwords. "There is no way that I, or anyone else in the government, can solve our energy problems if you are not willing to help," the president said. "All of us must learn to waste less energy. Simply by keeping our thermostats, for instance, at 65 degrees in the daytime and 55 degrees at night we could save half the current shortage of natural gas." Carter was pushing on an open door. High prices were already undermining oil demand in the United States, inspiring conservation and efficiency. People not only endured uncomfortable indoor temperatures, but they insulated their homes and invested in more efficient capital equipment, swapping the gasoline-guzzling Cadillac for a fuel-sipping Toyota.

The 1979 Iranian Revolution sent oil prices soaring again, and this reinforced the behavioral changes already underway. Fuel switching became a global movement. Homeowners scrapped furnaces that burned expensive heating oil and switched to natural gas. Where gas was unavailable, they turned to woodstoves. Governments around the world did the same thing on a macro scale. Much of Western Europe scrambled for nuclear power. France leveraged the brainpower of its engineering class, enabling it to generate 80 percent of its electricity via nuclear reactor. Japan and South Korea also went nuclear. America did too, while revitalizing coal and natural gas. Solar panels began to appear on rooftops, including that of the Carter White House.

When the dust settled from the Iranian Revolution, world oil demand had dropped by 10 percent, the largest amount in modern history, from 64m b/d in 1979 to under 58m b/d in 1983. The biggest changes in demand didn't stem from temporary adjustments of the thermostat but from structural reductions based on investment in alternate fuels and more efficient capital equipment—Toyotas, wall-cavity insulation, and nuclear power. Oil had been pushed out of the electricity sector completely—with the exception of the small island states, where there was no other option, and the Middle East, where it was subsidized. But while demand for oil slackened elsewhere, in the Gulf it grew profoundly. In 1973, oil consumption in the Gulf was less than 500,000 b/d, or less than 1 percent of the world total. Forty years later, the Gulf states, with just 0.5 percent of the world's population, consumed 6 percent of humanity's oil, 6m b/d.

Growth in energy demand is normal in countries undergoing industrialization. Japan, China, Germany, and South Korea all displayed fast energy-demand growth rates during their boom years. But while the energy boom years in Japan, Germany, or China lasted a decade or maybe two, the fast pace of demand in the Gulf has continued to build for nearly a half-century (see table 5.1).

Put in context, the Gulf monarchies now get through more oil than Japan, India, Russia—or the entire continent of Africa.[3] This huge growth

TABLE 5.1 Average yearly growth, 1971–2015

	Primary energy demand	Oil demand only
UAE	9.5% per year	11.3% per year
Qatar	8.9%	11.1%
Oman	13.4%	10.6%
Saudi Arabia	10.1%	9.4%
Bahrain	7.2%	7.4%
China	4.0%	6.1%
South Korea	6.0%	5.8%
Kuwait	3.8%	5.2%
USA	0.5%	0.4%
Japan	0.9%	0.1%
Germany	0.0%	−0.5%

Source: International Energy Agency, "World Energy Balances," statistics database (Paris: IEA, 2018).

in demand means that nearly a quarter of GCC oil production is now diverted to domestic use. At the time of the 1973 oil spike, that figure was around 4 percent. The German economist Eckart Woertz describes it succinctly: "The region is not only the world's petrol station; it has also become its own best customer."[4] Despite the implications of regional demand displacing exports from the world's foremost energy supply region, this growth in consumption went unnoticed until 2008, when the International Energy Agency released a special report declaring the need to come to grips with this "under-anticipated" trend.[5]

Growth may have slipped under the radar because Middle Eastern hydrocarbon reserves are big enough to produce for many more decades. Saudi Arabia's oil-reserves-to-production ratio (the length of time proven reserves can produce at current rates) stood at 59 years in 2017. The UAE had 66 years remaining; Kuwait had 88. Qatari oil reserves were at a modest 36 years, but Qatar has enough gas to produce at 2017 levels for 134 years.[6] Underground reserves, as we will see, are of little help to a government giving away its production.

The stakes are highest in Saudi Arabia, which consumed 3.9m b/d in 2017, a third of all the oil and natural gas liquids it produced that year.

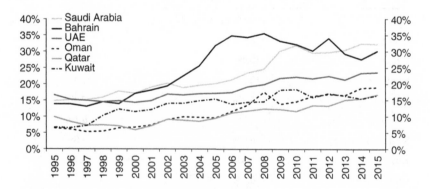

FIGURE 5.1 Domestic oil consumption as a percentage of domestic oil production, 1995–2016. Includes natural gas liquids, or NGLs.

Source: BP, *Statistical Review of World Energy 2017* (London: BP, 2017); IEA Oil Information database, International Energy Agency, Paris, 2018.

Twenty years ago, when output was substantially lower, the kingdom consumed 15 percent of its production (figure 5.1).

Saudi Arabia has vaulted up the ranks of global oil consumers. In 2016, the kingdom was the world's fifth-largest oil consumer, despite a population that ranked forty-seventh. That same year, oil demand in Saudi Arabia surpassed that of Russia, the world's largest country by area and a peer oil producer with a much larger population and economy (see table 5.2).

Saudi Arabia's oil consumption has grown at nearly the same pace as that of India, the world's third-largest consumer and a fast-developing behemoth with 1.3 billion people and an economy more than three times the size of Saudi Arabia's. Saudi oil consumption is approaching that of the world's fourth-highest consumer, Japan, which has a highly developed industrial and manufacturing economy. Among all the world's countries, in fact, only China (ranking second) and the United States (ranking first) consume significantly more oil than Saudi Arabia.

A major reason Saudi consumption is so high is because, while crude oil and diesel have long been banished from the power sector nearly everywhere else, the kingdom still burns oil to generate electricity. During the summer months, the Saudis burn an average of 700,000 b/d[7] and sometimes as much as 900,000 b/d.[8] That's an enormous amount, equal to the average daily consumption for the entire country of Turkey.

These stunning summer numbers stem from the region's ubiquitous air conditioners, which account for the lion's share of electricity consumed—around 70 percent of total power.[9] Electrification came so late in the Gulf that older residents remember the days before air conditioning, when they slept outdoors to stay cool. From a base of nearly zero, electricity demand quickly grew to lead the world.

Residents of Kuwait, Qatar, Saudi Arabia, and the UAE consume more electricity, on average, than Americans (see figure 5.2)—and the vast majority of this power is generated by fossil fuels. Generation growth averaged 10 percent per year between 1973 and 1999, slipping to 7 percent per year between 2000 and 2010, which was slightly faster than the average GDP growth that decade of 6.5 percent.

TABLE 5.2 The world's largest oil consumers

	Oil consumption rank	Oil consumed 2016 (MMb/d)	GDP 2016 (billion US$)	Population 2016 (million)	Oil consumption per capita (bbl/year)
USA	1	19.6	16,866	323.1	22.2
China	2	12.4	9,505	1378.7	3.3
India	3	4.5	2,465	1324.2	1.2
Japan	4	4	6,046	127	11.6
Saudi Arabia	5	3.9	691	32.3	44.2
Russia	6	3.2	1,628	144.3	8.1
Brazil	7	3	2,248	207.7	5.3
South Korea	8	2.8	1,305	51.2	19.7
Germany	9	2.4	3,766	82.7	10.6
UAE	25	1.0	379	9.3	38.9
Kuwait	38	0.5	143	4.1	44.9
Qatar	45	0.3	171	2.6	48.2

Source: "Worldwide Governance Indicators," interactive dataset (Washington: World Bank, 2017), http://info.worldbank.org/governance/wgi/. BP, *Statistical Review of World Energy 2017* (London: BP, 2017)

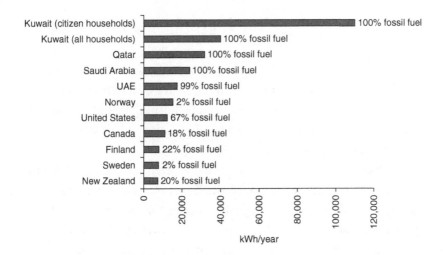

FIGURE 5.2 Top ten countries ranked by 2014 household electricity demand.

Kuwait's average household consumption in 2016 (foreign and citizen customers) is provided alongside that of citizen households only. Among the top ten, only the Gulf monarchies and the United States consumed electricity that was generated predominantly by fossil fuels. Fossil fuel proportion is for 2014 or 2015.

Sources: Consumption data: World Energy Council 2016, Kuwait Ministry of Electricity and Water; World Bank World Development Indicators database (2017).

In Kuwait, power demand in citizen homes has reached levels that beggar belief. A typical Kuwaiti family occupies a 6,000-square-foot villa, with live-in staff and sometimes an extended family. In such homes, average consumption is 110,000 kWh per year,[10] more than *nine times* the average US household demand of 12,000 kWh/y and an incredible *thirty-six times* the power consumed by the average German household, which uses just over 3,000 kWh/y.[11] Kuwaiti citizen households alone consume 48 percent of the country's *total* electricity output, far outpacing the more numerous expatriates (17 percent) as well as the commercial/governmental sector (28 percent) and industrial users (7 percent).

The seasonality of demand, with huge summer peaks that might see twice as much consumed as in winter, adds to the expense of power generation in the Gulf by mandating investment in infrastructure that is only used a few months per year.

FOSSIL-FUELED DEMAND

While the Gulf is one of the few regions still to use oil for electricity, it doesn't rely only, or even mostly, on oil. In 2018, more than 99 percent of electricity in the Gulf was generated by burning fossil fuels: 40 percent from liquid fuels such as crude oil, diesel, and heavy fuel oil and 60 percent from natural gas.[12]

The perceived value of natural gas has evolved considerably from the days it was considered a nuisance and flared off. Over time, associated gas (gas found alongside oil deposits) became the central source of supply for the power sector and an important industrial feedstock. For more than thirty years, there was plenty of domestic associated gas to meet the growing demand for electricity and desalinated water in all of the Gulf monarchies.

Gas took on a role akin to that of a Hollywood stuntman: performing dramatic roles but getting little of the credit. Oil provided the rents that underpinned state budgets, but natural gas was the workhorse that enabled the expansion of the air-conditioned and water-intensive lifestyle in the region's homes, malls, and offices. Put simply, natural gas made the searing Gulf fit for modern human habitation.

As with oil, the Gulf monarchies represent a world-class repository of natural gas. The six GCC states alone harbor a more than a fifth of the world's conventional gas reserves. Add in Iran and Iraq, and the share rises to beyond 40 percent of the world's known supply, roughly 80 trillion cubic meters (see table 5.3).

Despite these abundant reserves, the Gulf is a bit player in the global gas trade. Saudi Arabia exports no natural gas whatsoever, and even Iran, which holds more reserves than any other country in the world, exports very little. Qatar is the only real Gulf participant in global gas markets; boasting the third-largest reserves in the world, it was the second-largest exporter in 2015.[13]

The remaining five monarchies produced 217 billion cubic meters (bcm) in 2016 and consumed even more, 227 bcm, which meant they *imported* 10 bcm. The UAE and Kuwait are the main sources of this

TABLE 5.3 Gas reserves in the region

Natural gas reserves of the Gulf and Arabian Peninsula	Size (Tcm)	Share of world total
Iran	33.5	18.0%
Qatar	24.3	13.0%
Saudi Arabia	8.4	4.5%
UAE	6.1	3.3%
Iraq	3.7	2.0%
Kuwait	1.8	1.0%
Oman	0.7	0.4%
Yemen	0.3	0.1%
Bahrain	0.2	0.1%
GCC total	41.5	22.2%
Region total	79.4	42.5%
World total	186.6	100%

Source: BP, Statistical Review of World Energy 2017 (London: BP, 2017).

imbalance. With ever-larger domestic needs in power generation, desalination, and industry, they became net gas importers in 2008. As the UAE and Kuwait prepared themselves to import gas, the IEA warned the world that the Gulf region had transformed itself into a major energy-consuming region and that the supply of cheap associated gas that helped lead development had run its course.[14]

How did some Gulf countries get to the point of becoming net *importers*—an idea that would have seemed absurd half a century ago?

WHAT CAUSES HIGH DEMAND?

Basic energy economics teaches us that energy demand is a factor of a handful of variables: population, income, technology, climate, and price.

Population growth in the Gulf has been a big factor. The number of inhabitants has quintupled over four decades, as a result of high birth-rates and large-scale immigration. Combined population in the six states rose from 8.2m in 1971 to 54m in 2016, an annual growth rate of 4.3 percent—nearly triple the global average.

Rising individual income is another key predictor of demand growth. When incomes rise, people buy more energy-consuming devices and can afford more fuel and energy services. In the Gulf, income growth has compounded the effect of rising population. Per capita GDP in the Gulf has grown by an average of 2.2 percent per year since 1981. Since 2000, the rise in oil prices drove up per capita incomes by an average of 4.9 percent per year (see table 5.4).[15]

The effects of the hot and humid climate in the Gulf also play a role, especially in encouraging the use of air conditioning. The climate hasn't changed much over time, but in combination with rising populations and incomes, preferences have. Residents now have the money and the inclination to buy air conditioners and swimming-pool pumps, and large-scale immigration has brought new arrivals with lower heat tolerance.

TABLE 5.4 Growth in GDP per capita and oil demand since 1971

	GDP per capita 1971 (curr US$)	GDP per capita 2016 (curr US$)	Yearly growth rate	Oil demand 1971 (Mb/d)	Oil demand 2015	Yearly growth rate
Bahrain	$8,584*	$22,354	2.7%	15	64	3.3%
Kuwait	$4,784	$28,975***	4.2%	70	435	4.2%
Oman	$397	$14,982	8.4%	25	187	4.7%
Qatar	$3,280	$59,331	6.6%	2	252	11.5%
Saudi Arabia	$1,127	$20,029	6.6%	307	3,415	5.6%
UAE	$27,590**	$37,622	0.8%	3	835	13.6%

Source: "Worldwide Governance Indicators," interactive dataset (Washington: World Bank, 2017), http://info.worldbank.org/governance/wgi/. International Energy Agency, "Oil Information" (Statistics database, Paris: IEA, 2017). (*1980, **1975, ***2015)

The Gulf's broadening industrial structure also contributes, given the profusion of energy-intensive businesses in petrochemicals, fertilizer, and aluminum, along with the oil and gas sectors themselves. In Qatar, for example, the energy-intensive process of converting gaseous methane into liquefied natural gas (LNG) for export has added a huge source of energy demand.

Even the hydrology of the Arabian Peninsula influences energy use. There isn't a single natural river or lake on the peninsula and virtually no perennial surface water that is drinkable. Since so much of the Gulf's fresh water is produced through energy-intensive seawater desalination, water consumption is more directly tied to energy in the Gulf than almost anywhere else.

Another reason that the Gulf monarchies consume so much oil and gas is because it is readily available from local sources owned by the state and because the cost of production is low.

All these factors contribute to the high rates of demand in the Gulf. But it is *prices*—set at low, subsidized levels by the state—that play the biggest role. Energy prices affect demand in three important ways. First, prices directly influence consumers' decisions about how much fuel, electricity, or water they are willing to buy. When prices are low, people buy more—sometimes deliberately, sometimes through careless behavior. Low electricity prices enable residents to afford more indoor cooling, either by acquiring a larger home or opting for colder indoor temperatures on hot days, or both. Cheaper water allows consumers to splash out, by installing swimming pools or water-intensive gardens. Cheaper fuels enable poorer people to drive personal vehicles when they might otherwise opt for public transport.

Second, prices affect demand in an indirect way, by influencing purchases of energy-consuming equipment and its level of efficiency. When energy prices are low, consumers have little incentive to replace low-efficiency air conditioners or dishwashers or to buy high-efficiency appliances in the first place. Same goes for vehicles. As in America, when gasoline prices run low, vehicle sizes run large.

Third, low prices also allow people to operate energy-consuming equipment more often. Rather than running your swimming pool pump for three hours, you can run it for eight hours. Motorists can drive more often, commute longer distances, or leave their vehicles running (with the a/c on) while they shop.[16]

In the oil-importing world, the high prices of the 1970s transformed consumption, steering consumers toward more energy-efficient equipment and behavior. But in the Gulf, residents received the opposite message. When international oil prices were high, Gulf rulers awash in windfall oil rents often took the opportunity to spread the wealth. They granted even deeper discounts on electricity and fuel prices that were already divorced from reality. Later, when international prices fell, cash-strapped Gulf governments bent over backward to maintain fixed energy prices and hold up their end of the social contract.

In short, regimes shielded their people from pricing signals. There was no downsizing, no insulating of homes, no technology upgrades, and no fuel switching because there was no local understanding of the true value of the energy on offer. Generous welfare benefit schemes, which included subsidized water, electricity, and fuel, were important components in rulers' plans to jumpstart growth during the nationalization period. But subsidies also encouraged demand for the resources themselves, which were sold at prices that allowed consumers to use energy without concern for efficiency or the environment—or really without much thought at all.

Rising incomes in oil-exporting countries would have ignited energy consumption on their own. The combination of incredible income growth and low, fixed prices created extraordinarily fertile conditions for demand growth. For the onetime nomads who had conditioned themselves for survival in one of the earth's harshest environments, it was time to relax. "There was a feeling that after a long period of deprivation and poverty it was about time that we enjoyed ourselves," says Abdulkhaleq Abdulla, an Emirati political scientist. "The government's duty was to establish the best subsidized welfare system on earth."[17]

As time wore on, state-owned utilities found themselves trapped in a game of catch-up, making continuous capital investments to meet galloping electricity demand. As expenditures rose, fixed tariffs recovered fewer and fewer of the increasing costs involved in providing power. The subsidy portion grew over time to become a major burden on government budgets.

While the initial motivations were sound, the system of energy pricing in the Gulf lacked foresight. Once fixed, prices that might have covered costs in the 1970s or 1980s stagnated or were reduced. Bahraini electricity prices started out in 1961 at 10 fils (2.7 US cents) per kilowatt-hour (kWh) and were cut in half in 1974 after the oil embargo produced windfall profits.[18] By 2005, Bahrain was selling power for an average of 5.4 fils per kWh, less than half of its breakeven cost (13.5 fils).[19]

Residential electricity prices in Saudi Arabia have been reduced six times since 1950. By 2015, Saudi electricity sales revenue covered just 17 percent of costs.[20] Kuwait was even worse off. Electricity costs have been fixed at 2 fils (0.7 US cents) per kWh since 1966; by the Kuwaiti government's own estimates, customer payments in 2017 covered less than 5 percent of the cost of providing electricity.[21] Transportation fuel prices followed the same trajectory. None of the Gulf states indexed prices to inflation. Saudi Arabia actually reduced gasoline prices twice, first in 1992 and again in 2006, when policy makers felt that high oil revenues required a grand gesture from the king.

Over time, the gap between sales revenues and the cost of provision of energy products grew into a chasm. By 2014, spending on energy subsidies reached 9.5 percent of GDP in Saudi Arabia, 4.4 percent in the UAE, 5 percent in Kuwait, and 9 percent in Oman.[22] As a portion of the total economy, that's more than the 3.3 percent of GDP that the United States spent on defense in 2015. Gulf citizens often had no idea that the government was paying for their energy benefits.

The downside of subsidies went well beyond the expense and difficulty of expunging them. For oil exporters, subsidizing oil amounted to economic cannibalism. On average in the Gulf, oil export revenues cover roughly 80 percent of government budgets and provide about 40 percent of GDP. Subsidies threatened that revenue stream by encouraging domestic demand for oil—oil that would fetch a much higher price abroad. The revenue lost by distributing oil at home rather than selling it abroad is its opportunity cost. For Saudi Arabia, the opportunity cost of subsidizing oil at home can be enormous. It was nearly $30 billion in 2015 and even more the previous year, when international prices were higher (table 4.1). At times when oil production was flat, growth in domestic demand inevitably meant diverting exportable crude into the domestic market. The opportunity cost of domestic consumption rose for each tanker that wasn't loaded and sent steaming through the Strait of Hormuz.

For regimes reliant on oil rents to stay in power, this was a pyramid scheme. Trading away exports in favor of domestic consumption began to strangle the rent stream. As figure 5.3 shows, the process played out in a self-reinforcing loop of negative feedback. Practices meant to bring political legitimacy to the regime undermined the economy, which, in turn, undermined the regime's wherewithal to maintain political legitimacy.[23] The rentier governance practices of the 1970s had become a big problem.

But oil exports are not only the linchpin of the economy and political systems; they are also the region's biggest strategic asset. Crude exports

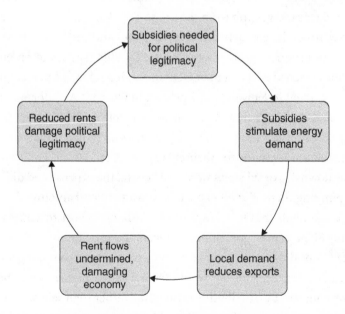

FIGURE 5.3 The negative feedback loop created by subsidizing energy in autocratic petrostates.

provide the foundation for strong relations with the United States, which come with significant security benefits. America spends $50 to $100 billion a year to protect the Gulf monarchies from external threats.[24] In return, the Gulf states are expected to keep the global economy supplied with oil.

For Saudi Arabia, spare oil production capacity is an important strategic asset, which plays a key role in maintaining US interest and support. If Saudi domestic consumption eats the kingdom's spare capacity, Washington may grow less willing to maintain its side of the oil-for-security arrangement,[25] exposing Saudi Arabia and the other monarchies to the vagaries of unshielded competition with unfriendly neighbors like Iran as well as nonstate Islamist opponents that command some internal support. High demand has security implications as well.

The early decisions by the Gulf monarchies to provide heavily subsidized energy triggered a process of path dependence, which placed the region on a downhill track to energy intensity. All sectors contributed to the growth in demand. Investors seized competitive advantage by moving energy-intensive industries to the Gulf. High-paying jobs and the low cost of living attracted foreigners, enlarging the population. Planners given swatches of empty desert designed low-density cities of big homes and spacious and inefficient office buildings based on assumptions of cheap energy. Cheap energy allowed developers to cut costs on building materials and disregard public transport in favor of personal vehicles. Over time, high individual rates of consumption were locked in.

A HYPOTHETICAL PRICE INCREASE

How can we be sure that it's low prices and not the other factors mentioned that are the main driver behind the Gulf's energy-demand quandary? One way to test this hypothesis is by comparing demand in two places with many similarities but where prices are different.

Take Abu Dhabi and Arizona. Both have hot climates (average temperature 81°F [27°C] in Abu Dhabi and 75° F [24°C] in Phoenix) and high incomes (2016 GDP per capita of $98,000 in Abu Dhabi is still more than double the $40,000 in Arizona). Comparing Abu Dhabi and Arizona allows us to isolate the effects of price, since income and climate are similar. Any large differences in per capita electricity demand must be caused by something else—probably different price levels. Indeed, electricity prices in these two places are *very* different. Arizonans paid an average of 9.7 cents per kilowatt hour (kWh)—about seven times as much as Abu Dhabi nationals, who paid just 1.4 cents, and a bit more than twice as much as expatriate residents in Abu Dhabi, who paid 4.1 cents.

How important are prices to demand for electricity? Since my hypothesis is that prices play a *large* role in consumption behavior, we should see a large discrepancy among demand in Arizona when compared with the two customer groups in Abu Dhabi.

Again, there are *huge* differences in consumption. Arizona households consume just a *fifth* as much electricity as households made up of Abu Dhabi nationals and about half as much as expatriate homes in Abu Dhabi. The demand differentials roughly correlate with the pricing differentials. And, despite consuming so much less electricity, the average Arizona household paid a higher annual bill than its typical counterpart in Abu Dhabi.[26]

These very simple results suggest that prices are a major influencing factor on decisions to consume electricity.

What if we wanted to quantify the effect of price? We could try an experiment: what would happen to electricity demand in Abu Dhabi if prices were increased to Arizona levels? To answer this question, we first need to determine how sensitive Abu Dhabi's electricity use is to prices. In other words, will Abu Dhabi households use less energy if prices go up, or will they simply pay more money and maintain the same usage?

Economists believe that energy demand is resistant to price increases in the short run, since energy products like electricity have few substitutes. Rates of consumption are linked to existing infrastructure, which itself is based on past energy prices. If your house has an inefficient air-conditioning system, it isn't easy to reduce your exposure to a rate increase without feeling uncomfortably warm. Over time, however, energy demand is more elastic. When the time comes to replace your a/c system, higher utility bills might prompt you to upgrade to more efficient technology. Given time, consumers and product developers find ways to economize.

However, many economists remain skeptical that price increases in the wealthy Gulf would be sufficient to reduce energy demand. They expect that high personal incomes would enable consumers to pay more without adjusting consumption. In the jargon of economists, the price and income elasticity of energy demand is assumed to be low.[27] A 100 percent increase in price would have a smaller corresponding effect on demand, which might only drop by, say, 30 percent.

Let's assume this relatively low estimate of price elasticity, expressed as a ratio of 1 to −0.3 (this is within the range of estimates deemed realistic among energy scholars), is basically correct and calculate how demand might then respond to price increases.[28] Abu Dhabi nationals were paying about one-seventh the price paid by Arizonans. Using our price-elasticity ratio of 1 to −0.3, this indicates that if prices were raised to Arizona levels, demand will decrease from 71,000 kWh/year to 40,000 kWh/y. That's a 44 percent decrease—a substantial drop, but it still leaves Abu Dhabi nationals consuming almost triple the 14,000 kWh/y in Arizona. For Abu Dhabi expatriates, who are only paying half as much as Arizonans, demand would drop by about a quarter, from 26,500 to 20,000 kWh/y—still above but closer to Arizona's energy use.

This suggests that, while price contributes considerably to demand, at least three other factors are also important. First, while average temperatures and incomes are similar between the two places, they are both higher in Abu Dhabi. Second, homes and households are typically much larger among Emirati nationals, since they often house domestic workers and extended families. Arizonans' homes and those of expatriates are smaller on average. Both these would help explain higher demand even in the face of equalized unit costs. Simply put, people in Abu Dhabi can afford more electricity, and they need more both because it is hotter and because their houses are bigger.

There is a third factor that would hinder Abu Dhabi's demand from fully adjusting downward: path dependence.[29] Over time, low prices have locked in higher demand *structurally*. For instance, because of higher energy prices, homes and buildings in Arizona are built with energy efficiency in mind. Most in Abu Dhabi are not. They typically lack insulation, efficient controls, shading, and energy-saving appliances. Even if an Abu Dhabi resident behaved in exactly the same way as an Arizona resident, she would consume more electricity.

Table 5.5 extends this method across energy products in the Gulf. It shows reductions in long-run demand that might be expected from raising fixed prices to world market levels. The hypotheticals provide some interesting findings. Kuwaitis undergoing a massive price increase to recoup the full costs of their oil-generated electricity might reduce their consumption by as much as 59 percent. While such a huge increase in price is unlikely, this calculation is useful in showing how

TABLE 5.5 Possible reductions in long-term demand

	Price (US$)	Unsubsidized price (US$)	% price increase to displace subsidy	% decrease in long-run demand at −0.3
Kuwait: electricity	0.007	0.135	1829	−59
Kuwait: gasoline	0.23	0.65	183	−27
Saudi Arabia: gasoline	0.16	0.65	306	−34
Abu Dhabi: electricity (expatriates)	0.041	0.089	117	−20
Abu Dhabi: electricity (citizens)	0.014	0.089	536	−43
Oman: electricity	0.026	0.1	285	−33
Oman: gasoline	0.31	0.65	110	−20

Note: Electricity prices are in kWh, and gasoline is priced per liter. Recent prices and estimates of unsubsidized prices compiled by author. Unsubsidized prices are based on those prevailing in 2014. Price elasticity estimate is based on the lower figure used in Pedro Rodriguez, Joshua Charap, and Arthur Ribeiro da Silva, "Fuel Subsidies and Energy Consumption: A Cross-Country Analysis," Kuwait Selected Issues and Statistical Appendix, IMF Country Report (Washington, DC: International Monetary Fund, June 2012). Demand effect calculations are based on energy demand formula in Rodriguez et al. (2012), which uses a nonlinear function that reflects effects of large price increases. Expatriates receive smaller energy subsidies in some countries. For calculations and formulae, see Jim Krane, "Stability Versus Sustainability: Energy Policy in the Gulf Monarchies," Energy Journal 36, no. 4 (2015), http://dx.doi.org/10.5547 /01956574.36.4.jkra.

the government's policy of leaving electricity prices untouched since 1966 has played out. Had prices been indexed to cost, Kuwaitis today might be using half as much electricity. This is a sobering thought for a government that constantly struggles to keep up with demand. Elsewhere, Omanis might respond to rationalized prices by cutting electricity demand by a third and gasoline demand by a fifth. Long-run gasoline demand in Saudi Arabia could drop by as much as a third, if prices reached 65 cents/liter, or $2.50 per gallon.

These results suggest that subsidies are responsible for *roughly a third* of the total demand for electricity and transportation fuel. A full reform of subsidies, all else constant, would probably bring about significant reductions in energy demand. Gasoline demand is typically less sensitive to price than electricity, so those declines might be smaller.

Raising prices to world levels, even if it didn't suppress demand to the world average, could still provide governments with relief. Reduced energy demand would slow the unsustainable tempo of building new power plants and refineries and the fuel purchases required to operate them. The government could direct this capital elsewhere. Reduced demand at home would also allow these countries to maintain oil and gas exports for longer. State budgets would benefit handsomely on both sides of the ledger. Treasurers would enjoy increased revenues from higher prices *and* reduced outlays for capital and operating expenses.

But price reform would not permanently halt increases in energy demand in countries where growth in population, wealth, and industrialization continues. Because today's consumption is based on prices and development decisions made in the past, path dependence on higher levels of demand—energy-inefficient housing, large residences, the lack of transportation alternatives—will hinder change. And if rentier theory is correct, price increases might even tempt citizens to demand democratic participation in government, which would provide regimes a strong disincentive to undertaking such reforms.

This hypothetical exercise provides us one further insight: it allows us to understand the long-term damage caused by energy policies set in place in the 1970s. In many ways, the Gulf's energy demand conundrum is a hangover from the euphoria over nationalization and the rent windfalls of 1973 and 1979. At the time, there was a sense that resources were in surplus. If natural gas that was going to waste could be captured and provided at cost, why shouldn't it be? Given the circumstances of the era, these attitudes were reasonable. But these early decisions about energy investment had ramifications that extended far into the future. Even if attitudes toward energy evolve, existing structures can undermine the effects of new policy.

The subsidies that helped pull Gulf populations out of poverty in the 1970s should have been rolled back—or at least indexed to inflation—long ago. Early undervaluation of these resources persisted, despite a sea change in the understanding of their value. The current generation now faces the consequences of inefficient demand habits, construction methods, and capital equipment. In other words, natural resources are "too cheap for the good of future generations," to borrow from the American economist Harold Hotelling's still relevant 1931 argument, and "in consequence of their excessive cheapness they are being produced and consumed wastefully."[30]

What looked like sensible development in the 1970s nowadays looks like waste: natural capital squandered with little or no remuneration. But it isn't just waste that Gulf policy makers must contend with. Petroleum exports form the bedrock of the region's political economies. Hydrocarbons help ruling families buy political support domestically and also provide regimes with economic viability, through export revenues. For the system to continue functioning, resource revenues from abroad must not be displaced by resource demand from inside the country. Without reform, the old rentier system could unravel. Five of these monarchies face an increasingly acute conflict between sustaining exports and maintaining subsidies on electricity, desalinated water, and fuels. Increasing production of oil and gas cannot solve the problem. While some states—Kuwait, the UAE, and Saudi Arabia—may be able to undergo the huge investment required to increase production capacity, rulers cannot justify those investments if the output is given away domestically.

Converging pressures have forced regimes to contemplate the one action that they have resisted for so long: cutting subsidies.

6

WE HAVE A SERIOUS PROBLEM

bu Dhabi's annual International Petroleum Exhibition and Conference (ADIPEC) is one of the industry's most eagerly awaited trade shows. The Abu Dhabi government bankrolls the convention, flying in guests from around the world and putting them up in five-star splendor in the towers that crowd the emirate's skyline. The proceedings unfold inside the luxurious Emirates Palace Hotel, where oil executives and petrostate officials discuss the latest research in oil and gas. Attendees dig into shrimp and steaks at sumptuous buffets, looking for opportunities to mingle with ruling family members. The big prize is a piece of the seemingly bottomless market in the Gulf.

The ostentatious ADIPEC conference is an odd venue for a Gulf technocrat to assume the mantle of Jimmy Carter and call upon fellow citizens to make personal sacrifices. But that is exactly what happened in 2013, when Oman's energy minister, Mohammed bin Hamad al-Rumhy, strode to the podium inside the Emirates Palace and pleaded for Gulf nationals to stop wasting energy. Dr. al-Rumhy, an energy scholar and longtime petroleum engineer, was appointed to lead Oman's Ministry of Oil and Gas in 1997. He had worked his way to the top of the Omani energy pyramid by way of a doctorate from London's Imperial College, followed by management of drilling operations at Petroleum Development Oman, the sultanate's national oil company. He took those experiences back to academia, serving first as a professor and then as an associate dean of engineering in Oman's top university.

Al-Rumhy understood too well how energy subsidies had metastasized throughout Gulf society and how crucial it was to purge them from the politician's sheaf of patronage tools. The incendiary effects on demand—and the untold billions required to increase fossil fuel production so that subsidies could be maintained—meant that continuing these giveaways was a fools' errand.

"I think we have a serious problem," al-Rumhy said in his plenary address in the conference hall. "We are wasting too much energy in the region. And the barrels that we are consuming are becoming a threat now, for our region particularly." The minister's call for restraint must have grated on the buoyant mood at ADIPEC. Al-Rumhy pointed to the subsidies underpinning expectations for "endless growth" that made the trade show so spectacular and described these policies as the enemy of any sensible Gulf technocrat. Prior to al-Rumhy's call, few political figures ever dared attack such a key pillar of political stability for the Gulf ruling families. "What is really destroying us right now is subsidies," the Omani minister boomed. "We simply need to raise the price of petrol and electricity. In some countries in our region electricity is free and you leave on your air conditioning for the whole summer when you go on holiday. That is really a crime. Our cars are getting bigger, our consumption is getting bigger and the price is almost free. So you need to send a signal to the pockets of the public."[1]

Energy technocrats in the Gulf had quietly been making similar statements for years; al-Rumhy's 2013 speech made the open discussion of dismantling energy subsidies politically palatable. Besides challenging the standard governing calculus, al-Rumhy's quest to rein in demand stood at odds with four decades of academic work on the rules of governance in his own country and those like it. If raising prices would end the long-running feast on domestic energy products, why don't rulers simply go for the quick fix? Gulf regimes have the autonomy to enact policy without consulting their citizens; shouldn't Kuwait's ruling emir simply impose on his subjects an 1,800 percent increase in their electricity rates (the amount by which current prices must rise to reflect actual cost) and be done with it? The problem is, according to rentier theory, energy subsidies are also inviolable components of the social contract between state and society. Rulers provide them in exchange for political support. One can no more retract subsidies in a rentier state than one can retract the right to vote in a democracy.

Beblawi and Luciani wrote in 1987 that the specter of rentier governments clinging to "detrimental" spending policies that "very clearly cannot be sustained in the long run" was a symptom of the weakness of their states.[2] Samih Farsoun in 1988 warned of the attractions of subsidies: over time they metamorphose from ruler's gift into "a political right of the citizen." Jill Crystal cautioned during the oil bust in 1990 that the combination of low oil rents and cutbacks in welfare benefits would create a "source of future instability" and bring "demands for representation."[3] Dismantling subsidies, echoed Farsoun, "will likely trigger movements of opposition against the regime."[4]

There is undoubtedly some truth to these arguments. A sudden eighteen-fold increase in electricity prices would probably push Kuwaitis to riot. If things went badly, the emir could find himself out of a job. But is *any* reform off the table? Can there be no compromise to the energy subsidy quandary in which the Gulf finds itself?

Academics have long argued that these types of regimes have little to no flexibility on subsidies. Rentier theory considers benefits such as subsidies on energy, food, housing, health care, and land as vital components of citizenship, which, collectively, comprise the citizen's biggest incentive for consent to his government's rule. The predominant message is that benefits cannot be retracted without offsetting their loss with a corresponding increase in democratic participation. To do otherwise would challenge the basis of the state.

Whether these scholarly prohibitions are accurate is another matter.

CAN YOU REMOVE SUBSIDIES?

As mentioned in chapter 4, a key issue in the rentier social contract is the rejection of taxation and other forms of extraction from society. Not only are autocrats unable to tax citizens, theory holds, but they also cannot take away their benefits. According to Beblawi and Luciani, subsidies, once extended, become rights. Weak and legitimacy-deficient rentier states could neither retract them nor restrict them to the poor. "Cutting subsidies," they wrote, is "not qualitatively different from raising taxes: either of the two is feasible only if the state enjoys solid democratic legitimation, justifying the degree of repression which may on some occasions be necessary."[5]

What I provide next is just a brief sketch of the academic "prohibitions" on the kind of reforms advocated by al-Rumhy and other technocrats; I have also done a much deeper treatment elsewhere.[6] The view of state welfare functions as "rights" was endorsed by the political scientist F. Gregory Gause III in his 1994 book on the Gulf states. After two decades of oil-derived state benefits, he argued, "a substantial part of the citizenry has ceased to regard these benefits as temporary benefices from their rulers, and has come to see them as rights of citizenship."[7]

Attempts to unwind social benefits, such scholars claimed, would invite demands for democracy or incite opposition. "Were the Gulf monarchies to find themselves unable to meet their end of the economic bargain with their citizens, the future of their political systems could be called into question," wrote Gause.[8] Cutting subsidies "holds the risk of alienating large portions of their populations who have come to expect extensive welfare state benefits as their right as citizens."[9]

Later scholarship only intensified the subsidy-as-rights theme. Authors portrayed the state's obligations as growing increasingly rigid, alongside rising citizen expectations and incomes. "The Gulf Arabs feel an entitlement to their share of the countries' oil wealth," wrote Michael Herb in 1999. Citizens do not feel gratitude to ruling families for sharing oil rents, because they "think that they themselves, as citizens, own the oil, not the ruling families. . . . Few are particularly grateful on receipt of something they think is theirs in the first place."[10] Kiren Aziz Chaudhry argued in a 1997 book that in Saudi Arabia, "welfare programs defined citizenship." She illustrated the principle by showing how citizen opposition forced the Saudi government to reverse an attempt to cut subsidies on fuel, water, and electricity during the oil bust in 1988.[11]

Regime survival, these scholars agreed, entailed safeguarding patronage no matter what—even in the face of two decades of sustained low oil prices that followed the high-price heyday of the 1970s and that put severe pressure on state finances. Indeed, while the price spikes of 1973 and 1979 brought the monarchies a huge influx of cash, high oil prices had two additional pernicious consequences. First, they killed off demand in importing countries (as we saw in chapter 5); second, they incentivized the discovery of alternative oil supplies. The international oil companies that had been kicked out of the developing world soon found new drilling grounds—and with oil prices so high, they worked hard to produce and sell as much oil as possible. The next frontiers for oil and gas moved to the freeze-blasted tundra of Alaska's North Slope, the hurricane-ridden Gulf of Mexico, and the storm-lashed North Sea. As a result, oil entered a long period of lower prices, a manifestation of the cyclical nature of crude oil pricing that has only grown more familiar. From the mid-1980s until 2003, with few exceptions, oil remained within a price band of ten to twenty dollars a barrel. This long "oil bust" caused ruling sheikhs in the petrostates of the Middle East to reassess their freewheeling spending.

Even with oil revenues collapsing and debt rising, the sheikhs' options were limited. A chorus of scholarly voices saw benefit reform as impossible. Books and articles assessing the bust period steadfastly maintained that "populations were unwilling to countenance any reductions in welfare spending"[12] and that "welfare services to the local population can be seen as the single most important source of political legitimacy."[13] Cutbacks might bring political change, even the collapse of the state.[14]

A few authors warned about these accumulating fiscal commitments and their effects on energy demand. Even so, tinkering with social spending was said to be freighted with political risk. Hertog and Luciani addressed—and dismissed—the possibility of rationalizing energy prices, conceding that raising residential electricity tariffs was nigh impossible because "reduced prices have traditionally been perceived as part of the ruling bargain and attempts to increase them have been repeatedly reversed."[15]

More recently, after international oil prices returned to higher levels, Gause noted that the monarchies proved their resourcefulness and durability by surviving the oil bust and the Arab Spring. But he argued that reforming the rising energy consumption that besets Saudi Arabia will be tricky. The policies other governments might respond with—reducing spending or imposing taxes—are unavailable to the Saudi regime, in Gause's view, since they would "challenge the basis of the oil state the al-Saud family has built since the early 1970s, with uncertain political consequences."[16]

Whether stated outright or inferred, the subsidies-as-rights theme remains a bedrock tenet of rentier scholarship: Benefits such as energy subsidies are sacrosanct. My price elasticity exercise in the previous chapter—showing the potential for dramatic reductions in energy demand—is a pipe dream. Or is it?

By 2010, the bloated Gulf social contract was headed for its first stress test. Years of oil prices near $100 per barrel had brought temporary relief but had also further cemented the Gulf regimes' dependence on cash from oil and gas exports. Meanwhile, their growing populations were clamoring for more of those same export commodities. Regimes were locked into providing increasing amounts of exportable energy at prices that, for the most part, didn't even cover their costs. Rulers had painted themselves into a corner. The more energy they gave away at home, the less they could sell at market prices. Al-Rumhy was right. Subsidies were a governance trap. Left unaltered, they could strangle the economy.

Rulers were forced to address subsidies. But they didn't need to reduce or abolish *all* welfare benefits, only the most damaging ones. And to see which are most damaging, we have to look deeper at the fundamental difference between subsidies on energy and other welfare benefits, such as subsidized housing or state jobs. It's a distinction that may prove central to the survival of the monarchies.

ENERGY SUBSIDIES ARE DIFFERENT

There are important differences between the distribution of *rents* and the giving away of in-kind *resources*. Both represent sources of fiscal pressure on governments, which become especially relevant at times when oil export earnings are down. But the domestic distribution of exportable commodities is fundamentally different than rent-funded benefits such as housing, education, and subsidized food staples. The energy burden manifests itself not only in terms of *cost* (what the government spends) but also in lost *revenue* (what the government earns).

States have temporary policy options to help them cope with fiscal burdens. They can cut spending or issue debt. Coping with a loss in revenue is tougher. If the state forces national oil companies to divert a portion of their output into the domestic economy—where it is given away or sold at reduced prices—the profitable export portion shrinks (see figure 6.1).

The situation with natural gas illustrates the danger. Despite the abundance of gas in the region, the Gulf—outside of Qatar—is now a net gas importer. Low prices (fixed at around one to two dollars per million BTUs) stimulated demand but also stifled production. Making matters worse, gas production in the Gulf is getting more expensive. The supply of "associated" gas—that produced with oil—is no longer sufficient. Countries are increasingly turning to unconventional gas, including geologically difficult "tight" gas, bound up in low-porosity rock, as well as

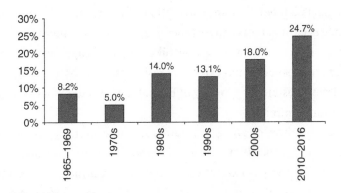

FIGURE 6.1 Average percentage of GCC oil production consumed domestically, per decade.

Domestic demand as a portion of oil production has crept higher over the decades.
This chart depicts average oil demand growth for the GCC per decade.

Source: BP, *Statistical Review of World Energy 2017* (London: BP, 2017).

toxic "sour" gas, laced with hydrogen sulfide. Production costs for these "nonassociated" sources start at around $3 and range as high as $8 per MMBtu.[17] Since gas produced is nearly always destined for the subsidized domestic market, rather than the more lucrative export market, no one wants to invest. There is simply no money in it. Fixed local prices are below the cost of production.[18]

Qatar is the exception. Qatar's successful launch of LNG shipments in 1996 has allowed the tiny monarchy to rise above the low-value mindset of its region and trade with countries, particularly Japan and South Korea, willing to pay market price. Timely investments that came toward the end of the oil bust allowed Qatar to build its LNG infrastructure affordably, making its unit costs by far the world's lowest. LNG prices began rising in 2005, with Japanese import prices averaging $13 per MMBtu in 2008 and nearly $17 in 2017. Qatar's ability to meet demand with its low-cost supply made the tiny monarchy incredibly rich. For the rest of the Gulf, the big difference between oil and gas is that gas has never been an important source of rents. The onset of shortages and gas imports has not destroyed their economies. But becoming an oil importer easily could.

For regimes seeking legitimacy, distribution of energy *products* is also a less flexible practice than distribution of energy *rents*. When energy revenue is falling, rents can be generated from myriad nonhydrocarbon sources. Dubai, now a fully non-oil economy, reaps rents from fees charged to businesses and expatriate residents. Distribution of these fee-based rents sustains the loyalty of Emirati citizens to Dubai's ruling al-Maktoum family.[19]

By comparison, oil and gas resources are finite. Even if reserves remain large in four of the six monarchies, it's no easy matter to raise oil production. Oil and gas extraction is subject to technical and economic limits. Increasing output requires investments in the tens of billions of dollars. No rational policy maker will spend that kind of money only to hand over the yield to citizens—and smugglers—at prices below the cost of production. Finally, energy subsidies also contaminate the national economy. They increase its energy intensity and encourage dependence by domestic industry in ways that make it uncompetitive.

National oil companies take the hit. Their cash flow is reduced, which damages their wherewithal to reinvest.

If petrostates cannot reduce growth in demand for oil and gas, then, simply put, their exports will be displaced along with the all-important rents they generate. If no one intervenes, the entire system will fail. In fact, the outcomes of oil subsidization resemble the effects of the so-called resource curse but with a second stage that compounds the damage. First, as that theory holds, oil helps perpetuate autocratic rule by providing regimes with rents and subsidies to exchange for political support.[20] States that follow these practices tend to subsidize energy, which brings about the second-stage effect of raising per capita energy demand. Thus, the resource curse also works in reverse. Oil supports autocrats in power and, in turn, autocrats support demand for oil. It's a two-way curse. Oil-exporting states tend to be both autocratic *and* energy intense.[21]

Adding to the litany of evils attributed to fossil fuel subsidies is the unnecessary environmental damage they encourage. Cheap gasoline and diesel fuel incentivize driving. Civil servants in Saudi Arabia, Qatar, Bahrain, and the UAE spent 1 percent or less of their monthly salary to fill their SUV's fuel tank in 2016; an equivalent civil servant in the United Kingdom had to devote *ten times* as much salary to fuel up.[22] Increased driving exacerbates traffic congestion, pollution, and accidents, which, in turn, raise public health costs. Higher consumption of fossil fuel also increases carbon dioxide emissions, contributing to the warming of Earth's climate. Per capita carbon emissions from the Gulf already lead the world.

Combined, the Gulf monarchies are sending nearly as much CO_2 into the atmosphere as Japan, despite a population less than a third the size.[23] The IEA and IMF have begun stressing the role of fossil fuel subsidies in climate change. In 2015, the IEA called on Middle Eastern governments to take action on carbon by reducing energy subsidies, oil's use in power generation, and the flaring of natural gas.[24] The subsidy problem is shifting from the domestic to the global arena.

The climate damage wreaked by the Gulf's energy intensity is starting to hit uncomfortably close to home. As temperatures rise, the region is emerging as a cautionary example of the dangers of the new climate. Summers in the Gulf are already about as hot as they can get and still support human life. Coping, for now, involves more fossil fuel–based cooling, creating a climate-damaging feedback loop. If temperatures continue to climb, summers that are now at the upper end of unpleasant will become unbearable. Climate scientists predict that by 2070 or so, global warming will push high temperatures in the Gulf beyond levels that humans can tolerate. Residents will eventually be forced to flee to cooler parts of the world.[25] The summer of 2016 was a harbinger. On July 22, the daytime high temperature in Kuwait reached a smothering 129.2°F (54°C), setting a new record for the Eastern Hemisphere.[26] At those levels, air conditioners become life-support systems. A power outage is more than an annoyance. It can be fatal.

What actions have Gulf regimes taken? One of them—a move toward the generation of renewable electricity in the UAE and Saudi Arabia—has produced a lot of hype, mostly unwarranted. BP data show that in 2016, the UAE consumed 137 TWh of electricity, of which just 0.3 TWh was generated by solar technology. Saudi Arabia's solar share was even less, just 0.1 TWh of a total of 330 TWh. In other words, the two monarchies leading the way in Gulf renewables provided *less than one-tenth of 1 percent* of total power via those means. None of the other Gulf monarchies produced enough nonfossil power even to reach statistical relevance.[27]

In coming years, zero-carbon solar and nuclear power—and later, wind—will make important contributions to electricity production in the Gulf. But these developments will be overshadowed by continued expansion of the fossil fuel grid. Exhibit A is Dubai's giant 4.8 GW Hassyan coal-fired power plant, funded and built by China. By 2023, Dubai will import more than 10 million tons of coal per year to power the first 2.4 GW of capacity.[28] The 20 million tons of CO_2 Hassyan sends into the atmosphere each year will push the Gulf's carbon footprint to new heights.

The fact that Dubai is turning to coal, the only fossil fuel not found on the Arabian Peninsula, illustrates the tension created by demand growth and subsidy reform. Once considered preposterous, coal use in the Middle East is growing quickly. The UAE's coal consumption grew by 24 percent in 2016, leading every other country in the world except Singapore.[29]

OPTIONS FOR THE FUTURE

The Gulf monarchies have four broad policy choices to deal with their energy dilemma. Three of them attack the problem from the supply side.

First, they can *invest upstream* (upstream meaning the point of production, with refining as downstream) to try to raise oil and gas production beyond current levels. Increased supply would, at least temporarily, accommodate growing domestic demand alongside exports.[30] Second, they can *diversify their supply.* Instead of generating electricity solely from oil and gas, they could develop alternate sources such as nuclear, renewables, or coal. These would offset the continually growing demand for oil and gas. Third, they could *diversify their economies beyond hydrocarbons,* seeking alternate sources of rent that can compensate for future reductions in exports. Post-oil Dubai has shown that diversification can take place without altering the character of governance.

The fourth option is to attack *demand.* The Gulf monarchies can try to stop or at least slow the relentless growth in energy consumption. Reining in demand—cutting growth from, say 7 percent a year to 2 percent— would allow them to maintain exports for a few more decades. The most effective way to reduce demand is to make energy less attractive by decreasing subsidies and raising prices on fuels, desalinated water, and electricity.[31] Once prices are raised, conservation and efficiency programs can ease the burden of increased pricing.

In reality, the monarchies are exercising all these options, at least in part. But the fourth option, demand-side reforms that target energy subsidies, has long been seen as impossible by political scientists and regional elites. On-the-ground reality has, until recently, backed their assertions. Previous attempts to raise electricity prices on the citizen residential sector, the most politically sensitive consumer group, have failed; Saudi Arabia imposed electricity tariff increases in 1985 and 1999 that were quickly reversed, and a 2010 attempt also failed.

It's not hard to see why monarchies might be hesitant to pull back subsidies (or why scholars have viewed subsidies as necessary for regime survival). Under any political setting, subsidies are described as asymmetric: easy to enact, difficult to retract. Governments usually intend for subsidies to provide a helping hand to a struggling (or politically connected) community or business sector. What policy makers don't realize is that their benevolent policy winds up creating a new bloc that can turn against them. Subsidies create solidarity among beneficiaries who organize to protect their interests. When their benefits are put at risk, this bloc can rise up and threaten the political leadership. Welfare societies like those in the Gulf therefore maintain a constant potential for mobilization that raises the stakes of reform.[32]

It's also worth noting that citizens in the 1970s were not clamoring for cheap energy. Governments decided to provide it. Electricity and fuels are cheap today because autocratic governments require a source of legitimacy for their rule that does not involve a mandate from the ballot box. In other words, subsidies exist not because citizens remain unable or unwilling to pay but because the state has been unwilling to charge them.[33]

The highly centralized nature of Gulf regimes poses an additional barrier to reform. When authority is concentrated, so is accountability. Monarchs that dare reform are exposed to the full force of public reaction. Everyone knows that there is no one to blame but the ruler. This makes subsidy reform an especially agonizing prospect for a ruling sheikh. Since regime survival is the ultimate priority, rulers try to push through unpopular measures when they can be shielded from blame.[34] Low oil prices, for instance, can give political cover for belt tightening.

Monarchs may also be dissuaded from taking action by watching backlash from other countries. Angry hordes flooded the streets and overthrew regimes after reforms that included fuel price increases in Venezuela in 1993 and Indonesia in 1998. More recently and closer to home, rioters greeted fuel price hikes in Jordan in 2012 and Yemen in 2006. Yet while rulers may fixate on the times reform caused an uprising, unrest is not the typical outcome. All but five of twenty-eight substantial energy subsidy reforms documented by the IMF in the past two decades met with some success.[35] Among energy exporters, Indonesia, after failed attempts in 1997 and 2003, successfully raised fuel prices in 2005 and 2008 and reduced its subsidy load from 3.5 percent of GDP in 2005 to 0.8 percent by 2009. Yemen also managed small reductions in fuel subsidies, which, however, still accounted for 7.4 percent of 2009 GDP. Mexico eliminated gasoline subsidies in 2014 after raising them at various times, including in 2005 and 2006.[36] Mexico's attempts to cut electricity subsidies between 1999 and 2002 failed, however, and in 2016 the government was still paying half the cost of residential electricity.[37] Malaysia underwent a series of attempts to reduce fuel subsidies, some of which were reversed following public outcries. By 2014, however, Malaysia managed to eliminate price supports amid low global oil prices.[38] Nigeria's fuel price reforms of 2011–2012 triggered antigovernment unrest but still managed to reduce subsidy costs from 4.7 percent to 3.6 percent of GDP.[39] A further Nigerian reform in 2016 eliminated price supports.[40]

Can the Gulf monarchies come to grips with the consequences of their long hiatus from market prices? Two pioneering cases provide clues. Iran and Dubai both launched ambitious price reforms, with mixed results. I'll explore these in the next chapter and in chapter 8 will turn to Saudi Arabia to study a young leader's attempt to take on this knotty problem that his predecessors avoided. Chapter 9 unveils the near-simultaneous changes in energy prices in the rest of the Gulf, from low-level tinkering in Kuwait to a foreigner-focused approach in the United Arab Emirates.

7

IRAN AND DUBAI LEAD THE WAY

D own through the centuries, Gulf Arabs have taken numerous cues from Persia: in poetry, architecture, music, carpet weaving, and their common diet of grilled meats and herbed grains. In energy as well, Iran blazed a trail that was followed by its Arab neighbors. The first commercial oil in the Middle East flowed a hundred years ago in southwestern Persia, after the 1908 strike at the Masjed-e-Soleyman field demonstrated there were viable resources in the shadow of the Zagros Mountains. Oil from Iran provided the bunker fuel behind the British Royal Navy's 1911 conversion from coal to oil and led to the creation of the international oil company now known as BP. The strategic value of Iranian petroleum brought Western wildcatters to explore both sides of the Persian Gulf.

Iran also led the region in nationalizing its industry and in developing an oil-based rentier state. The term itself was coined in 1970 by an Iranian, Hossein Mahdavy, an economist who documented how oil provided Iran's monarchy with the means to develop, while reducing the urgency to pursue advancement, particularly in education.[1] Subsidies weren't enough to prevent the shah from being swept aside in the 1979 revolution. Even so, the revolutionary state led by Ayatollah Khomeini retained parts of the shah's rentier playbook, including low, fixed prices on energy.

IRAN'S DRAMATIC REFORMS

By 2010, subsidies on energy had pushed Iran into the advanced stages of economic cannibalism. Runaway demand for gasoline and diesel fuel had transformed a country with the fourth-highest global oil reserves into a net importer of refined fuels. Iran found itself that year buying gasoline at world wholesale prices of around US$2 per gallon and then reselling the fuel domestically for 38 US cents.[2] Domestic demand was not only draining away exports of crude oil, the Islamic Republic's chief source of hard currency. It was also encouraging too much driving, which led to traffic congestion, air pollution, collisions, and all the attendant public health problems. Fuel was so cheap that Iranian smugglers weren't just moving it to Pakistan and Turkey. They were even loading it on boats and reselling it across the Gulf, in Oman, where fuel was also subsidized, just not by as much.[3] Giving away energy was costing Iran $100 billion a year, a quarter of its GDP.[4]

Iranian leaders understood the political risks involved in taking away social welfare benefits, but by 2010, with oil near $100 a barrel, the economic distortions had outweighed the risk. On December 18, 2010, Iran's president, Mahmoud Ahmadinejad, went live on national TV and told the nation that he had ordered "economic surgery" to be performed on an energy subsidy program that had been bleeding the Islamic Republic dry.[5] "We've been giving out these subsidies in an unjust manner for fifty years," Ahmadinejad said. "We're now using four times more energy than necessary for our current standard of living. With a little effort, we can reduce our energy consumption so that Iran can become the most advanced country in the world."[6]

The president ordered drastic increases in fixed prices that had never been indexed to inflation and had grown cheaper in real terms over the years until they were among the world's lowest. Ahmadinejad and his policy makers built public support by pointing out how subsidies encouraged waste. Seventy percent of the subsidy was captured by the rich, with their fleets of personal vehicles and large homes. Iranian economists devised tiered prices that kept modest amounts of electricity and fuel cheap, while targeting the wealthy with drastic increases for wasteful consumption. "Some of them are using cheap energy to keep the water warm in their swimming pools, and meanwhile a young student told me that his school's roof was falling in," the president confided. "Those whose consumption levels are low, the price will be cheap. As consumption levels go up, the price will go up. The energy and the wealth of the country belong to the people."[7]

Ahmadinejad sold his reforms using populist rhetoric that appealed to his political base. But the design of the new pricing scheme was an economic masterstroke that might have been devised by free-marketeers at the University of Chicago. Instead of simply wiping away the subsidies by raising prices, Iran acted strategically to placate the public. It replaced benefits with cash. Preparations included the creation of bank accounts for each household. The state deposited two monthly payments, each worth about $40, into every account before raising prices. Recipients could only access those payments after the reform was launched. This increased support among the poor for the forthcoming price hikes.[8]

Economists have long encouraged cash transfers over in-kind subsidies, arguing that cash handouts—while still carrying some negative side effects—are far more efficient.[9] For a short time, Ahmadinejad, the ultra-conservative antagonist of the West, became the darling of monetary economists. The 2010 reform managed the rare achievement of positive welcomes from both the IMF and the Iranian public. It made Iran the first major energy-exporting country to cut energy subsidies at such a drastic level as well as the first country in the world to replace handouts of energy products with handouts of cash.[10]

The scale of the price increases, in many cases, was huge (see figure 7.1). The cost of diesel fuel leaped from 6 cents to $1.40 per gallon, an increase of more than 2,000 percent, although this was still not enough to reach world wholesale prices, which were near $2.50 at the time. Electricity rates also jumped, particularly for large residential consumers. While the base price of electricity rose only slightly, from 1.6 to 2.7 cents per kilowatt-hour, for consumption in excess of 600 kWh per month (about two-thirds of what the average US household uses), the price rocketed to 19 cents per kWh (a rate nearly double the average US price in

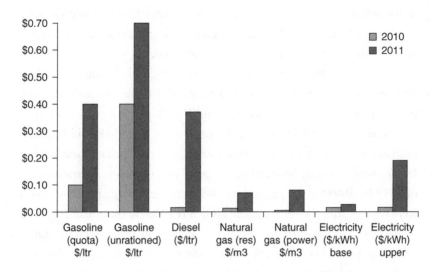

FIGURE 7.1 Before and after comparison of energy prices in Iran, 2010 vs. 2011.

Note: Liquid fuels are given in dollars per liter, or "US$/ltr."

2018). Rising price bands were designed to encourage conservation and protect the poor.

The price increases halved Iran's $100 billion subsidy burden and brought a 10 percent short-run reduction in domestic energy demand.[11] Best of all, a 133,000 b/d drop in oil consumption allowed Iran to increase its oil exports, albeit temporarily; the increase in exports was soon blocked by international sanctions and an embargo targeting Iran's nuclear program.[12]

After the promising start, Iran's subsidy reform stalled in 2012, beset by rising inflation and a lack of parliamentary support.[13] Initial plans called for prices to be increased to 90 percent of international levels over five years, but that goal was soon forgotten, eclipsed by the confrontation over uranium enrichment. The sanctions crisis also made it difficult to discern the macroeconomic effects of raising energy prices. The embargo contributed to the inflation that roiled the Iranian economy, which quickly unwound the subsidy measure. Since energy prices had not been indexed to inflation or to world prices—a major shortcoming—inflation reduced prices in real terms. Inflation also undermined the value of the replacement cash transfers.[14] By 2013, Iran's energy consumption was back to prereform levels.

Since then, Iran has renewed its efforts, gradually hiking fuel prices and removing 3 million wealthy households from the cash-transfer program. In 2014, Iran pushed through a 75 percent price increase, followed by another 20 to 40 percent in 2015. The IMF said the new increases—aided by the halving of international oil prices—meant that Iran's energy subsidy burden had dropped precipitously, from a quarter of GDP in 2010 to just 4 percent in 2016.[15] Further energy price increases were written into the Iranian state budget released at the end of 2017, and President Hassan Rouhani sought a 50 percent increase in gasoline prices, in part to combat urban air pollution by discouraging driving. "You cannot leave the prices unchanged and expect to counter the air pollution," Rouhani said.[16] However, ensuing violent demonstrations called those reforms into question, and prices had not changed as of May 2018.

Among policy makers in the Arab monarchies across the Gulf, there was little public commentary on the changes underway in their archrival Iran. Despite the silence, the Islamic Republic's actions resonated deeply. In Saudi Arabia, an adviser told me that Iran's achievements were being studied as a serious path toward efficiency.[17]

Experts and some policy makers I have interviewed tend to assume that tinkering with benefits such as electricity subsidies is only possible if there is a quid pro quo—a replacement benefit, as Iran provided. One prominent Saudi energy official told me: "The residential electricity tariff is part of the social agreement between the royal family and the people. If you touch it, you have to repay it somewhere else."[18] Iran did this with cash, a technique that provides the highest level of economic efficiency. Free cash is still a subsidy and still has a distorting effect on productivity and consumption. But it is more efficient than regressive subsidies on energy that flow mainly to the rich. More importantly, cash handouts also allowed Iran to cut subsidies without triggering social unrest—until late December 2017. That said, Iran's subsidy burden remains among the largest in the world (recall table 4.1).

The need for replacement benefits may not be universal, especially for less ambitious reforms that eliminate a smaller portion of the subsidy. Just across the Gulf from Iran, Dubai pushed through a modest increase in energy prices without offering any incentive. The public reaction was altogether different.

DUBAI STEPS BACK FROM THE BRINK

In 2009, Dubai was in trouble. The city had just capped off a six-year boom that had not only cemented it as the region's premier non-oil-based economy but turned it into a destination for jet-set opulence. As the emirate's slate of projects grew more outlandish and expensive—palm-shaped islands dredged from the sea and forests of gleaming office towers—its debt grew to alarming levels. When the 2008 global financial meltdown came, Dubai succumbed. The financial crisis triggered a sudden crash in Dubai's real estate market, and in 2009 the city lapsed into a painful economic recession.

Most alarming was the declaration by a Dubai-owned conglomerate that it was unable to meet terms on a portion of the emirate's $100 billion or so in sovereign debt. The November 2009 "debt standstill" announcement ignited worldwide fears that the global financial crisis could intensify. The emirate narrowly avoided default by securing a bailout from neighboring Abu Dhabi and renegotiating repayment. The crisis pushed Dubai into austerity mode. Policy makers imposed tough spending restrictions to stabilize the city's finances, cancelling projects and firing masses of expatriate workers. In this context, ruling elites decided to stanch the bleeding caused by longstanding energy subsidies.

Unlike neighboring Abu Dhabi, Dubai never had much oil. When Dubai struck oil offshore in 1966, there was some promise of oil wealth, but when these oilfields were assessed in the mid-1970s, Dubai learned that it held less than 4 percent of the UAE's roughly 100 billion barrels of oil. Nearly all the rest was in Abu Dhabi (which is also the largest emirate by far in terms of land area). The emirates of Sharjah and Ras al-Khaimah found paltry deposits, and the other three sheikhdoms found nothing.[19] Even so, oil earnings dominated Dubai's economy for about a decade. In 1975, oil rents provided two-thirds of Dubai's GDP, the highest level it would ever reach. Production peaked at 420,000 barrels per day in 1991 and has been dwindling ever since. These days, Dubai's daily draw is in the low tens of thousands of barrels. Abu Dhabi's is around 4 million.[20]

Thankfully, Dubai could count on energy supply from its cousins next door. Over the years, Abu Dhabi provided a seemingly bottomless supply of cut-rate natural gas for power generation and industry.[21] But by 2008, Abu Dhabi was facing a demand crunch of its own. It could no longer increase gas supplies to Dubai. Confronting continued increases in electricity demand, Dubai was forced to turn to market-priced imports. That year—just as the financial crisis unfolded—the UAE became a net importer of natural gas.[22]

The new reality of more expensive energy dawned in Dubai before it did in the rest of the Gulf. In 2008, Dubai began to pass those increased prices along to consumers. The Dubai Electricity and Water Authority (DEWA) raised power and water rates to cost-reflective levels on commercial, industrial, and foreign residential customers. Citizens, who make up just 5 percent of the city's overall population, were exempt.

This left foreign residents paying rates that were roughly quadruple those of UAE nationals—and meant that Dubai citizens continued feasting on subsidized energy as if the boom had never ended, undermining the austerity needed to prevent Dubai's financial collapse. In 2010, Dubai had to start importing liquefied natural gas (LNG) at around $10/MMBtu, five times what it paid Abu Dhabi. The crisis pushed Dubai's leadership to opt for another increase in utility rates.

Dubai's ruler Sheikh Mohammed bin Rashid al-Maktoum agreed that citizens also needed price signals to change their consumption behavior. Despite perceptions of citizen entitlement to subsidies, the ruler approved a 30 percent increase in electricity prices. Half of that increase would be imposed through a 15 percent hike in electricity consumption tariffs on all customer classes, including citizens. The other half would take the form of a surcharge to cover imports of LNG. The ruler also imposed the first-ever limits on citizens' receipt of free municipal water, which had to be desalinated at high cost in the same gas-fired cogeneration plants that produce electricity.[23]

Enforcing these directives was left to the Dubai Supreme Council of Energy, a regulatory body created to impose efficiency on a city in which infrastructure and habits had been shaped by forty years of cheap energy. The council's director was Nejib Zaafrani, a Tunisian former Shell executive and board member on Abu Dhabi's state-owned oil and gas firms. Zaafrani declared that Dubai was now an importer of energy and that its residents should behave accordingly. He set out to reduce projected electricity demand in 2030 by 30 percent. This, he said, would allow Dubai to forgo construction of 4 gigawatts of generation capacity.[24] Raising prices would be complemented by new efficiency standards on buildings and appliances. Zaafrani warned that efficiency programs could not function unless subsidies were cut. No one, for example, would replace an inefficient air conditioner without a strong price signal.[25]

With Sheikh Mohammed's blessing, DEWA imposed Dubai's tariff increase on January 1, 2011. The new prices were not subject to public debate. Even inside government, there appears to have been very little consultation outside the ruler's *diwan* and energy council.[26] The price hikes surprised policy-making staff in the Dubai Executive Council, the body normally tasked with evaluating and implementing policy.[27]

DEWA's increase took effect during the winter, when electricity demand is at its lowest. It initially raised few objections among the majority expatriate community. As the weather warmed and people turned on their air conditioners, they started to notice. They not only paid higher rates for power and water, but the LNG surcharge weighed heavily on their bills because of the seasonal increase in demand.

Dubai's foreign residents were effectively cross-subsidizing citizens. A story in Dubai's *Gulf News* was flooded with more than two hundred comments from foreign residents shocked by the increases. "I can attest to the tremendous and horrifying increase in my DEWA bill," one resident wrote, offering comparisons of summer 2010 and 2011 invoices, which showed increases of 70 percent or more, from $144 in July 2010 to

$245 a year later. Expatriate complaints elicited little official sympathy. DEWA executives advised them to "stop wastage of precious resources."[28]

Rising prices created a more worrying stir within the ranks of citizens. Dubai nationals commonly own businesses, and many merchants complained of simultaneous increases in their business and living costs. Angry citizens brought bills to DEWA headquarters and demanded relief. "The uproar came as a surprise," one official said. "The government didn't realize that people would complain so much. They didn't have a plan for managing this. [Citizens] were coming to the head of the DEWA billing department and complaining. For some of these people it was the first time they had ever looked at their electricity bills."[29]

Other citizens vented their outrage to tribal leaders, who approached Sheikh Mohammed to pass along word of the discontent. "People went to the sheikh and complained. There were a lot of articles in the press," a second Dubai official said. "After a few days the sheikh ordered the increased prices to be waived for certain segments. People were coming to the government asking for increased social benefits to pay their bills because they couldn't afford the new rates."[30]

Citizens reserved their most vehement indignation for the new water payments, the first time Emirati nationals had been asked to pay for water since the municipal water system was built in 1968. The revised tariff structure gave citizen households a free allotment of 10,000 gallons per month. (By contrast, average household consumption in Tucson, Arizona, is around 7,000 gallons per month.) For consumption beyond 10,000 gallons, DEWA imposed a modest fee. Expatriates, who were already paying higher rates and not getting a free allotment, also received a price increase.

Securing water for the population had been a longstanding duty of every Gulf ruling sheikh. In the pre-oil era, water provision was a key indicator of a sheikh's stature.[31] The onset of desalination ended the era of scarcity, allowing water consumption in Dubai to grow unfettered by the limits of its small underground aquifer. The city began developing golf courses, water parks, and horse tracks. Crews lined roads with flower gardens and date palms. Since water was being given away, consumers had no understanding of the cost. People planted water-intensive gardens around their swimming pools. They hosed down cars and walkways to keep down the dust. "Forty years ago drinkable water was hard to access. The leadership of this country offered people water for free. That's very honorable," Zaafrani said in an interview. "But that was forty years ago. It's a different world today."

Angry citizens complained to the Arabic press and radio talk shows and launched a spate of illegal well drilling.[32] Prominent Emiratis began complaining to Zaafrani, often in person. "The ones who made much more noise after we made the increase were UAE nationals," he said. "For UAE nationals, water is not free anymore. Human beings do not want to be told to pay more. People came to me and said, 'We are being penalized!' I said, 'No, we're trying to save energy and raise awareness.'"

Dubai's elites might have managed to hold the line against such complaints, except that the increases had the misfortune of coinciding with the Arab Spring, which began in Tunisia and Egypt just as prices were raised in Dubai. By February, political unrest had swept into neighboring Bahrain and Oman.[33] Policy makers became much more sensitive to citizen opposition.[34] The ruling al-Maktoum family began to back away from the price increases. Ruling elites decreed three separate retractions of parts of the 2011 tariff reform, all of which affected *only* the citizen residential sector. Government officials portrayed these retractions as ad hoc decisions, again made without consulting the usual policy channels. First, Sheikh Mohammed quietly rolled back electricity prices to previous levels for low-income households receiving social benefits.[35] Second, one of the ruler's sons announced that the government would pay LNG surcharges on behalf of citizens.[36] And in October, the Dubai ruler relented on the increase in water prices and announced a doubling of the free water quota for citizen households to 20,000 gallons per month.[37] No price relief was offered to noncitizens or business and industrial customers. "This is what happens when you announce the policy with no proper analysis or consultation," a government policy maker said, in response to the climbdowns.

Raising prices was one side of subsidy reform. Collecting payment was another matter. DEWA had a record of effective bill collection, uncharacteristic in a region where paying utility bills used to be understood as optional, since enforcement by disconnection was unusual. DEWA, however, took a hard line, giving customers just forty-seven days to pay before turning off their power and water—unless those customers were UAE citizens or "certain designated institutions" (presumably linked to the ruling family, security forces, or prominent tribes). A 2013 financial-risk prospectus accompanying the issue of a Dubai bond noted that "UAE nationals are required to pay their own electricity bills."

But for water, the bond prospectus told a different story. "While the government encourages UAE nationals to pay their own invoices, the Government issues credit notes to cover any unpaid residential water invoices of UAE nationals."[38] Two years after imposing a charge for water, the government's representatives put in writing that citizen payments for water were voluntary. These policy retreats underscore the complexity of subsidy reform in an absolute monarchy and the resilience of social contract provisions enshrined in rentier theory. In Dubai, even during a financial crisis, the regime lacked the clout to enforce an across-the-board increase in citizens' utility rates.

Although the loss of benefits triggered a rash of complaints, it did not appear to inspire demands for democratic representation, as predicted by academic theory. A UAE-wide petition calling for increased political participation did emerge shortly after the price increase, but it seemed inspired by the onset of the Arab Spring, not Dubai's tariff measure.[39] One petition signer told me that the issues of subsidy reform and political participation were not linked in the way described in the rentier literature. He said energy subsidies were a vestige of the UAE's emergence from poverty a generation ago and were now more detrimental than helpful. Participating in political life was a natural aspiration of an enlightened citizen.[40]

Subsidy reform also exposed Dubai's ruler to public anger, including direct petitions by prominent citizens. Welfare reforms are best pursued when centralized regimes are either secure enough to absorb the political consequences or when a budgetary crisis or external pressure shelters leadership from blame. In Dubai's case, the 2008 financial crisis provided a helpful shield that enabled the increased prices. But the Arab Spring intervened. The uprisings reduced the regime's sense of security and changed its calculations.

The fact remains that Dubai's 15 percent increase in electricity tariffs stayed in place for the majority of citizens, and citizens were—in principle—expected to pay *something* for excessive water consumption. By the end of 2011, the increase in electricity and water prices reduced power consumption by an average of 3 percent per account and water consumption by an average of 7 percent. The tariff hike saved Dubai the equivalent of around six shipments of LNG that year, worth some $300 million.[41]

Dubai's electricity tariff increase breached an important barrier: that subsidies—once extended—are understood by citizens as rights that cannot be retracted. Whether or not Dubai citizens felt entitled to their subsidies on power and water, a portion of that entitlement was taken away. Only indigent citizens on income support avoided increased electricity rates, which amounted to targeting the subsidy toward the poor. Even this result represents a theoretical breach of sorts, as rentier states are supposed to be unable to retract subsidy entitlements or even restrict their delivery to only the poor.[42] For households and citizen-owned businesses that lost benefits, the regime offered no replacement, as Iran did, nor any increase in political participation, as prescribed by rentier theory. Citizens protested, but the regime was never endangered. Public satisfaction with the rule of the al-Maktoum family appears intact.

Dubai's reform was also important for another reason. The permissive emirate holds the unofficial role as the Gulf's test bed for controversial policies and investments. When one of Dubai's ventures succeeds, one or more of the surrounding monarchies inevitably copies the idea. Dubai's launch of an airline, free-trade zones, and tourism sectors are examples. Subsidy reform was another Dubai-tested policy that would soon be adopted by its neighbors.

ERRING ON THE SIDE OF CAUTION

In their willingness to snatch back long-held social benefits Dubai and Iran were in the vanguard. Their situations were acute. Dubai's ruling family was teetering close to financial default. Iran had boxed itself into a corner from which there was no other way out. The rest of the Gulf found itself in similar, albeit less urgent, circumstances. Might these countries, too, break the social compact and retract benefits? Answering that question depended on what citizens were willing to accept.

I decided to find out. In 2011, I worked with the polling firm You-Gov to conduct a public survey in all six Gulf monarchies. We polled 730 Gulf nationals on the subject of electricity pricing and willingness to pay full cost. My results suggested that citizens don't feel as reflexively entitled to subsidized energy or as adamantly opposed to paying higher prices as academics or regional elites think. I concluded that the successful subsidy reforms that took place in Iran and Dubai could indeed be replicated.[43]

Nearly half of survey respondents (49 percent) did not oppose paying the full cost of electricity when they were informed that the national interest depended on them paying more and using less. By contrast, 32 percent did oppose higher prices. (The rest had no opinion.) When asked how they felt about an Iran-style deal that traded an alternate benefit for giving up electricity subsidy, 51 percent either supported or did not oppose the idea.

Further, only a minority of citizens, albeit a significant minority—42 percent of respondents—maintained that they were entitled to subsidized electricity, as academic theory holds.[44] This suggests that the academic understanding of the social contract may be off base. The results weren't categorical. A significant minority of around a third of respondents remained opposed to higher prices no matter how I phrased the question. For Gulf citizens, then, the door to subsidy reform was partly open.

In a second survey, I asked energy experts, policy makers, and academics about the prospects for subsidy reform. I selected all participants—seventy-six in total—because their expertise included knowledge of Gulf energy issues. This survey produced entirely different results. For the experts, the door to reform was all but closed. Their responses showed that they had done their homework—by reading the scholarly literature. Experts expected citizens to be overwhelmingly opposed to higher prices, and 80 percent of experts (61 of 76) agreed that citizens consider subsidies as "rights of citizenship," backing up the academic claims.[45]

These two surveys point to a chasm in the perceptions of the autocratic social contract in the Gulf. Citizens' feelings about their own energy benefits diverged starkly from the understanding of experts and the literature. Elites held a conservative view that citizens expected the state to provide subsidized energy because it was their birthright (or the government's duty) to do so. Citizens held more flexible views. Some expected free energy. Others were OK with paying the full cost, if doing so was good for the country.

For policy makers, this finding suggested that what happened in Iran and Dubai might be duplicated. There may be a way out of the subsidy pyramid scheme after all.

THE DICTATOR'S DILEMMA
AND THE POPULIST PARADOX

These research findings suggest that regional elites were guilty of a costly misreading of public opinion. In part, this is a shortcoming of autocratic governance. Autocrats like those in the Gulf typically find it difficult to learn what society thinks. Scholars describe it as a "dictator's dilemma." Policy makers in democracies enjoy a stronger awareness of public preferences because institutions offer avenues for criticism and amendment of unpopular measures. These range from freedoms of speech and press, independent judiciaries, and opportunities to vote for the opposition.[46] Citizens in autocracies, on the other hand, tend to be reluctant to signal their displeasure with policy. The more repressive the regime, the less citizens are willing to speak out. Anxiety isn't confined to the ruled. Autocratic rulers are likely to overcompensate. Since they lack information on public opinion, they proceed with extreme caution.[47]

The information deficit is also attributable to the scarcity of common consultative practices such as survey and focus groups that can illuminate public preferences. A UAE official said policy proposals are normally debated in traditional family-tribal networks and then simply launched: "Policy making isn't very mature in the government. People will just brainstorm around an idea, take it to the legal department, and draft a law. From legal it goes to the *diwan* [ruler's court] and then to the sheikh. He will discuss whatever proposal they bring him. Most [policy makers] don't see the value in consultation." [48]

But while avenues of citizen protest are not institutionalized in the Gulf, they still exist, as we saw in Dubai. Complaints filter into the media and social networks. Prominent citizens go directly to the ruler or his agents. When the outcry is sharp enough, politics trumps economic expediency, and the law is adjusted. As the same official stated: "We don't have a mechanism for public complaints. We hear about it through the newspapers and our own social connections. We need channels of communication." [49]

In addition to the "dictator's dilemma" that makes it difficult to know what subjects think, subsidies in autocratic settings have been described as a "populist paradox." Autocratic regimes do not face electoral pressure that might lead them to manipulate energy prices for votes—but they *do* fear instability. Generous subsidies reduce the risk of revolt among a population that has few means for letting off steam and are a "carrot" that regimes can use instead of the "stick" of violence to stay in power.

Large resource endowments relative to the size of the population can allow generous welfare spending and public salaries, which tend to ease the use of repression. [50] (Table 7.1 shows how this has played out.) The Arab Spring uprisings that ousted leaders in Tunisia, Egypt, Libya, and Yemen demonstrate what can happen to autocrats who lose public support—but few rich rentier autocracies found themselves combating Arab Spring uprisings. There is a strong link between subsidies and regime security, which provides yet another explanation for the durability of otherwise counterproductive energy policy.

With the dictator's dilemma making it difficult to assess citizen attitudes and the populist paradox exposing the attractiveness of subsidies for stability's sake, it's no wonder these price supports have been so durable. Yet, with the regional economy on the line, the monarchies need to

TABLE 7.1 Public employment, political repression, and unrest (annual average: 2000–2007)

Country	Rent per capita US$ thousands	Public Wage Bill per capita US$ thousands (PPP)	Index of Political Repression 0 = most repressive, 8 = least	Unrest (2010–2012) 1 = regime change; 2 = major conflict; 3 = minor conflict; 4 = little to none
GCC Countries				
Qatar	40,446	11.9	6.8	4
Kuwait	25,007	8.1	5.9	3
UAE	15,556	9.2	6.4	4
Bahrain	8,584	3.5	5.9	2
Saudi Arabia	8,239	3.9	4.5	3
Oman	6,975	2.1	7.3	3
GCC Mean	**11,898**	**6**	**6.1**	**3.16**

(*continued*)

TABLE 7.1 Public employment, political repression, and unrest (annual average: 2000–2007) *(continued)*

Country	Rent per capita US$ thousands	Public Wage Bill per capita US$ thousands (PPP)	Index of Political Repression 0 = most repressive, 8 = least	Unrest (2010–2012) 1 = regime change; 2 = major conflict; 3 = minor conflict; 4 = little to none
Populous Arab Oil Exporters				
Iraq	1,775	0.5	0.3	n/a
Algeria	1,563	0.4	3.3	3
Syria	532	0.1	2.9	2
Egypt	313	1.9	2.8	1
Sudan	288	0.1	0.6	3
Yemen	—	0.1	2.9	1
Non-GCC Median	**532**	**0.2**	**2.8**	**2 (mean)**

Notes: Libya was not analyzed. Units: Rent per capita is in thousands of current US dollars, with data from Paul Collier and Anke Hoeffler, "Testing the Neocon Agenda: Democracy in Resource-Rich Societies," *European Economic Review* 53, no. 3 (2009): 293–308, https://doi.org/10.1016/j.euroecorev.2008.05.006, who use data from the World Bank's adjusted savings project. Public Wage Bill per capita is in thousands of real PPP dollars, from the IMF's World Economic Outlook database. Political repression is measured by the index of Physical Integrity Rights: David L. Cingranelli, "The Cingranelli-Richards Human Rights Dataset Version 2008.03.12," http://www.humanrightsdata.org, 2008.

Source: Omer Ali and Ibrahim Elbadawi, "The Political Economy of Public Sector Employment in Resource Dependent Countries," Cairo: ERF Working Paper, 2012; unrest index estimates made by author.

take a new approach. My survey data suggests two lessons: First, governments need to find ways to float proposals for public discussion. Citizens are more likely to get behind painful policy if it's explained and makes sense. Gulf citizens understand how important natural resources are to their well-being. When people are told that higher prices can increase oil and gas exports, many accept the need for personal sacrifice. Second, policy makers are probably being too cautious. They may have more scope than they believe for raising prices. If ruling elites level with their people, like Iran did ahead of its monumental subsidy reform, they might find citizens will accept hardship if it is distributed fairly.

In Saudi Arabia, rulers seem to have internalized these lessons; there, a long era of caution in energy policy was coming to an end.

8

SHIFTING GEARS IN SAUDI ARABIA

Abdullah bin Abdul-Aziz ibn Saud was eighty-two when, in 2005, he was crowned king. Abdullah had already effectively governed Saudi Arabia for a decade as crown prince. King Fahd, his brother, had suffered a debilitating stroke in 1995, and Abdullah took the reins in all but title. When Fahd passed away a decade later, Abdullah's rule became official.

For many Saudis, King Abdullah was a refreshing change from his more flamboyant kin, including Fahd. These were royals with a taste for the fast life, lavishing cash on yachts and parties and flying entourages to Marbella on royal jets, with each given a Mercedes on arrival.[1] By contrast, Abdullah was a modest, cautious man committed to maintaining the sociopolitical status quo. On his watch, Wahhabi restrictions on gender segregation remained intact. Women continued to be banned from driving or even sitting in the main lounge of a coffee shop. Religious police roamed the malls to ensure Saudis behaved and dressed modestly.

King Abdullah likewise refused to tinker with the long-held social contract. He made sure Saudi citizens received their subsidized services, including energy. This meant keeping the prices of electricity, water, and gasoline at rock bottom. King Abdullah did authorize some innovations, including an institute empaneled to explore nuclear and renewable electricity, but by and large, energy policy stagnated.

Energy technocrats understood the danger posed by the kingdom's yearly 6 percent growth in oil consumption, which had compounded in the decades since the oil sector had been nationalized. Saudi Arabia's population had nearly quintupled since the 1970s. Wealth per capita rose almost ninefold. The country's energy-intense industrial structure added complexity and further sources of demand. But policy had not kept pace. Saudis were paying an average of just 3.7 cents per kWh for electricity that cost the kingdom nearly 22 cents to generate, given the world price of the crude oil and diesel fuel used as feedstocks.[2]

The losses being racked up by the domestic energy business were shocking—and embarrassing. Engineers and economists inside government ministries, universities, and especially at the national oil company, Saudi Aramco, were frustrated by the king's caution. "The king is a very old man. He is like a grandfather. He doesn't want to be troubled with the intricacies of policy debates," a Saudi oil sector technocrat told me over mocktails in an al-Khobar restaurant in 2012, during Abdullah's reign. "No one knows what can be done."

Just as in Iran, the kingdom's subsidies were exacerbating inequality. The rich were capturing disproportionate shares of subsidized energy. The effects damaged long-cherished institutions like *asabiyya*, the longstanding tradition of Bedouin egalitarianism. Tribal code considered leaders who shared similar fatherly lineage as equals, with the ruling sheikh considered "first among equals." Now, subsidies were aggravating once minor differences in social class and status.

Subsidies also led arbitrage opportunists to take advantages of price differences in neighboring countries. Saudi diesel fuel that sold for the equivalent of 27 cents per gallon was being trafficked from Turkey all the way to Oman. "We're actually smuggling the subsidy," lamented Majid al-Moneef, a prominent Saudi energy economist and member of the Shura Council, which serves to advise the king. "We're subsidizing all the trucking that goes into the GCC. All the trucks that come from Turkey, Jordan, Lebanon, Syria, and Iraq, they all come into Saudi Arabia, and they fill up on the way in and the way out. We're sending our subsidy not to our needy, not to Yemen, but to Qatar and the UAE! These are very rich countries."[3]

Time and again, King Abdullah's ministers and energy advisers brought up the necessity of reform. The ruler did not want to hear it. "The king would look at it and might say, 'Don't anger the people with new-fangled economic theories. Why raise prices? Aren't we a rich country? Give the people what they want!'" the technocrat said.[4] "He thinks the ministers are trying to gain influence and channel the benefits to themselves." Unfortunately, the technocrats needed the king's signature to raise energy prices. There was no way the Shura Council would approve such a confrontational rearrangement of the terms of the social contract without the king's approval.

Abdullah was perhaps more cautious given the failure of the two previous attempts to raise electricity prices in the kingdom, in 1985 and 1999. Both times the leadership backed down amid public outcries and reversed the increases for households. Abdullah had authorized one price hike during his rule, in 2012, but that, too, was restricted to commercial customers. Antagonizing Saudi households looked too politically risky.[5] Since the residential sector was the largest, consuming nearly half of all power generated, the inability to raise prices on Saudi homes became a major impediment to demand management.

The king wasn't the only point of opposition. Wealthy Saudis had raised hell over the 1999 increase, making the politically effective but false argument that the new pricing amounted to an attack on the poor. In reality the pricing scheme—which would have kept rates unchanged for modest levels of consumption—was aimed at profligate consumers. Saudis in the largest homes consume more than 10,000 kWh per month, around what the average American household consumes in a year and more than double the average yearly consumption in Britain.

THE REGULATOR

The architect of the failed subsidy reform of 1999 was Abdullah al-Shehri, the Saudi electricity regulator and a member of the Shura Council. Al-Shehri was a classic Saudi "meritocrat" who leveraged education to climb the ranks. He grew up in fog-shrouded Abha, a remote mountaintop town near the Yemeni border, and left to study electrical engineering at King Fahd University of Petroleum and Minerals. KFUPM is a masterwork of the 1970s brutalist architecture style that was in vogue across the Mideast during the first oil boom. The university sits at the base of the dome-shaped hill in Dhahran crowned by the Saudi Aramco headquarters. The school feeds a constant stream of graduates up the rocky hill into Aramco and to ministries dealing with oil, electricity, and water.

Al-Shehri didn't take the trip up the hill. Striving for a keener understanding of the power systems he would one day help restructure, al-Shehri sought his graduate degree at Oregon State University, a world away from the Aramco campus, a place where near-constant rainfall fed trees that soared higher than any building then constructed in the kingdom. Al-Shehri returned home in 1985 with a PhD in electrical engineering, starting his career at a time when power infrastructure was still being built out. Al-Shehri taught at his alma mater, KFUPM, and eventually became dean of graduate studies. It was when he was appointed governor of the kingdom's electricity and water regulator, the Electricity and Co-Generation Regulatory Authority of Saudi Arabia (ECRA), that he began informing ruling elites about the kingdom's self-destructive practices.

Al-Shehri, alarmed by the public's increasing thirst for the kingdom's main export commodity, became an advocate for subsidy reform as a way to reduce the kingdom's runaway energy demand. The 1999 reform that he engineered had a tiered tariff structure that reserved high prices for upper levels of consumption to nudge wealthy Saudis to find ways to avoid waste. "There aren't many people who are consuming more than 10,000 kWh a month, but they are the ones with the flexibility to reduce their consumption without sacrificing their comfort," al-Shehri told me over tea in the 1970s-era Dhahran International Hotel, among a lobby full of thobe-wearing men stubbing cigarettes into giant brass ashtrays. Figures from 2016 back this up, showing that over 50 percent of households use less than 2,000 kWh per month, while only 2.4 percent use more than 8,000.[6] Improving efficiency is a relatively simple matter. For instance, three-quarters of the kingdom's buildings lack insulation.[7] Many also lack double-glazed windows. But without the incentive of higher prices, few people are willing to make capital investments required to reduce demand.

However, any policy that suggested hardship for poorer Saudis—even if untrue—was a nonstarter. Al-Shehri was ordered to drop the new tariff. "It was in place for six months, and then there were a lot of complaints that the poor people were being affected. There was a big cry from the rich. And then the price was reduced," al-Shehri said. "They always use the poor as an excuse. But the reduction did not benefit the poor. It benefited the rich." The failed quest instilled in him a disdain for "fat cats" who refused to pull their own weight. The constant battles left al-Shehri, who wears wire-rimmed glasses and a dyed black beard in the Gulf style, with an ingrained skepticism that disguises an otherwise patient demeanor.

Al-Shehri wasn't ready to give up, and he began to lay the groundwork for his next attempt. This time he worked with the Saudi Ministry of Social Affairs to identify poor Saudis, those receiving some form of financial support from the government. Al-Shehri arranged for the monthly electricity bills of those customers to be paid directly by the state—in full, if they managed to keep their consumption below a reasonable threshold.[8] The program was fully supported by King Abdullah, who reserved particular paternal compassion for the poor. By 2015, 414,000 Saudi households were receiving government support with their bills. The poor were protected.[9]

But their protector was unwell. On January 23, 2015, after spending three weeks in the hospital with pneumonia, King Abdullah died at the age of ninety-one. After a brief period of mourning, a city ambulance transported Abdullah's body to the al-Oud cemetery in a rundown section of old Riyadh. The king's male relatives carried the shroud-wrapped body through the crowds and lowered it into an unmarked grave, a fitting resting place for a humble ruler.

For Saudis, the end of an era was at hand. Not only had they lost King Abdullah, but his death coincided with the end of the decade-long boom in the world price of crude oil. For most of that boom, and right up until

September 2015, oil had hovered near $100 a barrel. At the time of Abdullah's death in January, the price of a barrel had crashed into the $40s. Many Saudis would find themselves unprepared for the resulting changes. Not al-Shehri. His plan was ready.

"It's difficult to find a solution that will not make pain for some groups," the regulator said. "But that pain is worth it."

THE GRANDSONS

Salman bin Abdul-Aziz al-Saud, half-brother of King Abdullah and former defense minister and Riyadh governor, took over as king. Salman, seventy-nine at the time of accession, would be the last in a long line of sons of Ibn Saud to rule the lands his father conquered and named for himself in 1932. Shortly after taking power, King Salman appointed the first pair of crown princes from the third generation, the grandsons of Ibn Saud. These grandsons not only wielded increasing power and influence, but they maintained a less paternalistic understanding of the duties of a ruler.

Salman initially chose his nephew Muhammad bin Nayef, then fifty-five, as crown prince, his direct heir. Muhammad bin Nayef, the former interior minister, was well known among elites in the kingdom. In Washington and other capitals, he was considered a safe pair of hands, a potential ruler with government experience and a Western education.[10] Salman did not stop there. He also named a backup—a deputy crown prince—selecting another of the thousand or so grandsons of Ibn Saud, who had had twenty-two known wives and at least forty-five legitimate sons.[11] This time, the choice was a wildcard. Salman selected his favorite son, Muhammad bin Salman.

MbS—as he is known among English speakers—had little governing experience in the kingdom and even less exposure to the accepted protocol for a Saudi ruler in the capitals of the West. He was not the "safe pair of hands" that observers had come to expect from the tightly managed succession process. The choice was a jolt to the kingdom and its watchers. For starters, Muhammad bin Salman was just thirty years old. Many Saudis said he resembled his grandfather, both physically and in the force of his determination. Prince Muhammad combined the vigor of youth with a work ethic that kept him and his aides formulating policy until the desert birds started their chorus at dawn.

Most importantly, MbS enjoyed his father's complete confidence. Despite what many observers considered an insufficient pedigree—for instance, he attended King Saud University rather than a top school in the West—the king entrusted his son with powerful new positions. MbS became chief of the royal *diwan*, which controls access to the king. He landed controlling roles in the economy and energy sector as the head of the new Supreme Council for Saudi Aramco. Most significantly, MbS was named minister of defense.

Saudis and observers were deeply divided on the wisdom of handing so much power to such a young man. Many argued that MbS was unprepared. He had not paid his dues by governing a province, leading a ministry, or serving as an ambassador or chief of one of the security services or intelligence branches. Many qualified candidates had been leapfrogged by the headstrong prince. Anonymous letters purportedly written by disgruntled royal family members began circulating, warning of divisions within the al-Saud and threatening that a palace coup could be the result.

But MbS had strong backing too. Besides his father, Muhammad built up a cadre of top advisers and consultants, men like Khalid al-Falih, the former CEO of Saudi Aramco (who would soon become oil minister), and Mohammed al-Sheikh, a Harvard-educated World Bank lawyer. To ordinary Saudis, Muhammad's lack of international experience looked more like a lack of Western taint. He was a real Saudi who spoke like them, a man at ease in power and comfortable in his own skin, not afraid to debate policy with Western journalists and be photographed informally, relaxing without his *gutra* headscarf.

Best of all, MbS was of the younger generation. Many Saudis felt deeply frustrated that decades of sclerotic rule had made policy making too risk averse, holding back the potential of an emerging power. Saudi Arabia is one of the youngest countries on earth, and grassroots changes have been percolating up from a tech-savvy society despite the anemic pace at the top. Young Saudis embraced Twitter and Facebook at a level unmatched nearly anywhere else. The religion-inspired ban on cinema (only lifted in 2017) combined with excellent internet connectivity allowed Saudis to become the world's top per capita consumers of You-Tube videos. The average Saudi watches at least six internet videos a day, or 190 million daily for the kingdom.[12] These tools allowed Saudis to fraternize with the opposite sex and, for a time, to shed their inhibitions about criticizing the regime.

Western academics and other Saudi-watchers had long identified the jump between generations as a potential trigger mechanism for a "succession crisis" that could bring down the monarchy.[13] Others, including some in the region, saw the opposite. Saudi Arabia needed a jolt out of its lethargy, someone who could realign its system with reality. Initially, MbS convinced many that he was the right reformer for the job. He won over skeptics by increasing social freedoms, allowing women to drive. But gains were soon eclipsed by reckless actions, including repression of critics and a clampdown on political speech.[14]

This combination of power and support soon allowed MbS to over-turn dramatically the hierarchy of succession that his father had set in place. In June 2017, Muhammad bin Salman and others within the royal family forced the removal of the crown prince, Mohammed bin Nayef. Muhammad bin Salman assumed his uncle's role as crown prince, positioning himself a heartbeat from the throne. Royal family sources told the press that Nayef's dismissal had not come as a result of a naked power grab but stemmed from Nayef's inability to end his stubborn addiction to morphine, a painkilling drug he had been prescribed after being wounded in a 2009 assassination attempt.[15] Whatever the case, MbS continued to consolidate power in early 2018 by ousting or detaining key opponents.

THE PRINCE AND THE PRICE INCREASES

As Muhammad bin Salman came into power, the kingdom's rising energy consumption assumed the urgency of an impending train wreck.

The outlook was sobering. The kingdom needed an estimated $133 billion to keep up with electricity demand, which was expected to more than double over the coming decade.[16] On top of those direct costs was the even more onerous opportunity cost—the potential revenue squandered by burning so much oil and gas rather than exporting it at market prices. Saudi Arabia could not afford to continue along this ruinous trajectory much longer.

Most of the growth was being driven by simple demand for air conditioning. Despite the damage to the kingdom's financial and environmental health, almost no individual consumer was willing to spend the money to insulate buildings or upgrade windows, either of which would cut household demand by a third. Since electricity was so cheap, contractors complained that the additional 5 percent cost in weatherization expenses went uncompensated. One frustrated official said the refusal to insulate buildings was costing the kingdom 30 million barrels of oil per year.[17]

Water use was another big concern. Daily consumption had reached 66 gallons (250 liters) per person, versus a global average of just over 20 (80 liters). Officials complained that Saudi Arabia, without a single river or natural lake, consumed water at rates nearly as high as Canada, a country with fresh water covering 9 percent of its surface area.[18] The distortions caused by underpricing threatened the very foundations of the Saudi state. The "untouchable" cradle-to-grave subsidies on energy began to look like teetering anachronisms.

Would Muhammad bin Salman feel that his legitimacy depended on maintaining the big energy giveaway? King Abdullah hadn't even been buried a year by the time Saudis learned the answer. On December 28, 2015, King Salman's cabinet announced that a full roster of energy price increases would take effect across the kingdom in four days—on January 1, 2016. The price hikes increased the costs of all forms of energy and affected all customer classes, from factories to shops, government offices to homes. Saudi citizens would see their household electricity and water costs rise, as would the price of transportation fuels. Al-Shehri's preparations ensured that poor Saudis could be exempted from the increase as long as they kept their consumption within reasonable bounds.

Muhammad bin Salman followed up with an announcement that, over the next five years, energy subsidies would be totally abolished.[19]

As the Saudi public digested the news, the authorities gave a grim demonstration of their appetite for dissent. On January 2, a day after the price reform took effect, the government announced it had executed forty-seven Saudi prisoners, including the outspoken Shiite religious sheikh Nimr al-Nimr. The executions overshadowed the subsidy retractions, causing an international uproar. Enraged Iranians overran Saudi diplomatic missions in Iran, leading Riyadh to break off diplomatic ties. At least one observer speculated that the executions were timed to obscure the kingdom's increase in energy prices.[20]

In December 2016, al-Falih added further detail to the reform plans. The energy ministry would gradually raise energy prices to international levels and, in the future, compensate Saudi citizens with monthly cash deposits.[21] The kingdom began registering people in a new distribution scheme called the Citizen's Account program. The amount of compensation would vary according to income, with the poorest Saudis getting 100 percent of the subsidy value and the very richest receiving nothing. Foreign residents who had previously benefited from subsidized energy would also receive nothing.

As it turned out, the success of Iran's subsidy reform had not escaped notice in the kingdom. The MbS plan resembled that of Ahmadinejad, except that the Saudi treasury would capture a larger portion of energy sales revenue, because cash handouts would be tilted toward the poor. Iran made the costly blunder of giving out payments indiscriminately.

The Saudi reform was the most sweeping to date in the Gulf monarchies. Residential electricity and water prices rose for the first time ever. Water charges increased by more than 400 percent for the average household, and the price for electricity went up for consumption beyond 4,000 kWh per month. Water and electricity rates for commercial and industrial consumers increased at all tiers of consumption. Commercial water users in the kingdom were handed rates more than double those in Arizona.[22] Saudi Arabia also raised prices on gasoline, diesel, and other refined oil products by an average of 122 percent.

On the other hand, as table 8.1 shows, most prices remained heavily subsidized and well below international benchmarks. Unlike Dubai's across-the-board increase to electricity prices, residential rates in Saudi Arabia were initially only raised on higher consumption brackets to discourage waste. The target was the "fat cats," the rich households in sprawling villas consuming disproportionate shares of subsidized electricity.[23]

The jump in water prices caused the biggest outcry.[24] When Saudis complained, the minister of water and electricity, Abdullah al-Hasin, suggested they drill their own wells. Not only was al-Hasin's statement an empathy-deficient "let them eat cake" moment, but an increase in well drilling would only put more pressure on already overstressed aquifers. King Salman quickly fired al-Hasin.[25] Soon after, his ministry was reorganized.

In 2018, the Saudi government acted on subsidies a second time, raising some prices significantly and leaving others alone. Gasoline and electricity prices saw the biggest increases. High-octane gasoline began selling inside the kingdom for an unheard-of $2.09 per gallon, approaching prices in the United States. Most surprising was the hike in electricity prices for small amounts of consumption; a measure meant to protect the poor had fallen by the wayside. The price rose 260 percent, from 1.4 cents to 5 cents per kWh.

But the poor had not been abandoned. A week before the price increases went into effect, the government launched the Citizen's Account program, distributing $533 million in cash replacement benefits for low- and middle-income families. Inaugural monthly payments went to 3 million households (13 million Saudis), a bit more than half of the citizen population. Checks ranged from $80 to a maximum of $250. A fifth of the families that registered for a Citizen's Account received nothing, presumably because their income was deemed too high.[26] The cash stipends were aimed to assuage some the sting of higher energy prices as well as the introduction of another allegedly taboo policy, a value-added tax.[27]

The government held firm on both rounds of price increases. Although Saudis did not pour into the streets in protest, they made their grievances known on Twitter. Some Saudis argued that subsidy cuts were the

TABLE 8.1 Price changes of Saudi energy products after January 1, 2016

Product	2015	2016/2017	2018	% change (2015–2018)	Current benchmark (US$) (source)	Saudi 2018 price as factor of international benchmark
Crude oil for power generation (US$/bbl)	$4.23	$5.87	$5.87	39%	$54.20 (2017 Brent)	11%
Heavy fuel oil for power generation (US$/mmbtu)	$0.36	$0.66	$0.66	82%	$6.26 (2016 US no.6 Residual fuel oil)	10%
Natural gas (methane) (US$/mmbtu)	$0.75	$1.25	$1.25	67%	$4.69 (2016 NBP)	27%
Natural gas (ethane) (US$/mmbtu)	$0.75	$1.75	$1.75	133%	$4.69 (2016 NBP)	37%
Gasoline (91 octane) (US$/gallon)	$0.46	$0.77	$1.40	204%	$2.53 (2017 US)	55%
Gasoline (95 octane) (US$/gallon)	$0.61	$0.92	$2.09	240%	$2.53 (2017 US)	82%
Diesel (US$/gallon)	$0.26	$0.48	$0.48	88%	$2.65 (2017 US)	18%
Diesel (industry use)	$0.26	$0.34	$0.39	51%		15%
Water (nonresidential) (US$/cubic meter)	$1.62	$2.43	$2.43	50%	$1.02 (2018 Tucson, AZ, US)*	238%
Water (residential) (US$/cubic meter)**	$0.03	$0.04	$0.04	50%	$0.61 (2018 Tucson, AZ, US)	7%
Electricity (residential, low consumption) (US$/kWh)	$0.01	$0.01	$0.05	260%	$0.13 (2017 EIA)	37%
Electricity (residential, moderate consumption) (US$/kWh)	$0.03	$0.05	$0.05	50%	$0.13 (2017 EIA)	37%
Electricity (residential, high consumption) (US$/kWh)	$0.04	$0.08	$0.08	100%	$0.13 (2017 EIA)	62%

* Base rate for commercial users.
** Saudi 2016 price covers first 15m³/month only; Abbreviations: bbl, barrels; mmbtu, million British thermal units; NBP, National Balancing Point; EIA, Energy Information Administration.

result of economic mismanagement. One common refrain was that poor Saudis were being forced to pay more to underwrite the billions of riyals spent on questionable weapons purchases, ill-conceived wars in Syria and Yemen, and aid for Egypt's military. Government corruption and royal family privilege was another thread. "When oil went up to $120 a barrel, what did the general population gain? How can we justify increasing the cost burden on the public today?" one disgruntled Saudi tweeted. "Whoever fails to manage these affairs properly should resign."[28]

Others supported the reform on the basis that the prior distribution of subsidies was an even bigger injustice. Reforms disproportionately targeted the rich. "Imagine if the government decided to give a billion riyals to citizens, but 80 percent of this billion goes to the richest 40 percent of the population and the remaining 20 percent share goes to the poorer majority. Right now that is exactly what is happening under the current subsidy system," the commentator Essam al-Zamel argued in a YouTube video that preceded the reform. Al-Zamel maintained that government outlays for energy subsidies were more than double those aimed at poverty reduction. "We are taking from the poor to give to the rich. The optimal situation is that everybody pays the real price and you target the poor with cash."[29] Despite al-Zamel's backing for the reform, he was one of several prominent commentators swept up in mass arrests in September 2017. Muhammad bin Salman's consolidation of his power base included a crackdown on preachers, scholars, intellectuals, and activist Saudis, many of whom were jailed for speaking out against changes in government policies or in favor of political reforms or opposition groups.[30]

Intensified repression probably helped dissuade Saudis from taking to the streets. But other factors also calmed the masses. When the poor were hit with higher rates in 2018, they received cash compensation. Further, new water and power rates were skewed toward commercial rather than residential customers. Finally, Saudi officials had wisely publicized the wasted resources.[31] By the time the subsidy cuts came, at least some members of the public understood that their loss in benefits was in the national interest.

EFFECTS ON DEMAND

There are any number of terrific reasons for abolishing fossil fuel subsidies, whether for climate benefits, reduced local pollution and traffic congestion, better health (both physical and fiscal), and improved social equity. But the biggest prize for the Gulf petrostates has been the hope that higher prices will begin to throttle down the relentless growth in energy demand and, as a consequence, extend these countries' ability to export.

A simple hypothetical exercise that holds all variables constant other than consumption offers basic insight. At an average annual increase in domestic oil demand of 7 percent, Saudi Arabia would consume all of its 2015 oil production of 10.2mbd by 2035. Reducing that rate to 2 percent pushes the date out to 2085.[32] The lower the growth rate of domestic demand, the more breathing space the kingdom has to diversify its economy before oil exports come to an end.

When the price increases hit, Saudis faced a choice: they could maintain their habits and pay more for energy or reduce their consumption and pay a similar amount. Would higher prices start to budge demand? Would people insulate homes or downsize vehicles? The answer is yes. Electricity demand declined for the first time in the sixteen-year history of the Saudi Electricity Company.[33] Peak load in 2016 dropped 2.3 percent over 2015, and the average per customer consumption was down by just over 5 percent (figures 8.1 and 8.2).[34] The data must have cheered the technocrats at Saudi Aramco: behavior seemed to be responding to higher prices.

Demand for transportation fuel also responded. The 88 percent increase in diesel prices played havoc on Saudi consumption, which dropped by 10 percent in 2016 and fell another 16 percent in 2017. In the first three months of 2018, diesel demand continued downward, dropping another 14 percent compared with the same period the year before. As for gasoline, the price increase produced a less dramatic response. Gasoline demand remained flat in 2016 and rose by nearly 6 percent in 2017. However, the major price hike in 2018 finally convinced

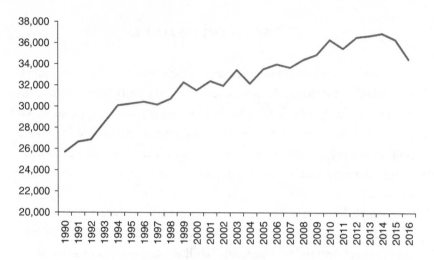

FIGURE 8.1 Saudi electricity demand: kWh/customer.

Saudi power demand per customer shows a decline in 2016,
with the first decline in peak load since 1991.

Source: Electricity and Cogeneration Regulatory Authority, "Electricity
and Cogeneration Regulatory Authority (ECRA) Data and Statistics," regulatory report
(Riyadh: ECRA, 2017), http://www.ecra.gov.sa/en-us/DataAndStatistics/NationalRecord
/HistoricalData/Pages/Home.aspx.

Saudi consumers to change their behavior. Gasoline demand in the
first quarter of 2018 dropped by 7 percent over the same period in 2017.
Overall, Saudi oil consumption grew by just 1.6 percent in 2016, a
fraction of the 5.7 percent average for the decade. In 2017, oil demand
actually shifted into reverse, dropping by just over half a percent—the
first drop in yearly demand since the mid-90s.[35]

The reforms under King Salman went beyond price changes. The king
also decreed a long-overdue rearranging of the institutions of energy
governance, starting with the Ministry of Petroleum and Minerals under
its long-serving leader Ali Naimi. Naimi is one of the more colorful characters in the kingdom; his life is emblematic of the transformation of
the kingdom from a hermetic backwater to global powerhouse. Naimi
was raised in a Bedouin family that grazed livestock in the desert around

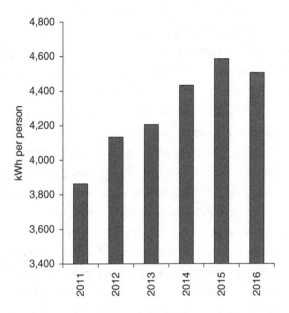

FIGURE 8.2 Per capita consumption of electricity in the Saudi residential sector.

The Saudi residential sector also saw a small decline in per capita consumption in 2016.

Source: Electricity and Cogeneration Regulatory Authority, "Electricity and Cogeneration Regulatory Authority (ECRA) Data and Statistics," regulatory report (Riyadh: ECRA, 2017), http://www.ecra.gov.sa/en-us/DataAndStatistics /NationalRecord/HistoricalData/Pages/Home.aspx.

al-Hasa, the same area in which American prospectors found oil in the 1930s. At the age of eight, he started English school at Aramco's Dhahran camp and, by the age of twelve, in 1947, young Ali landed his first job in the oil sector, as an Aramco office boy. By 1995, Naimi had clawed his way to the pinnacle of the Saudi energy bureaucracy, becoming minister of petroleum and minerals. The energetic oil minister soon became the most internationally recognizable Saudi, a man with a penchant for forcing interlocutors to join him for a vigorous hike, during which he would provide his thoughts. During OPEC meetings, Naimi did the same thing with the international press, holding court with a coterie of reporters he persuaded to wake early and join him for a jog around

Vienna. Those who ran alongside were rewarded with scraps of detail for their stories.[36] By 2016, after nearly seventy years in the Saudi oil sector, Naimi was finally allowed to retire. But instead of simply appointing a replacement minister, King Salman leveraged the opportunity to fix another problematic aspect of Saudi energy governance. He merged Naimi's ministry with the Ministry of Electricity and Water, whose director, Abdullah al-Hasin, had been fired.

Combining the two discordant fiefs of Saudi energy policy was another move that Saudi technocrats had been dreaming of under King Abdullah. The two ministries had long worked at cross purposes. Naimi's oil ministry had been externally focused, concerned mainly with producing enough oil for export and managing international market strategy. The oil minister had no control over domestic consumption of oil and gas in power generation, which fell under the purview of al-Hasin's electricity ministry. Al-Hasin's objective was to meet domestic demand for electricity and water, no matter what the effect on exports. The crucial matter of demand management had fallen through the cracks.

The new body, the Ministry of Energy, Industry, and Natural Resources, now governed the entire energy landscape. It could see that internal needs were met while also guaranteeing that Saudi demand didn't conflict with exports or the industrial strategy that underpins the kingdom's GDP. Picked to run the "super ministry" was the former Saudi Aramco CEO Khalid al-Falih. A mechanical engineer schooled at Texas A&M, al-Falih had deftly scaled the ranks inside Saudi Aramco. On the world stage, al-Falih's competence was so obvious that many observers considered the Dammam native to outshine the CEOs of the big Western oil firms that had created Aramco so many years ago.

Al-Falih had long spoken in support of price reforms. As minister, he would now oversee them. In August 2016, it fell to al-Falih to declare the first sign of success of the January price increases: a drop in the kingdom's summer "crude burn," the peak period when crude oil is burned to power the kingdom's millions of air conditioners. Saudi burning of crude oil averaged 572,000 b/d in 2015. In 2016, it fell to 497,000 b/d. In 2017, it fell again, reaching 458,000 b/d.[37] "The efficiency program that we adapted during the last three years has started bearing fruit, especially that now efficiency measures have been combined with higher electricity and oil product prices, which had the desired effect of slowing demand growth," al-Falih said. He attributed the drop in crude oil demand to the subsidy reforms and to increased production of natural gas, which substituted for oil in power generation.[38]

Higher prices curtailed a few egregiously wasteful practices. One was the widespread use of diesel-powered generators to provide electricity to commercial buildings. Diesel had been so cheap that owners of shopping malls saved money by disconnecting from the central grid—where commercial electricity rates had risen in 2012—and generating their own power. The practice of running noisy, smoke-belching generators all day and night exacerbated oil demand and local air pollution and enlarged the Saudi carbon footprint. The steep drop in diesel demand showed that such practices were being abandoned.

Aramco officials hoped that higher gasoline prices might also discourage joyriding and car accidents. Fuel was so cheap that young men drove aimlessly to pass time, which aggravated pollution, traffic congestion, and oil demand.[39] The joy of driving often brought tragedy. Reckless driving had given Saudi Arabia the grim title of world leader in per capita deaths from car crashes, the leading cause of death for Saudi males aged sixteen to thirty-six.[40] Smuggling was another major focus of the reforms, but Aramco's hopes that higher prices would undercut fuel trafficking only went part way. Neighboring countries also increased prices. Saudi diesel fuel still carried a hefty discount in comparison with prices in the UAE, Oman, Jordan, and other neighbors.

In January 2016, a few weeks into the new price environment, I discussed the subsidy reforms with several prominent Saudi merchants, the heads of big family business groups in the Eastern Province. Their responses, over dinner in Dhahran, were mixed. While some said the reduction of smuggling and waste was in the national interest, others said the reforms would inevitably bring on inflation. One young Saudi merchant, the head of a dairy business, told me he would be forced to pass along the increased business costs in the form of higher prices for milk and butter. Higher diesel prices meant that trucking his products to market was more expensive. Costs for air conditioning his cow barns had risen, as had the price of water used for "misting" the cows to cool them. "I have no choice," he said.[41] Inflation did bump abruptly upward that January, but Saudi central bank data revealed it to be a one-time price adjustment that lasted about a month.

By 2018, following the second round of energy price increases, the Saudi demand conundrum finally began to appear resolvable. The elite who upended previous price reforms had lost their touch. With MbS's oversight, new prices were brusquely shoved through. In February 2018, most Saudis I met with had grown used to the notion that energy services had to be paid for. "We Saudis have been getting a fantastic deal for more than 40 years," said the owner of a real-estate business. "We're not used to paying more. But we must." Surprisingly, a succession of Uber drivers I queried seemed unfazed by the new gasoline prices. Not everyone was so blasé. A prominent Shia from the Eastern Province, a young man who asked that his name not be used, reported high levels of dissatisfaction in poorer Qatif. "The government is asking far too much, too quickly. They cannot keep pushing people so hard. Reforms are necessary. But the poor are not ready for this."[42]

Sweeping price reforms in Saudi Arabia represented another sort of milestone: a recasting of commonly held assumptions about energy in the world's fossil fuel heartland. Dubai demonstrated that prices could be changed without triggering riots. But post-oil Dubai operates under a different set of conditions than does Saudi Arabia and the other oil monarchies. Dubai extracts rents from foreign businesses and from the expatriate residents that dominate its population. The presence of so many foreigners—all paying at least triple the citizen price for electricity and water—insulates the Dubai government against an outcry by citizens.

Reforms in Saudi Arabia were more politically fraught. Ordinary Saudis considered themselves stewards of the kingdom's colossal resource base, and many appeared to believe that their special status should be reflected in the prices and availability of energy. When prices rose, many Saudis took to social media to voice their dissatisfaction with King Salman's energy policy. Some railed against the government or even criticized individual ministers by name, a risky tactic in an autocracy known to jail dissenters. Others chose a more subtle but still effective technique: They posted the portrait of King Abdullah, the cautious paternalist who had never burdened his people with such policies.

As one of the key architects of the reforms, al-Shehri had dealt often with such critiques. Reflecting on the progress the kingdom had made since King Salman's accession, he offered a diplomatic response. "The era of King Abdullah was good one. He achieved a lot of development," al-Shehri told me during a 2018 meeting in ECRA's Riyadh office tower. "The era of King Salman is about sustaining that development—and preparing for the future."

Sustainability is the mantra of subsidy reform. If price increases could go ahead in Saudi Arabia, what about its neighbors? Most of them were in the same boat. Could they squeeze similar concessions from their social contracts?

9

THE POLITICS OF REFORM

The Imam Jafar al-Sadiq Mosque is one of the oldest in Kuwait, with a moss-green dome covered in eight-pointed stars and a coating of orange dust. Bracketing the dome is a pair of balconied minarets that rise among the aging skyscrapers in the old heart of Kuwait City. The mosque, named for a Medina-born Islamic jurist descended from the Prophet Muhammad, is a favored house of worship for Kuwait's large Shia population. Since Kuwait lies adjacent to deeply Shiite southern Iraq and western Iran, Shia have long constituted a significant minority. But unlike in some of the other Gulf monarchies, Shia enjoy deep integration and prominent roles in Kuwaiti society. Worshippers frequenting the Imam Jafar Mosque include many Hasawi Shia, so named because they migrated in the late nineteenth and early twentieth centuries from the al-Hasa oasis in what is now eastern Saudi Arabia.

On June 26, 2015, during the holy month of Ramadan, two Sunni Muslim men challenged this relatively harmonious state of affairs. The pair—Fahd al-Gabaa and Abdulrahman Sabah Saud—sat in a car outside the Imam Jafar Mosque as the imam's Friday sermon blared out over the parking lot. Al-Gabaa, a twenty-three-year-old Saudi with a bushy beard and intense eyes, sat in the passenger's seat. He wore a bomb taped to his chest and clenched a detonator in his fist. Saud, a twenty-six-year-old stateless Kuwaiti, sat in the driver's seat. Both men had pledged allegiance to the Islamic State, or ISIS, which was then in the midst of a gory Ramadan offensive. On the same day, Islamist attackers also struck a factory in France, a beach resort in Tunisia, a Kurdish village in Syria, and a peacekeeping base in Somalia. The pair had been ordered to commit an attack that would "shake Kuwait up." Al-Gabaa and Saud targeted the mosque, knowing that ISIS reserved a particular disdain for adherents of Shiism, the second-largest of Islam's two main branches.

More than two thousand worshippers had streamed into the downtown mosque for Friday prayers, mainly men in white *kandoura* robes. The sanctuary was packed beyond capacity. At some point toward the end of the sermon, when the attackers determined that the crowd had reached its peak, al-Gabaa stepped out of the car and bid his companion goodbye. The young Saudi threaded his way into the rear of the mosque, still gripping the detonator in his fist. As his co-conspirator drove toward the Saudi border, al-Gabaa made his way among the last two rows of kneeling worshippers. He at last unclasped his fist. An enormous blast erupted, obliterating al-Gabaa's body and ripping open the ceiling and the rear wall of the mosque. The explosion killed twenty-six worshippers, mainly Kuwaitis but also Iranians, Indians, and others. Among the 227 injured was the Kuwaiti parliamentarian Khalil al-Salih. He had noticed al-Gabaa walk into the mosque with his left arm curiously crossed over his torso. "I saw him with my own eyes," al-Salih said.[1]

For Kuwait, the bombing was an alarming step in the wrong direction. The tiny sheikhdom was a haven of prosperity. Kuwait was so safe it was considered boring, particularly among expatriates irritated by its ban on alcohol. Even so, Kuwaitis understood the fragility of stability better than most, given the vagaries of survival next to Iraq, a neighbor prone to periodic threats of invasion (and actually carrying one of them out, in 1990). Other than a few minor bombings in the 1980s and small-scale shooting attempts—one on US troops—Kuwait had no experience with terrorism and certainly not with a mass-casualty attack like the bombing of the Imam Jafar al-Sadiq Mosque.[2]

Kuwait's emir, Sheikh Sabah, visited the mosque immediately after the blast, stressing unity in the face of a widening sectarian rift. The attack was deeply symbolic, given the Saudi citizenship of the bomber and the Saudi ancestry of the Shia Hasawi victims. The emir knew that if he was not careful Kuwait's precious stability could unravel. "National unity is a protective fence for the security of the nation," Sheikh Sabah told reporters at the scene. Justice Minister Yaqoub al-Sanea declared that the chaos of surrounding states would not be allowed to infect Kuwait. He swore that "Kuwait will remain an oasis of security for all groups of Kuwaiti society and all sects."

The mosque bombing in Kuwait did not attract much attention in the West, with media crews focused on the attacks in Tunisia, Syria, and France. But it resonated deeply in the Gulf. Was chaos closing in on the Persian Gulf region, the last remaining bastion of stability in the Middle East?

Five years after the start of the Arab Spring, the initial euphoria among democracy advocates had soured. Popular uprisings had dragged Libya, Syria, and Yemen into civil war and tipped Iraq back into chaos. Repressive dictatorships reemerged in Bahrain and Egypt, and the Islamic State took control of much of Iraq and Syria, muscling into the oil business. ISIS deployed a slick media operation that turned young men against their rulers and the West. Young Saudis appeared particularly susceptible. The kingdom suffered dozens of attacks starting in 2002 not just from ISIS terrorists but from cross-border incursions by Shia Houthi forces in Yemen, mostly in retaliation for the Saudi-led campaign to dislodge them from power. Citizens in the Gulf were rightly worried.

Contributing to the sense of siege was the 73 percent plunge in oil prices between late 2014 and the end of 2015—from $112 to $30 a barrel. By 2016, all six Gulf monarchies were in fiscal trouble. They needed high oil prices to balance their budgets (see figure 9.1), ranging from a low of $49/bbl in Kuwait to an untenable $108/bbl in Bahrain. In 2016, all the Gulf monarchies, even ultra-rich Qatar, faced budget shortfalls of at least 30 percent.[3]

To young technocrats angling to cut energy subsidies, the combination of a crash in the price of oil and civil unrest provided the beginnings of a pretext. As mentioned, centralized states are at a disadvantage when

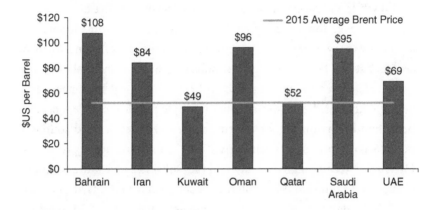

FIGURE 9.1 2015 breakeven oil prices in GCC.

Oil prices needed to fund 2015 government budgets fully were above the prevailing Brent price in all but Kuwait and Qatar.

Source: International Monetary Fund, "World Economic Outlook" (Washington: IMF, October 2016).

it comes to reforming subsidies or other benefits. Everyone knows who is behind any painful policy decision. Therefore, centralized regimes try to restrict unpopular reforms to periods when they can deflect blame.[4] A crisis presents a useful excuse. The old governing adage "never let a crisis go to waste" is apt.

The Kuwait mosque bombers probably had no idea that their attack would make it easier for governments around the Gulf to raise prices on fuel, electricity, and water, but that is essentially what happened. Citizens rallied around their ruling sheikhs as bulwarks against the depredations of ISIS. Fear of unrest put citizens in a more understanding mindset.

A few years earlier, Dubai's ability to retract citizen electricity and water subsidies was seen as a "special case," given the peculiarities of that post-oil city-state. Now, the prerequisites for retraction began to materialize across the GCC. Keeping citizens awash in cheap fuel was not as important as keeping them safe from ISIS. Since crumbling oil prices had shattered government budgets, social spending could at last be tackled.

But while a fiscal crisis and a security crisis might have been enough political cover for ordinary centralized states, the Gulf monarchies aren't ordinary. They are *absolute monarchies*, an extreme form of centralization. For these regimes, subsidies are crucial tools that are exploited to preserve social peace *and* rulers' political legitimacy. Tinkering with subsidies is so risky that multiple political enablers need to be in hand. Fortunately for reform-minded regimes, a third source of political cover presented itself, arriving in the form of outside pressure—international campaigns to end fossil fuel subsidies and address climate change and pollution. Multilateral agencies such as the G20, the IMF, the World Bank, and the Paris climate agreement of 2015 intensified pressure on countries to end price supports for carbon-rich fuels. Saudi Arabia, a G20 member, explicitly tied its Paris pledge to its ability to reduce domestic energy demand by raising prices.[5]

Thus, we can say that reforms in the Gulf appear to have been catalyzed by the combination of extreme instability and deepening fiscal crisis, with an added dose of external pressure. These factors should be considered *convenient political cover* that helped launch reforms; they were not the driving rationales for changes in energy prices. The real reason reforms went ahead, of course, was that policy makers simply needed to rein in the growing diversion of exportable oil and gas into domestic markets.

In the previous chapter, we looked at some of Saudi Arabia's reforms— but they weren't the only ones. The other five sheikhdoms also took action.

KUWAIT

Of all the Gulf monarchies, subsidy reform faced its stiffest challenge in Kuwait. By the mid-2000s, per capita energy demand in Kuwait had reached staggering levels, particularly for power consumption in the homes of Kuwaiti citizens. This led to a defining moment in 2008, when

Kuwait's shortage of natural gas forced the monarchy to begin importing LNG at world market prices. Even so, ever-larger amounts of crude oil were still being diverted into the power sector. Liquid fuels accounted for 60 percent of power generation at the end of 2016, the highest share in the Gulf. [6]

This predicament was entirely of the government's own making. Electricity prices had been fixed for fifty years at a rate that ranks among the world's lowest. Charges were so tiny that, despite consumption at world-leading rates, most households were billed once a year, rather than monthly. Even so, the Ministry of Electricity and Water only managed to collect payment for about 55 percent of the electricity it sold.[7]

Stymieing reform was the structure of politics in Kuwait, which featured the unproductive combination of an autocratic monarchy and an elected legislature endowed with the power to spoil monarchical initiatives. Kuwaiti elections tended to bring populists to parliament, politicians who view it as their duty to clamor for more rent distribution, not less. A tariff increase in Kuwait would first have to be approved by the emir and his cabinet and then face the unlikely prospect of passage in parliament.[8] Several parliamentarians declared they would fight any such proposals.

Despite the opposition and hurdles, Kuwait succeeded in raising some energy prices (table 9.1). Kuwait hiked diesel prices in January 2015 from 69 US cents to US$2.15 per gallon, but within a month it readjusted the price to US$1.32 per gallon. Businesses with "heavy demand" continued paying the original price.[9] In 2016, Kuwait increased gasoline prices by 41 percent—the first increase since 1998—and pledged to adjust fuel prices in line with market shifts every three months. Regular gasoline rose from 77 US cents to US$1.07 per gallon, while premium jumped from 81 cents to $1.35 per gallon.[10]

And in late 2017, Kuwait at long last raised electricity and water prices—but just for commercial and government customers. Rates for nonresidential users jumped from two to 25 fils, or from less than one US cent to about 8 US cents per kWh. Water prices for the same customers also rose substantially, from $2.65 to $13.25 for 1,000 gallons.[11]

TABLE 9.1 Fuel price increases around the GCC

	Diesel (US$/gallon)			Gasoline (US$/gallon)		
	2014/2015	2018	% change	2014/2015	2018	% change
Bahrain	1.00	1.61	61%	0.80	1.40	75%
Kuwait*	0.69	1.32	109%	0.77	1.07	41%
Oman*	1.44	2.45	71%	1.12	2.12	89%
Qatar*	1.02	2.10	106%	0.87	2.04	134%
UAE*	2.96	2.77	−6%	1.65	2.49	51%

After oil prices fell in the international market, Kuwait, Oman, Qatar, and the UAE linked gasoline and diesel prices to international market prices, adjusting them monthly. Increases occurred in all the countries reviewed here except for diesel fuel in the UAE, which was adjusted downward in line with falling international prices.
* Fuel prices are linked to global market prices; adjusted monthly 2018 prices were retrieved from media and government sources in June 2018; price for 90 octane (or approx.) was used for gasoline price.

Source: Compiled by Baker Institute from regional media and government publications.

QATAR

The only Gulf monarchy with cheaper electricity than Kuwait—and less pressure to reform prices—is Qatar. Qatar is the richest of the Gulf monarchies and in 2018 was the wealthiest country in the world on the basis of per capita income. For Qatari citizens, electricity is free, as is water. For expatriate residents who dominate the population, however, electricity prices have been rising for the last decade, including a bump in October 2015 from 2.16 to 2.43 US cents per kWh for consumption between 2,000 and 4,000 kWh. Even so, the cost of electricity to the government was about twice as much, 4.2 cents per kWh.[12] Under the same reform, expatriates' water charges jumped from US$1.20 to at least US$1.50 per cubic meter for consumption beyond 20 cubic meters per month.[13]

Qatar's increased fuel prices (table 9.1) also appear to have reduced 2016 demand by 11 percent for gasoline and 2 percent for diesel. Qatar's small increases in expatriates' utility rates were insufficient to reduce overall demand but may have contributed to small declines in per capita consumption—which for electricity dropped 2 percent in 2015 and 4 percent in 2016 and for water dropped 2 percent and 3 percent over the same period.[14]

For Qatari citizens, electricity and water will probably remain free. The country produces huge amounts of natural gas relative to its population. Domestic demand remains too small to threaten exports anytime soon. Only 7 percent of gas production is consumed in the power sector; 80 percent is exported.[15] With an absolute monarch dependent on citizen support, Qatar appears comfortable giving citizens unlimited free utility services.[16] "The locals have this right to free power and water," said an expatriate manager within the electricity sector. "For the foreseeable future it won't change."[17]

OMAN

Oman is in a much tighter spot than either Kuwait or Qatar and arguably is worse off from an energy standpoint than any of the other Gulf monarchies. Average 12 percent yearly growth in electricity consumption has tripled power demand in just a decade.[18] Despite this scorching growth, per capita consumption in Oman remains the lowest in the Gulf, since Oman got off to such a late start in development.

Oman's electricity regulator has warned that the sultanate, with modest hydrocarbon reserves, cannot tolerate the indulgent levels of power and water demand seen in the other monarchies. The fear is twofold. First, subsidies have locked in high rates of demand by encouraging an energy-inefficient building boom. Second, this path dependence is being set in place at a time when the costs to provide these services are rising dramatically.

Oman's oil and gas production has been shifting away from the sultanate's small and depleting conventional reserves to its technically challenging deposits of unconventional oil and gas.[19] Production costs have risen, but Omani policy makers have been reluctant to pass along those cost increases to customers, lest such reforms lead to unrest.

In 2011, the sultanate surprised the world—and Middle East scholars—by joining the Arab Spring.[20] Omanis, who had for so long been portrayed as grateful and docile subjects of Sultan Qaboos's modernizing drives, made it clear that the old order was starting to crack. A younger generation with no memory of the pre-Qaboos privations now formed more than 75 percent of the population. Rather than viewing their lot through the lens of their parents, younger Omanis benchmarked their privileges against the much greater largesse of the UAE and Qatar. Their awareness was enhanced by social media tools, which helped them organize protests and fire off lists of demands to Sultan Qaboos. High unemployment among young Omanis—half of whom do not work—probably contributed. Outside Bahrain, the uprising in Oman was the most virulent in the Gulf. Rioters burned a department store and attacked government buildings. Sultan Qaboos called in the army—while quickly creating state jobs, increasing employment benefits, and firing several members of his cabinet.[21] The sultan's moves temporarily restored order.

But even in the face of unrest, Oman was forced to pare back subsidies in order to avoid economic disaster. Amid persistent deficits and falling oil and gas revenue in 2015, the sultanate doubled natural gas prices for some industrial customers to $3 per MMBtu. In 2016, Oman increased prices for water, gasoline, and diesel fuel. Water prices were left as is for the residential sector, but those for the government, commercial, and industrial sectors rose by 17 percent.[22] The government also put commercial and industrial customers on notice that electricity prices would soon increase.

Following the example set in the UAE, Oman adjusted prices monthly based on world market levels. Gasoline prices initially jumped 23 percent to US$1.38 per gallon, and diesel rose by 10 percent to US$1.57 per gallon. However, the sultanate wavered in late 2017 as rising oil prices forced up prices at the pump, leading Omanis to picket the Ministry of Oil and Gas. The sultanate temporarily capped the price of regular gasoline at $1.82 per gallon—restoring a subsidy—until reversing course and raising prices in January 2018. By June 2018, Omanis were paying $2.12

per gallon for regular gasoline, almost 90 percent more than they paid in 2015.

The increases appeared to have had the intended effect on demand. After a decade of nearly 10 percent yearly consumption growth, transportation fuel demand dropped by 6.6 percent in 2016 and another 5 percent in 2017. Motorists switched en masse from premium gasoline to lower-priced regular fuel, and diesel demand saw a pronounced drop of more than 7 percent in 2016 and 2017 (see figure 9.2).

As of 2018, the politically sensitive residential sector remained insulated from increased power prices.[23] State-society relations continued to deteriorate, and the regime—like its counterparts across the GCC—has brooked less patience for dissent since the Arab Spring. Activists have been intimidated and jailed and demonstrators greeted by riot police and arrests.[24] Even so, senior energy policy officials say that Oman's residential electricity tariffs are not sacrosanct. "It's being discussed," said Zaid al-Siyabi, the former head of exploration and production at Oman's Ministry of Oil and Gas. "For higher consumption, maybe the subsidies will disappear."[25]

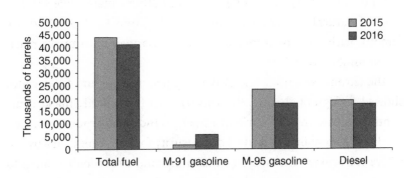

FIGURE 9.2 Domestic sales of fuels in Oman.

Drivers in Oman switched from premium (91) to (95) regular gasoline and consumed less gasoline overall in 2016.

Source: Oman National Center for Statistics and Information, 2017.

BAHRAIN

Bahrain is the Gulf state least able to afford subsidies but the one most politically dependent on them. The island kingdom is the most volatile country in the Gulf, as was demonstrated by its mass Arab Spring uprising in 2011. Bahrain remains politically and economically tethered to Saudi Arabia, which—in exchange for its influence over Bahraini affairs—has provided the tiny state with at least half the production of its giant Abu Safah oilfield since 1972. This has been crucial for Bahrain's survival, as it has very little of its own oil or gas.

However, as Saudi Arabia goes, so goes Bahrain. When the Saudi kingdom began to raise prices in 2016, Bahrain swung into line. In March 2016, the island kingdom launched a series of subsidy reforms targeting electricity, water, and transportation fuel. As in Qatar and the UAE, citizens were exempted from increases in household water and power prices, but water and electricity prices for noncitizens were to increase until they reflected actual costs sometime in 2019.[26] Since utility prices for citizens didn't change, expatriates effectively began cross-subsidizing the consumption of Bahraini nationals. Bahrain also raised transportation fuel prices for the first time in thirty years (table 9.1). The price of natural gas was also raised in 2015 from $2.25 to $2.50 per mmbtu, with an annual increase of $0.25 planned until prices reach $4 per mmbtu by 2021.[27]

The chronic sectarian unrest that has plagued Bahrain for decades showed no sign of abating. Protests by disenfranchised Shia citizens continued, and in 2017 a trio of underground rebel groups mounted small-scale bombings and attacks on security forces.[28] Unlike in Kuwait, where political violence inspired the ruling family to redouble efforts to maintain Shia integration, strife in Bahrain has only deepened marginalization. But since Bahrain's conflict has few, if any, links to subsidy retraction, authorities appear prepared to press ahead.

UNITED ARAB EMIRATES

Four years after Dubai's pathbreaking reform, described in chapter 7, the UAE federal government in Abu Dhabi acted to abolish UAE-wide subsidies on transportation fuels, allowing prices to fluctuate monthly based on world benchmarks. Abu Dhabi had planned to raise prices shortly after Dubai did in 2011 but shelved plans until August 2015, probably as a result of the Arab Spring. Ironically, the adjustment in fuel price initially *reduced* prices for gasoline and diesel, since they had been fixed at higher rates than those in world markets, which had fallen alongside crude prices. By late 2017, however, gasoline prices had risen back above $2/gallon, and the regime showed no signs of following the Omani example of capping prices.

Abu Dhabi also increased water and electricity rates. Once again, the biggest increases were handed to foreigners, who began paying *six times* the citizen price for electricity and four times more for water. Even so, nationals were still subject to groundbreaking price increases. In 2015, Abu Dhabi nationals saw tiny increases in electricity charges and a modest rise for water, which, like in Dubai, had always been given away free in unlimited quantities. The price increases for citizens looked less like a true fiscal reform than a warning that unlimited energy benefits would not continue in perpetuity.

In 2017, the regime made good on the implied threat. Expatriates and citizens received further increases. Over the two-year period, expatriate electricity costs nearly doubled from 4.1 US cents per kWh to 7.2 cents per kWh for small amounts of daily consumption. (For higher consumption by foreign residents, subsidies were eliminated. The price rose to a cost-reflective rate of 8.3 cents.) Citizen rates remained heavily subsidized but increased from 1.4 to 1.8 cents per kWh. Unit costs for water rose by a minimum of 270 percent for expatriates, from 59 cents to $2.12 per 1,000 liters, while citizens received water bills for the first time ever, at 56 cents per 1,000 liters.[29] The UAE's two remaining utilities, in Sharjah and the Northern Emirates, also raised prices, but only on foreign residents and industrial and commercial customers.[30]

In interviews I conducted before the Arab Spring uprisings, senior Abu Dhabi energy policy officials predicted that tariff increases would be needed to reduce peak electricity demand growth, which had reached 16 percent per year. Previously protected UAE nationals would not be exempt from increases.[31] One of the officials said:

> The government accepts that the rate should be hiked and that consumers should have the right pricing signals to help them with their behavior. There is no sense in the government that asking Emiratis to pay for electricity and water is *verboten*—just the opposite. I get the sense that they believe that individuals should pay, and more importantly that they should get the right signals, whether expatriates or nationals, that they should be more efficient in their consumption. There aren't really strong political barriers. There is some resistance.[32]

The official took issue with the view that citizen "rights" to cheap electricity were enshrined in a state-society social contract:

> I think it is more accurate to describe it as: this is how things always have been done. The precedent is that I'm changing electricity and water prices, rather than any kind of formal social contract that says these products should be free to the population. When Sheikh Zayed first set electricity and water prices, those weren't heavily subsidized. There was no sense that people should be getting a free ride. . . . What you see is an inattention to pricing . . . rather than a political commitment to free electricity.

UPDATING RENTIER THEORY

In one sheikhdom after another, Gulf citizens relinquished long-held benefits on fuel, electricity, and water. Each of the six monarchies raised prices on transportation fuel and on electricity and water for the commercial sector. In none of these countries was there much of a fight.

Outside Saudi Arabia's across-the-board price hikes, however, the reforms in the other five monarchies were less aggressive—unless you were an expatriate or owned a business. Foreign residents of the UAE, Bahrain, and Qatar were accustomed to their status as second-class temporary hirelings. Now, official discrimination in subsidy policy would widen the divisions between them and citizens. Gulf nationals would lose a small share of their social benefits, but in comparison to their noncitizen neighbors, they looked more privileged than ever. It was a clever trade of benefits for privilege.

Business owners were another prime focus for reforms. Like expatriates, private businesses enjoy little political clout. Firms are generally seen by the state as free riders. They pay little or no tax—since even business taxes are considered risky—and they hire few citizens because discriminatory labor laws mean citizens receive higher wages than expatriates. Businesses thus were easy targets.

Of course, discrimination in governance is a monarch's prerogative. The ruling sheikh enjoys policy flexibility unmatched by counterparts in republican systems, where all groups expect to be treated as equals. Playing favorites among subsidy recipients enabled rulers to begin reform without triggering a political backlash. As Homer and, later, Mel Brooks, put it: It's good to be the king.

But the significance of the 2015–2017 subsidy reforms extends beyond modest increases in price. The subsidy retractions represent a change in the understanding of the state-society relationship in the Gulf monarchies.[33] During the previous austerity period—the great oil bust that lasted from the mid-1980s until 2003—regime behavior was markedly different. Rulers in that era also slashed spending, but the focus was on projects and infrastructure. Saudi Arabia almost completely halted capital spending, allowing roads and infrastructure to rot until oil prices finally recovered in 2003. Social spending—especially government salaries and welfare benefits—was then understood as the glue that bound citizens to the regime. Governments did their best to preserve subsidies as long as they could.[34]

Things have changed. The pairing of fiscal and security crises has provided cover for Gulf regimes to launch permanent, structural drives to reduce welfare spending, especially on the energy subsidies that have undermined their export-led economies. Reforms weakened the notion that citizens were somehow *entitled* to the discounts they were getting. In most cases—and indeed everywhere until December 2017—prices were raised without replacement benefits.

That month, however, Saudi Arabia began distributing its Citizen's Account cash replacement benefits for low- and middle-income families. Outside Saudi Arabia, none of the other Gulf monarchies converted lost subsidies to cash. None of the sheikhdoms increased democratic participation either, as some scholars prescribed.

How could this happen, given that decades of scholarship suggest that such reforms are illegitimate? Were the scholars wrong? Or did something change on the ground? The correct answer is probably the latter. A new understanding of energy pricing has emerged. These days, subsidies' harmful effects on demand overshadow their beneficial effects on political legitimacy. At the same time, intervening circumstances provided political cover for reforms.

The chief driver for this momentous policy change is the unmistakable creep of domestic consumption into overall production, rising from 5 percent in 1973 to 14 percent a decade later, 18 percent in the mid-2000s, and 25 percent today (recall figure 6.1). The unmistakable and burgeoning threat to oil exports was itself a call to action.

A second factor is the cost of the subsidies, in fiscal terms. In late 2014, oil prices fell and stayed low for several years. Prices recovered somewhat in 2017 but remained far below earlier boom levels. Since governments in the region depended on oil revenues for up to 90 percent of their budgets, reduced oil prices created pressure to reduce state spending. Subsidies were the preferred target.

But oil prices don't explain the full story. Fiscal pressure was much more intense during previous periods of low oil prices, yet Gulf states left domestic subsidies untouched. In 2015, regimes responded to low prices quickly, launching subsidy reforms that technocrats had prepared in advance (see figure 9.3). Two of the wealthiest petrostates, Kuwait and Qatar, raised prices *despite fully funded national budgets*. Most of the others had crossed into deficit spending, but some retained substantial fiscal buffers. [35] By 2018, less than four years into the lower oil price environment, some countries had undergone multiple rounds of subsidy cuts, as figure 9.3 shows.

A third rationale for reforms is external pressure. Multilaterals have campaigned to end climate-damaging fossil fuel subsidies, formalizing this commitment in the Paris climate accord of 2015. These demands made it easier for ruling sheikhs to act, by providing convenient political cover that helped deflect blame for unpopular policy.

A fourth reason is the changing leadership in the Gulf. As seen in Saudi Arabia, the influx of younger leaders brought a push for change. The 2013 accession of then thirty-three-year-old Sheikh Tamim bin Hamad al-Thani in Qatar and the gradual assumption of power by fifty-five-year-old Sheikh Mohammed bin Zayed al-Nahyan in Abu Dhabi led to a reassessment of social benefits in those countries as well. [36] Sheikh Tamim decried the rentier mentality in a 2015 speech, saying that oil wealth had caused citizens to become dependent on the state "to provide for everything, which reduces the motivation of individuals to take initiatives and be progressive." He said the state could no longer deliver all of its people's needs in perpetuity. [37]

A fifth factor is the chaos that has crept across the region. The Kuwait mosque bombing was but one example. Islamic State terrorists and anti-government rebel forces held territory in neighboring countries—Yemen, Iraq, and Syria—and had launched attacks inside the monarchies. The violent spillovers rallied Gulf citizens around their ruling families for protection, increasing their willingness to sacrifice.

A final enabler is the realization that citizens would accept higher prices without acting against their governments or demanding an increase in democratic representation, as academics have long postulated.

It is important to state that the reforms have just begun, that prices on most energy products have not been fully rationalized, and that there remains plenty of opportunity for citizens to decry their lost benefits and demand replacements—or democracy. In 2018, Iran underwent its most fervent unrest since 2009, and the loss of subsidies—on food as well as fuel—was among the grievances cited. [38] There is no guarantee that Gulf citizens won't follow Iran's example.

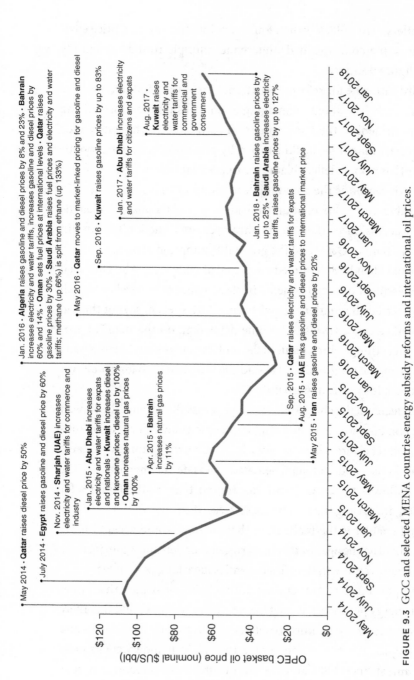

FIGURE 9.3 GCC and selected MENA countries energy subsidy reforms and international oil prices.

Governments began launching subsidy reforms in 2014. Most, but not all, came after the drop in oil prices in late 2014. Reforms continued through 2018 as oil market prices remained low.

Source: Glada Lahn, "Fuel, Food, and Utilities Price Reforms in the GCC: A Wake-up Call for Business," research paper (London: Chatham House, June 2016); Baker Institute research compilation; "OPEC Basket Price," Organization of the Petroleum Exporting Countries, 2018, http://www.opec.org/opec_web/en/data_graphs/40.htm.

Thus far, GCC citizens have not risen up en masse. Why? Two reasons. The evolution of Gulf society and economy is the first. The 1970s welfare state improved lives to such an extent that now "nanny state" benefits look like anachronisms from the era when people were swapping camels for Land Rovers. Economies have grown massively. High-salary job opportunities have made free energy unnecessary for many. Gulf citizens are healthier, more educated, and prosperous than ever before. A growing number understand the need to move beyond state-funded giveaways. But not everyone. Gulf citizens may have accepted their losses without resorting to violence, but many did not go quietly. A storm of protest erupted on social media, and benefit losses were partly behind strikes and protests in Oman.[39]

And this brings us to the second reason. Citizens have likely been dissuaded from action by the increase in state repression that coincided with the subsidy reforms. Authorities across the Gulf began to crack down on electronic dissent, including postings on social media that had once been tolerated. State security forces jailed activists in all six monarchies. Stepped-up surveillance and censorship of electronic communication was backed up, in each country, by legislation criminalizing dissent in the name of national security. Human Rights Watch and other groups noted the change, as did the human-rights data gathered by the US State Department. "Gulf states are intimidating, surveilling, imprisoning, and silencing activists as part of their all-out assault on peaceful criticism, but they are seriously mistaken if they think they can indefinitely block Gulf citizens from using social and other media to push for positive reforms," said Sarah Leah Whitson, director of HRW's Middle East section. [40]

The wave of repression was triggered by factors beyond subsidy reform, including post–Arab Spring insecurity, a campaign against the Muslim Brotherhood in some places, backlash against social liberalization, and younger leaders' more activist approach toward politics and regional relations. The 2017 blockade of Qatar by Saudi Arabia, UAE, and Bahrain contributed to the tightening of political control. Each of those regimes threatened to prosecute anyone publicly contradicting the official line on the embargo. Regardless, alongside dissent in general, complaints about subsidy reforms that may have been tolerated in the past became unacceptable.

In short, the evidence shows that neither governments nor citizens are following the script laid out by rentier state theory. Governments are taking away supposedly sacrosanct benefits, and citizens are not rising up and demanding democracy. These developments imply that rentier theory needs updating. First, as regards subsidy reform, we should acknowledge that the domestic subsidization of primary exports comprises an encumbrance on the economy. Left intact over the long term, domestic resource distribution can destabilize the governance structure. Regimes should be expected to take action to lessen the strain. Second, academics' central misunderstanding about subsidies is that they are inflexible. By portraying subsidies as rights, theory implies that they cannot be reformed without upsetting the stability of the entire system. Like Dr. al-Rumhy, the Omani energy minister, I argue that subsidies *must* be reformed to save the system. Indeed, as we have seen, governments alarmed by domestic demand have already moved against subsidies in the interest of preserving exports.

A simple amendment can bring theory into line with these developments. Academics should discard the portrayal of subsidies as "rights" and instead describe them as "customary privileges." (At some point, energy subsidies may become "former privileges.") This allows for retraction or replacement of social-contract benefits that are traded for regime support. These amendments provide theoretical allowance for the reforms that have already begun in the rentier heartland of the Gulf. Thus improved, theory can anticipate the likelihood for regimes to continue to streamline social welfare policies in the interest of preserving power.

SECURITY IS THE NEW DEMOCRACY

During the opening stages of the Arab Spring, as autocrats tumbled in Tunisia and Egypt without mass carnage, many Arabs, including some in the Gulf, found themselves attracted to the possibility of greater political participation. The attraction turned out to be fleeting. By 2014, the Arab Spring had morphed into grinding civil warfare and reprised dictatorship. Public opinion responded in kind. Many Arabs began equating democracy with sectarianism and instability. Even in Tunisia, the sole success story of the Arab Spring, support for democracy declined.[41] This shift brought relief to Gulf ruling families, who have proven unwilling to countenance the dilution of their monopoly over political control.

Insecurity led Gulf citizens to cluster around their ruling sheikhs. In Qatar, the proportion of citizens identifying "maintaining order and stability" as their top priority rose from 37 percent to 75 percent between 2011 and 2014, while only 8 percent of respondents chose "participation" as a top priority.[42] The accompanying crackdown on dissent probably made citizens even more reluctant to agitate, given the increased likelihood of prison time.

The social contract between rulers and ruled may actually have shifted. The contents of these compacts have never been enshrined in written laws, so no one is sure where the red lines lie. The limits wax and wane depending on context. During the Arab Spring, when people were inclined to join pan-Arab uprisings, regimes had less leeway to retract subsidies than they did after 2014, as oil prices plummeted, chaos spread, and people rallied around their rulers.

Broadly, the contents of the rentier social contract consist of a trade of welfare benefits for political support. Citizens seem to need a sense that living standards are rising, that government is responsive—even if there is no voting—and that rulers are effective domestically and internationally. Given these basics, citizens consent to ruling family control over the state.

Today's social contract might include a new clause: taxation in exchange for security (with loss of a subsidy seen as akin to imposition of a tax). Temporarily, at least, regimes can take away subsidies "in exchange for ensuring the security of citizens in an increasingly dangerous neighborhood," writes Sultan al-Qassemi, a Sharjah-based social commentator.[43] Even taxes themselves are no longer off the table.

In January 2018, Saudi Arabia and the UAE imposed the GCC's first-ever value-added tax, imposing an extra 5 percent price hike on nearly all goods and services. The remaining monarchies announced plans to impose VATs of their own in 2019.

New forms of supposedly illegitimate "extraction" from society were becoming business as usual in the Gulf. Depending on the level of chaos that persists in the Gulf and neighboring states, it's possible that citizens may even accept the long-avoided third rail of autocratic politics—personal income tax—if it protects their sheltered lifestyles. No democratic opening necessary.

FUTURE IMPLICATIONS

Taken together with Saudi Arabia's dramatic price increases, the modest subsidy reforms around the GCC—and the evidence that such subsidies indeed affect demand—suggest that the energy demand conundrum may be resolvable. The once-rigid social contract that confronted Gulf exporters' economic well-being has grown more flexible. Ruling families are finding that the advice of their technocrats is accurate: giving away ever-increasing amounts of energy products really is unsustainable. Furthermore, the public can grasp this notion. People may grumble, ruling family legitimacy may even be damaged in the eyes of some, but citizens appear to be moving on with their lives without trying to overthrow the regime.

My 2011 survey research, detailed in chapter 7, suggests that a hardcore group of about a third of the citizen population remains opposed to any sort of change in energy subsidies, even when told that increased prices are in the national interest.[44] For now, this large and potentially dangerous cadre of dogged opponents appears to have accepted its loss in benefits, probably grudgingly. Thus far, reforms have not impinged on ruling families' overriding concern: regime security. This, of course, could change. More survey work is needed to measure changes in attitudes as reforms are rolled out.

The farthest-reaching reforms have taken place in Saudi Arabia, the quintessential rentier state. The Saudi retractions provide the strongest evidence that subsides can be rolled back and therefore that they should no longer be described as rights. The theoretical prohibitions enshrined in the literature have been disproven by events on the ground. The Saudi social contract is undergoing deep experimentation through the Citizen's Account compensation, the imposition of VAT, and the steady drumbeat of increasing fuel and utility prices—with more hikes looming. The developments suggest that a new "Social Contract 2.0"—with increased regime flexibility in social policy—is being imposed from the top down.

According to rentier theory, this was supposed to be possible "only if the state enjoys solid democratic legitimation" that could justify the

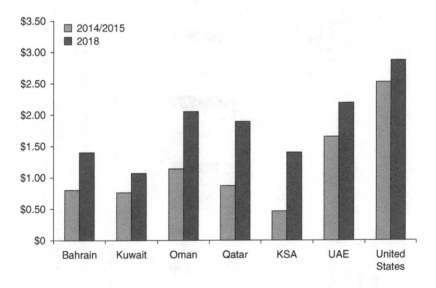

FIGURE 9.4 Change in regular gasoline price ($US/gallon) after subsidy cut.

Prices for regular-grade gasoline rose in all six GCC states as well as in other Middle Eastern oil exporters after 2015, but even by 2018 GCC prices still fell short of international prices, represented here by the United States, which imposes only a small amount of tax on gasoline sales.

Source: 2018 prices for the GCC were retrieved from media and government sources in March 2018, using prices for regular—90 or 91 octane—gasoline. US data are for February 2018, retail price for midgrade gasoline (88–90 octane).

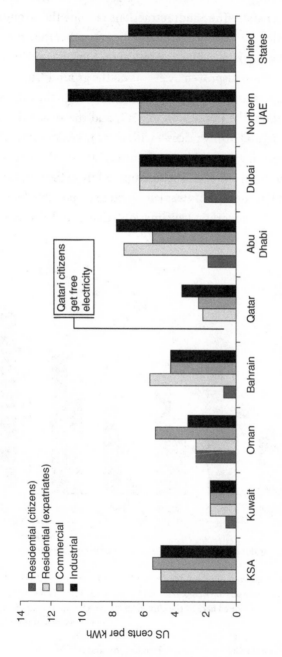

FIGURE 9.5 Retail electricity prices in GCC vs. the United States, 2018.

Despite recent increases, Gulf electricity prices remain well below average rates in the United States.

Source: Data compiled by the author and Baker Institute research staff; "Average Retail Price of Electricity, Monthly," US Energy Information Administration, 2017, https://www.eia.gov/electricity/data/browser/#/topic/7?agg=2,0,1&geo=g&freq=M.

accompanying repression.[45] Otherwise, benefit cuts and taxes risk "alienating large portions of their populations who have come to expect extensive welfare state benefits as their right as citizens."[46] The retractions mean "the future of their political systems could be called into question."[47]

Rather than weakening political systems, I argue that retracting unsustainable benefits—potentially destabilizing in the short run—is necessary to streamline and *strengthen* political structures. Since higher prices make oil products less attractive to domestic consumers, price reforms should comprise a key policy tool for avoiding the export death spiral depicted in the previous chapters. Fuel and electricity prices remained below those in the United States, a useful proxy for international pricing (see figures 9.4 and 9.5). Since energy demand is inelastic, it takes a large price increase to budge consumption, particularly on transportation fuels. Moving the needle will require a sustained assault on Gulf sensibilities. As the economist Partha Dasgupta argues, it takes a "big push" to escape path dependence.[48]

Even so, the accomplishments of Gulf reforms should not be underestimated. The history chronicled in this book shows how energy policy makers have overcome strong social and political barriers, taking away a long-held benefit deemed a central pillar of public support for ruling families. Gulf regimes recognize that they must end their use of cheap energy as a governance tool.

As subsidies are rolled back, regimes may resolve the contradictions between the Gulf's economic and political systems, so that domestic energy policy no longer works at cross purposes to exports. Citizens can still expect a generous social safety net in exchange for their support for the regime—as long as the world still needs oil and gas and as long as the Gulf monarchies remain major suppliers.

CONCLUSION

The Climate Hedge

The scruffy city of Jubail lies an hour's drive north of the Saudi oil metroplex around Dhahran, through a desert-industrial netherworld enveloped in wind-whirled trash and dust. The highway rumbles past camels gnawing at bushes, unfinished workshops sprouting re-bar, and the soaring flares of the Berri gas treatment plant. Filling station complexes dot the roadside, each with a mosque and a coffee kiosk, bidding truckers to dismount their battered cabs to refuel, pray, and recaffeinate. The drive nears its end amid makeshift labor camps where South Asian men live in portable trailers clustered in barracks-like rows.

The approach to industrial Jubail is one of the least picturesque settings imaginable, yet what it lacks in scenic beauty it makes up for in strategic importance. It is here, and in a few similar places nearby, where Saudi Arabia and the Gulf monarchies are staking their bets for the next phase of oil, and, if their preparations bear fruit, the next phase of monarchical rule.

Viewed from above, the Sadara Chemical Co. on Jubail's outskirts has a mesmerizing geometry. Thousands of miles of parallel pipes course alongside a grid of roads, connecting gleaming stainless-steel silos, stout storage tanks, windowless warehouses, and bewildering blocks of looped tubing, interspersed with steam-puffing vents and safety warnings.

Sadara, completed in 2017 as a $20 billion joint venture between Aramco and Dow Chemical, is the largest single-phase chemical plant ever built. Its four thousand employees convert Saudi oil and gas into a multitude of products, from polyolefin elastomers for car interiors to propylene glycol for toothpaste. For now, Sadara exports most of those precursors before conversion, in the form of resin or pellets that get shipped from Jubail's deepwater port. Soon, Sadara will deliver its polymers and pellets to a neighboring plastics-manufacturing district, where thousands of workers will convert the oil derivatives into finished goods, which will be exported instead. Sadara is but one bet on the future of oil. Another wager built of pipes, tanks, and valves sits just across the road. With the 400,000-barrel-per-day Satorp refinery, Aramco has teamed up with the French oil company Total to turn Saudi crude into high-value fuels, especially diesel, that meet stringent European emission standards.

Jubail and its environs are evidence of Saudi Arabia's shift away from simple exports of crude oil and into more complex "downstream" industries that transform oil and gas into usable products. Fixing the domestic demand problem plays directly into the kingdom's downstream strategy. Saudi Arabia and its neighbors aren't just confronting domestic consumption because they want to export more crude oil but because oil has more valuable—and more environmentally sustainable—uses than burning it in the region's cars and power plants. These regimes are looking to transform the *composition* of oil demand from simple to complex: converting raw oil and gas into high-value plastic merchandise and sophisticated refined products.

In Saudi Arabia, the campaign to beat back demand is moving alongside continuous investment to maintain or even increase Saudi Aramco's maximum sustainable production capacity at or above its longstanding 12.5m b/d threshold.[1] Saudi oil production hit an all-time record, 10.6m b/d, in June 2016 (see figure 10.1). Since the accession of King Salman and the rise of his son Muhammad, diversification into the downstream part of the oil business—refining and chemicals—has also accelerated. Similar efforts are underway in the UAE, Qatar, Kuwait, and Oman.

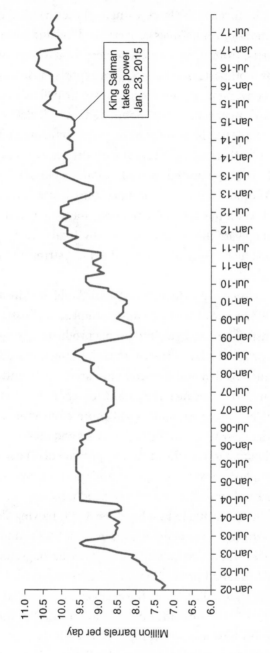

FIGURE 10.1 Saudi crude oil production since 2002.

Saudi crude oil production hit historic highs after King Salman's accession in 2015.

Source: JODI, "JODI Oil World Database," Statistical database (Joint Organisations Data Initiative, 2018), https://www.jodidata.org/oil/.

Saudi Aramco is now evolving into a global "integrated" oil company in the tradition of the Seven Sisters firms that spawned it. The giant oil company's most strategic downstream investments are taking place outside the kingdom, in countries with the strongest prospects for economic growth and consumer demand. Saudi Aramco is compiling ownership stakes in as much as 10m b/d of global refinery capacity. That is an enormous amount, double that held by ExxonMobil, the current top refiner, and roughly equal to all of Saudi Aramco's current oil production.[2]

Geopolitics has a role in this transformation. Saudi Arabia and its neighboring monarchies are moving toward a more diverse set of economic and investment ties with individual companies and countries. Washington remains paramount, but various forces have eroded relations with the United States.

One was the end of the Cold War, which took away a strategic rationale to the US-Saudi relationship that extended beyond oil; the two allies shared a common interest in countering the atheist and antimonarchy Soviet Union. US-Saudi cooperation reached its zenith in Afghanistan, when the mujahedeen drove out the Soviets with plentiful support from America and its allied kingdom. When the Cold War ended, US-Saudi relations lost much of their strategic justification.[3]

The September 11, 2001, attacks—planned and carried out by a group of mainly Saudi terrorists—added new stresses to the relationship. These were compounded by the US response to the attacks: the overthrow of Saddam Hussein in Iraq, which brought an Iran-friendly, Shia-led government to power. Deterioration in US-Saudi ties accelerated under President Obama, who openly disdained the relationship, once describing the Saudis as "our so-called ally."[4] Obama withdrew US forces from the region, sympathized openly with Arab Spring protesters in Egypt and Tunisia, and—to Saudi exasperation—was unwilling to intervene forcefully in the Syrian civil war. US participation in the successful 2015 Iran negotiations, which eased Western sanctions in exchange for Iran freezing nuclear development, only furthered tensions.

The shale revolution in the United States has added yet another complication. In just a decade, US oil production nearly doubled, jumping from 5m b/d in 2008 to 9.3m b/d in 2017.[5] The shale boom revived popu-list "energy independence" rhetoric, with pundits clamoring that shale oil could free Washington from dependence on Saudi Arabia and other "hostile" regimes. There is more heat than light here: the US remains a net oil importer, and there is no conceivable short-run combination of producers that could cover a disruption in the supply of Saudi oil. But taken together, these strains have made it clear that the monarchy must look to cement ties with other nations, most of them in the Far East.

Saudi Arabia is certainly not looking back. Important new ventures, particularly in refining, are tethering the kingdom to Japan, South Korea, and China, now the world's largest oil importer.[6] By configur-ing foreign refineries around Saudi crude oil, Saudi Aramco has locked up market share in countries expected to dominate the future of oil demand growth. Control of access to these growing markets also acts as a strategic hedge in the event of a climate-induced reduction in oil demand. In 2017, Aramco was negotiating further refinery stakes in China as well as in Indonesia, India, and Malaysia.[7] The Kuwait Petro-leum Co. did the same thing, buying a 35 percent share of a new refinery in Vietnam.

These investments promote deeper integration with importing coun-tries, converting them into stakeholders in the stability and security of the Gulf producers. Diversified refining ties also allow Saudi Arabia and its neighbors to guard against a future change of heart in Washington. Despite the recent tensions, the relationship with the United States is still a crucial one for Saudi Arabia, and the kingdom has taken steps to deepen its involvement in US energy security. The huge Saudi Aramco–owned Motiva refinery in Texas is the model. The refinery is configured around Saudi crude, and Aramco supplies a large share of the 600,000 b/d of crude oil that Motiva refines into gasoline and diesel. (Most of the fuel is sold under the Shell brand.) Saudi Arabia can point to Motiva and sim-ilar endeavors as a concrete rationale for the hard security Washington provides in the Gulf region.

In one way or another, the Gulf's internal stability and prosperity, and its external security and influence, all depend on oil.

CLIMATE CHANGE AND DEPLETION STRATEGY

Yet another threat to oil export looms, one far more ominous than creeping domestic demand: the changing climate. Climate change represents
a potential catastrophe for all of humanity, but the Gulf monarchies play
starring roles as both major perpetrators and early victims.

The problem is simple, the solution fiendishly hard. The burning
of coal, oil, and natural gas is responsible for about two-thirds of the
greenhouse gas emissions—mainly carbon dioxide—that are altering
the climate and warming the Earth. Reducing those emissions is therefore necessary. Doing so represents the mother of all collective-action
problems, because fossil fuels are so energy dense and selling them so
profitable.

For the Gulf monarchies, it must be frustrating. Just as they are enjoy-
ing some success demolishing longstanding energy subsidies—and
rearranging the social contract with their citizens—ruling families must
confront a new and even more complex challenge. The magical fluid that
dragged them from poverty and isolation just a few short generations
ago now threatens to render their already intense climate intolerable.
Foreign elites are suddenly less interested in trying to exploit their oil
than in forcing them to keep it underground.

A growing consensus of research concludes that about two-thirds of
remaining fossil fuel reserves must remain unburned if humanity is to
have a reasonable chance of weakening the advance of climate change.
Of course, rendering carbon "unburnable" endangers commercial activ-
ity based on fossil fuels. In the line of fire are some of the world's largest
firms (table 10.1), along with two dozen countries where exports of coal,
oil, or gas comprise more than 20 percent of GDP.[8]

The Gulf monarchies sit at the top of the list of carbon-dependent
economies. For them, climate action looks like a zero-sum game: the climate's gain is their loss, and vice versa. While subsidies threaten to damage exports from the *supply* side, climate action is a *demand-side* threat.
And it is global. Climate change undermines consumers' willingness to

TABLE 10.1 Current greenhouse gas emitters

Company	Current GHG emissions (% of global total 2010)	Historical emissions (% of global since 1854)
Saudi Aramco*	4.3	3.2
Gazprom*	3.8	2.2
National Iran Oil*	2.4	2.0
Coal India*	2.3	1.1
ExxonMobil	1.8	2.5
Pemex*	1.7	1.4
PetroChina*	1.7	0.7
British Petroleum	1.5	2.5
PD Venezuela*	1.4	1.1
Royal Dutch Shell	1.3	2.1
Chevron	1.2	3.5
Abu Dhabi NOC*	1.1	0.7
Sonatrach (Algeria)*	1.1	0.6
Total (France)	1.1	0.8
Rosneft*	1.0	0.2
ConocoPhillips	1.0	1.2
Kuwait Petroleum*	0.9	0.7
Petrobras*	0.9	0.4

Note: Saudi Aramco tops this list of companies and government entities. Note that Chevron, the former Standard Oil of California, or Socal, is the no. 1 holder of historic emissions. Socal was the original concession holder in Saudi Arabia and discovered oil in the kingdom in 1938. * Majority state-owned companies.

Source: Benoit Mayer and Mikko Rajavuori, "National Fossil Fuel Companies and Climate Change Mitigation Under International Law," *Syracuse Journal of International Law and Commerce*. 44 (2016): 55.

buy and burn fossil fuels, and it makes governments more likely to deny or discourage access to them.

Faced with the array of risks and threats posed by climate action, how might the Gulf states react? Saudi Aramco's oil market strategy gives a good indication. One of Aramco's strengths—and a source of pride—is the company's long-term outlook and cautious monetization of Saudi oil.

Aramco's production decisions undergo painstaking deliberation over the optimal pace of depletion. Aramco calibrates output from individual fields so that recoverable oil is exhausted gradually, over a minimum of thirty years.[9]

This strategy has had the effect of leaving oil in the ground for the benefit of future generations and, at the same time, constraining supply to the market. The kingdom's output has hovered at about 13 percent of global supply, a self-imposed limit that has forced oil prices up.[10] This restraint has allowed higher-cost "fringe" producers to meet remaining demand with costlier oil. The late King Abdullah gave voice to this strategy in 2008 when he reportedly ordered new reserves left for future generations. "I keep no secret from you that when there were some new finds, I told them, 'No, leave it in the ground. With grace from God, our children need it.'"[11]

Viewed through the lens of climate action, Aramco's disciplined strategy looks like a liability. Cautious monetization assumes there are no threats to the long-term value of crude oil. Yet, for at least a decade, Saudi officials have voiced fears about "security of demand," whether from climate factors or Washington's rhetoric around energy independence. US diplomatic cables released by WikiLeaks[12] revealed some of these concerns, as have Naimi's public statements[13] and those of an adviser, Mohammed al-Sabban, who predicted in 2015 that global demand would peak by 2025.[14]

In 2010, US Ambassador to Riyadh James Smith cabled Washington to describe Saudi fears over gathering threats to oil demand. "Saudi Arabia is concerned by the lack of clarity for [global oil] outlook, as forecasts have ranged from many prognosticating a year or two ago that oil production had peaked, to a growing consensus that perhaps demand has peaked," Smith wrote. "Uncertainties over what policies will be adopted to address issues like climate change play a big role in that uncertainty."[15] Those fears have only intensified in the years since Smith sent his cable.

The realization that the world is overendowed with hydrocarbon reserves that can never be produced is forcing a strategic alteration in oil market behavior. Oil and gas markets appear likely to grow more competitive, with states vying with rivals for market share and to differentiate themselves and their products based on climate criteria. My discussions with Saudi energy executives in January and February 2018, on condition of anonymity, revealed the outlines of Saudi Arabia's approach to the climate challenge.

A key component of this strategy is the one highlighted at the beginning of the chapter: petrochemicals. Converting crude oil and natural gas feedstocks into chemical form does not involve combusting those feedstocks. The carbon is locked inside the polymers and the final plastic goods produced. In this sense, petrochemicals are a "climate-proof" use of hydrocarbons, although lots of natural gas is combusted in the energy-intense process of creating the chemicals. (Plastic has other problems, particularly in regards to proper disposal, but those are more easily overcome than stanching emissions of greenhouse gases.)

It also turns out that the crude oil produced in Saudi Arabia and the Gulf is less damaging to the climate than competing grades. The climate advantage is based on the simplicity of lifting Gulf crude oil to the surface and transporting it to refiners. Carbon emitted in oil production is lowest in prolific reservoirs, like Ghawar, which enjoy high levels of natural drive pressure and minimize the use of energy-intense recovery techniques such as steam flooding or water injection. Saudi oil reservoirs also produce low levels of water, which means that a larger portion of the produced crude is usable. Low water content lightens the weight of the crude pumped to the surface and reduces the energy expended in surface processing and separation.[16] The Gulf monarchies have also phased out almost all flaring of natural gas, which further reduces the carbon footprint of their oil.

These advantages suggest that Saudi Aramco could position itself as a "responsible" oil supplier by highlighting the differences in carbon intensity between its crude and those of competitors, particularly heavy crudes from Canada, California, and Venezuela, which require energy-intensive extraction and processing. As countries begin to tax carbon, a tax that differentiates among crude types could actually *help* Saudi Arabia, by conferring its crude oil with a cost advantage over competing grades. The higher the tax, the larger the discount for "clean" crudes.

The kingdom also plans strategic investments that maximize the efficiency of oil's main technological partner, the internal combustion engine. If oil-fueled transportation remains cost competitive with electric vehicles, it prolongs the lifespan of gasoline. Over the long run, hybrids like the Toyota Prius, with its fuel-efficient internal combustion engine, look more like oil's salvation than a threat to demand. Vehicles that use no oil at all, like the plug-in Tesla, are where the risk lies. Further out, if threats to oil gain ground, producers might decide to step up production. With 260 billion barrels of proven crude oil reserves still underground, any reduction in global oil demand is a scary proposition in Saudi Arabia.[17] An increase in output could allow them to avoid being stuck with stranded reserves. The more you pump now, the less you abandon later.

Low-cost producers like those in the Gulf, where a barrel of oil costs around $10 to produce, might see an advantage in shortening the timeframe for converting underground reserves into aboveground assets.[18] This would, all else remaining constant, increase their market shares while reducing global oil prices and stimulating demand. For Riyadh, the cost advantages of "easy oil" could transfer the risk of stranded assets to producers needing high oil prices—say, around $70—to break even. High-cost producers include those in the Canadian oil sands, the Arctic, or Venezuela's Orinoco Belt.

If this phenomenon were caused by environmental policy such as climate action, it would mean that the dreaded "green paradox" had come to fruition. The so-called green paradox proclaims that environmental regulations aimed at discouraging fossil fuel could end up enhancing the fuels' attractiveness. If not designed properly, climate action could actually *incentivize* oil production and push down prices.[19] If such a scenario were to play out, the resulting oil glut might even delay the onset of peak demand, prolonging oil's dominance. Low prices might push emerging economies to increase their dependence on oil by making investments that "lock in" higher levels of long-term demand.[20]

The climate threat to the Gulf monarchies is moderated by two caveats. First, of the three fossil fuels—oil, gas, and coal—oil faces the smallest threat from climate action. Why? Because oil holds a near-monopoly as a transport fuel, and transportation services are vital. There are no fully viable substitute fuels that are cleaner than oil. Biofuels like corn-based ethanol are higher-carbon and lower in energy density.[21] Vehicles that run on electricity and fuel cells are a future possibility. But electric vehicles are only cleaner than oil-burning vehicles when the electricity grid that powers them is decarbonized. Other transport sectors, such as aviation, are nowhere close to decarbonization. The lack of substitutes makes oil difficult to dislodge. One influential paper finds that only 33 percent of global oil reserves will have to be left in the ground, even if humanity meets its goal in limiting the rise in temperatures to two degrees Celsius.[22]

Most of the climate risk falls on coal. Coal has many substitutes in power generation, all of them cleaner. One of those is natural gas, which emits about half the carbon per unit of energy consumed. But gas, too, has cleaner substitutes, including some, like wind power, which can compete on cost. Coal and gas are therefore more exposed to risk of abandonment. Oil simply does not face this level of competition—yet.

The second caveat relates to the possibility of technological break-throughs. New technology has pushed renewable energy to the fore-front of electricity capacity installation. But fossil fuel technology also benefits from periodic advances, as the US shale revolution demonstrates. A breakthrough that allowed fossil fuels to be burned without damaging the climate would be a game changer, reinforcing the energy status quo.

A green-paradox strategy of accelerated depletion might look like a short-term "win" for the Gulf monarchies. Longer term, it would be disastrous. One way or another, climate change is bound to disrupt life in the Gulf. If climate policies succeed, exporters' economies and political systems will be undermined and need amending. Rentier governance might not survive. If climate polices fall short, the Gulf faces an unwinnable confrontation with increasingly hostile summer temperatures and rising seas. The region may no longer support human habitation. This is the more depressing scenario.

WHERE NEXT?

The Gulf has come a long way since roughnecks from California tapped into a gusher at the foot of Jebel Dukhan in Bahrain. The oil business propelled the region into the modern world before it was ready, and it placed the Gulf at the center of the action.

Looking at the breadth of history, the Gulf monarchies face a familiar decision point. Will they remain linchpins of the global economy, providing not just energy commodities but services that capitalize on their location and sun-drenched climate? Or will they repeat the experience of the seventh century, when they briefly enjoyed the spotlight only to see the vanguard of their movement migrate elsewhere?

For now, the fate of the Gulf relies heavily on the fate of the oil business. And oil is entering an age of increasing risk. Progress on climate change endangers the dominance of fossil fuels in the global energy market. Although no one has yet devised a viable replacement for oil-fueled transportation, governments are increasingly demanding alternate fuels and technologies, regardless of oil prices. This understanding will most likely prompt at least some holders of large reserves, like those in the Gulf, to try to move their crude to market before the world moves on.

Where does that leave the ruling sheikhs of the Gulf? Undeniably, they face difficult choices. In the near term, it is hard to overstate the importance to the Gulf monarchies of defending their hydrocarbon export revenues. Despite modest success with economic diversification, energy exports still comprise the lion's share of GDP and government budgets. Oil and gas sales deliver the hard currency required to buy imported goods, to furnish social services, to build infrastructure for industry, and to create jobs for burgeoning workforces. They also underpin the strategic relationship with America.

The long-term remedy is well known but infuriatingly elusive. Economic diversification, the perennial recommendation of the IMF and the Washington consensus, has been scrawled at the top of every economic "vision" produced in the region since the 1980s. True diversification, other than in Dubai, has never overcome the monarchical institutions arrayed against it. Rentier states, with their two-track economies with separate rules for foreigners and citizens, with their quasi-functional rule of law and property rights, and the siphons of wealth to ruling-family accounts, have been unable to scrap the damaging vestiges of monarchical governance. Doing so would undermine the opaque institutions and discriminatory practices that keep the ruling families in power.

The sustainability of the Gulf economy and environment cannot be assured unless the demand conundrum is tackled by reforming energy subsidies. A country's political and economic systems cannot be permanently arrayed against one another. The subsidies that buttress political stability are undermining economic stability based on oil and gas exports. Ultimately, the rentier promise is a pyramid scheme.

The lapsing of the Arab Spring into protracted chaos has allowed unprecedented reforms to break ground in all six Gulf monarchies. The Arab Spring provided a trial by fire for the region's ruling families, long dismissed as fragile institutions. By and large, the monarchies passed the test. This bodes well for the next phase in their evolution. The streamlined social contract that was emerging appeared to provide regimes with more flexibility in policy making, perhaps restoring some of the families' elusive autonomy in governance. Flexibility will certainly be needed as these tribal autocracies and the enigmatic personalities who govern them prepare for another period of chaotic change: the post-oil age.

NOTES

INTRODUCTION

1. Some of the material in this book appeared in previous publications by the author. Among them: Jim Krane, "Reversing the Trend in Domestic Energy Consumption in the GCC: Consequences of Success and Failure," Abdullah bin Hamad al-Attiyah Foundation for Energy and Sustainable Development (Doha), November 2015, http:// bakerinstitute.org/research/reversing-trend-domestic-energy-consumption-gcc/; Jim Krane, "Guzzling in the Gulf: The Monarchies Face a Threat from Within," *Foreign Affairs*, December 19, 2014, http://www.foreignaffairs.com/articles/142692/jim-krane /guzzling-in-the-gulf; Jim Krane, "Stability Versus Sustainability: Energy Policy in the Gulf Monarchies," PhD diss., University of Cambridge, 2014, http://dx.doi.org /10.17863/CAM.5943; Jim Krane, "Stability Versus Sustainability: Energy Policy in the Gulf Monarchies," *Energy Journal* 36, no. 4 (2015), http://dx.doi.org/10.5547 /01956574.36.4.jkra.
2. Brad Bourland and Paul Gamble, "Saudi Arabia's Coming Oil and Fiscal Challenge," research report, Jadwa Investment (Riyadh), 2011, 20.
3. EDGAR, "Fossil CO_2 & GHG Emissions of All World Countries, 2017," Emissions Database for Global Atmospheric Research (EU), 2017, http://edgar.jrc.ec.europa.eu /overview.php?v=CO2andGHG1970-2016.

1. BEFORE OIL

1. Arnold Toynbee, "An Historical Outline to 1970," in *The Middle East*, Handbooks to the Modern World (New York: Facts on File, 1988), 224.
2. The first Portuguese interaction with a Gulf population came during the voyage of Pero de Covilha in the late fifteenth century; the first settlement dates to 1507. See

Joao Teles e Cunha, "The Portuguese Presence in the Persian Gulf," in *The Persian Gulf in History*, ed. Lawrence Potter (New York: Palgrave Macmillan, 2009), 209; John Wilton, "Saudi Arabia," in *The Middle East*, Handbooks to the Modern World (New York: Facts on File, 1988), 470–71; Juan Cole, *Sacred Space and Holy War* (London: I. B. Tauris, 2002), 37–39.

3. J. E. Peterson, "Britain and the Gulf: At the Periphery of Empire," in *The Persian Gulf in History*, ed. Lawrence Potter (New York: Palgrave Macmillan, 2009), 277–94.

4. Frederick Anscombe, "The Ottoman Role in the Gulf," in *The Persian Gulf in History*, ed. Lawrence Potter (New York: Palgrave Macmillan, 2009), 264.

5. Anscombe, "The Ottoman Role in the Gulf," 264–65.

6. Abdul Wahhab was an Islamic scholar in the early 1700s who promoted an austere monotheistic brand of Sunni Islam. His followers are known as Wahhabis or Salafis. The pact between the al-Saud and Abdul Wahhab dates to the 1740s.

7. Toynbee, "An Historical Outline to 1970," 226–27.

8. Vitalis contradicts this claim, pointing out that Ibn Saud conceded some sovereignty rights to Britain in a 1915 treaty in exchange for protection. Vitalis speculates that Ibn Saud, who initiated the treaty, may have sought British protection as a tactic to consolidate control over recently conquered parts of the peninsula that might have otherwise been taken by neighboring states. His acquiescence to Aramco's domination of the Saudi oil sector and the construction of a US airbase in Dhahran reveal a similar strategy when the mantle of regional protection passed from Great Britain to America. See Robert Vitalis, *America's Kingdom: Mythmaking on the Saudi Oil Frontier* (London: Verso, 2007), 5–6.

9. Chas W. Freeman, "The Arab Reawakening: Strategic Implications," *Middle East Policy* 18, no. 2 (2011): 29–36. A more sober assessment comes from Britain's military governor of Iraq, the historian Stephen Longrigg, who suggests that the region's autonomy stems more from a lack of interest by colonizing powers than the Arabs' ability to repel such inroads. See Brigadier Stephen Longrigg, "The Liquid Gold of Arabia," *Journal of the Royal Central Asian Society* 36, no. 1 (1949): 20–33.

10. More specifically, rulers must be from the lines of Mubarak's two immediate successors, his sons Salim and Jabir.

11. Jill Crystal, "Kuwait: Ruling Family," *Persian Gulf States: A Country Study* (Washington: Library of Congress, 1993), http://countrystudies.us/persian-gulf-states/26.htm.

12. Chief among these is Jill Crystal, *Oil and Politics in the Gulf: Rulers and Merchants in Kuwait and Qatar* (Cambridge: Cambridge University Press, 1990).

13. Michael Herb, *The Wages of Oil: Parliaments and Economic Development in Kuwait and the UAE* (Ithaca, NY: Cornell University Press, 2014).

14. Frauke Heard-Bey, *From Trucial States to United Arab Emirates: A Society in Transition*, 3rd ed. (Dubai: Motivate, 2005), 24. Archaeological finds reviewed by Peter Hellyer at the National Media Council in Abu Dhabi could point to a temporary population surge in the seventeenth and eighteenth centuries.

15. Historical British allegations of Qawasim piracy are disputed. Sharjah's ruling sheikh, Sultan bin Muhammad al-Qasimi, wrote a history on the topic as his PhD dissertation at Exeter University and argues that piracy was a pretext for Britain to take over

the Qawasim trade routes. See Sultan bin Muhammad al-Qassimi, *Power Struggles and Trade in the Gulf, 1620–1820* (Exeter: University of Exeter Press, 1999).

16. Jim Krane, *City of Gold: Dubai and the Dream of Capitalism* (New York: St. Martin's, 2009).

17. UAE figure is from "World Economic Outlook," International Monetary Fund, 2016; Abu Dhabi figure is from "Abu Dhabi Emirate: Facts and Figures," Abu Dhabi e-government portal, 2016, https://www.abudhabi.ae/portal/public/en/abu_dhabi_emirate/facts_figure_background.

18. Jim Krane and Steven Wright, "Qatar 'Rises Above' Its Region: Geopolitics and the Rejection of the GCC Gas Market," *Kuwait Programme on Development, Governance and Globalisation in the Gulf States*, London School of Economics, 2014, http://eprints.lse.ac.uk/55336/1/__lse.ac.uk_storage_LIBRARY_Secondary_libfile_shared_repository_Content_Kuwait%20Programme_Krane_2014.pdf.

19. "Qatar Economic Insight," Qatar National Bank, June 2016.

20. Lesley Walker, "Report: Qatari Families Earn Almost Three Times as Much as Expats," *Doha News*, June 18, 2014, https://dohanews.co/ministry-stats-show-average-qatari-household-earns-qr72000-monthly/.

21. By 1730, Oman's African colonies included parts of what are now Somalia, Kenya, and Tanzania, including the islands of Zanzibar and Pemba.

22. Francis Owtram, "A Close Relationship: Britain and Oman Since 1750," Qatar National Library, Articles from Our Experts series, n.d., http://www.qdl.qa/en/close-relationship-britain-and-oman-1750; Fred Halliday, *Arabia Without Sultans* (London: Saqi, 1974), 268–69.

23. Iran only relinquished its claim to Bahrain in 1972. See X. De Planhol and J. Kecheichian, "Bahrain: History of Political Relations with Iran," *Encyclopedia Iranica*, Iranica Online, August 24, 2011, http://www.iranicaonline.org/articles/bahrain-all#pt3.

24. "The Strategic Importance of Bahrain to Saudi Arabia," *Oil Drum*, June 29, 2011, http://oilprice.com/Geopolitics/Middle-East/The-Strategic-Importance-Of-Bahrain-To-Saudi-Arabia.html.

25. Krane, *City of Gold*, 35.

26. Sean Foley, *The Arab Gulf States: Beyond Oil and Islam* (Boulder, CO: Lynne Rienner, 2010), 16–22.

27. A large volume of literature on the resource curse includes Michael L. Ross, *The Oil Curse: How Petroleum Wealth Shapes the Development of Nations* (Princeton, NJ: Princeton University Press, 2012); Raymond F. Mikesell, "Explaining the Resource Curse, with Special Reference to Mineral-Exporting Countries," *Resources Policy* 23, no. 4 (1997): 191–99; Jeffrey D. Sachs and Andrew M. Warner, "The Curse of Natural Resources," *European Economic Review* 45, no. 4 (2001): 827–38; Paul Stevens, "Resource Impact: Curse or Blessing? A Literature Survey," *Journal of Energy Literature* 9, no. 1 (2003): 1–42; Michael L. Ross, "Does Oil Hinder Democracy?," *World Politics* 53 (2001): 325–61.

28. Michael Alexeev and Robert Conrad, "The Elusive Curse of Oil," *Review of Economics and Statistics* 91, no. 3 (August 2009): 586–98; Michael Herb, "No Representation

Without Taxation? Rents, Development, and Democracy," *Comparative Politics* 37, no. 3 (2005): 297–315; Stephen Haber and Victor Menaldo, "Do Natural Resources Fuel Authoritarianism? A Reappraisal of the Resource Curse," *American Political Science Review* 105, no. 1 (February 2011): 1–26.

2. THE OIL AGE ARRIVES

1. Wilfred Thesiger, *Arabian Sands* (Dubai: Motivate, 1994), 88–89.
2. Abdelrahman Munif, *Cities of Salt* (New York: Vintage, 1989), 67–68.
3. Munif, *Cities of Salt*, 85–87.
4. "Seven Wells of Dammam," *Aramco World* 14, no. 1 (January 1963): 18–21, http://archive.aramcoworld.com/issue/196301/seven.wells.of.dammam.htm.
5. The initial disappointing wells probed the Cretaceous zones that had proven fruitful in Bahrain. Well No. 7 aimed to penetrate a lower formation, the late Upper Jurassic zone. See R. W. Powers, L. F. Ramirez, C. D. Redmond, and E. L. Elberg Jr., "Geology of the Arabian Peninsula: Sedimentary Geology of Saudi Arabia," US Geological Survey Professional Paper 560-D, 1966, https://pubs.usgs.gov/pp/0560d/report.pdf.
6. Ray Vicker, *The Kingdom of Oil* (New York: Charles Scribner's Sons, 1974), 70.
7. "Seven Wells of Dammam."
8. Kuwait's National Assembly was not established until 1963 nor Bahrain's until 1973.
9. Eric Roach, "Saudi Arabia and Oil: What You Need to Know," Drillinginfo DI Blog, March 12, 2015, http://info.drillinginfo.com/saudi-arabia-oil-need-know.
10. Vicker, *The Kingdom of Oil*, 72.
11. Roach, "Saudi Arabia and Oil"; BP, *Statistical Review of World Energy 2016* (London: BP, 2016).
12. "Seven Wells of Dammam."
13. "Giant of the Sea," *Aramco World* 13, no. 10 (December 1962): 3–6, http://archive.aramcoworld.com/issue/196210/giant.of.the.sea.htm.
14. Thesiger, *Arabian Sands*, 87.
15. The Bahrain Petroleum Company operated the very first refinery in the Gulf, which opened in 1934, but its output was tiny.
16. "A Billion Barrels Ago . . ." *Aramco World* 13, no. 5 (May 1962): 3–6, http://archive.aramcoworld.com/issue/196205/a.billion.barrels.ago.htm.
17. Daniel Yergin, *The Prize: The Epic Quest for Oil, Money, and Power*, paperback ed. (New York: Free Press, 1991), 410–16.
18. As per the Achnacarry agreement of 1928. Yergin, *The Prize*, 243–50.
19. Toby Craig Jones, *Desert Kingdom: How Oil and Water Forged Modern Saudi Arabia* (Cambridge, MA: Harvard University Press, 2010), 49, 92.
20. Memo of conversation by Shaw, August 7, 1958, and attached memo by Duce, folder: General Subject Middle East Developments Arab Development Institution 1958 3, box 12, General Subject Files Relating to the Middle East, 1955–1958, Lot 61 D 12, RG

59, National Archives and Records Administration in College Park, MD (NARA). Provided by Nathan Citino of Rice University.

21. Jones, *Desert Kingdom*, 97–101; Robert Vitalis, *America's Kingdom: Mythmaking on the Saudi Oil Frontier* (London: Verso, 2007).

22. Figures from OPEC Annual Statistical Bulletin 2007, cited in Islam Y. Qasem, *Oil and Security Policies: Saudi Arabia, 1950–2012* (Leiden: Brill, 2015), 46.

23. Rachel Bronson, *Thicker Than Oil: America's Uneasy Partnership with Saudi Arabia* (Oxford: Oxford University Press, 2006), 65.

24. Vitalis, *America's Kingdom*, 27.

25. Thomas W. Lippman, *Arabian Knight: Colonel Bill Eddy USMC and the Rise of American Power in the Middle East* (Vista, CA: Selwa, 2008).

26. Aramco's 340-mile railway and its stations are still in use. For its history, see John C. Henry, "American Railroad on the Arabian Desert," *Popular Mechanics*, April 1952.

27. Osmel Manzano and Francisco Monaldi, "The Political Economy of Oil Contract Renegotiation in Venezuela," in *The Natural Resources Trap: Private Investment Without Public Commitment*, ed. William Hogan and Federico Sturzenegger (Cambridge, MA: MIT Press, 2010).

28. Multiplying current proven reserve figures of 267 billion barrels by a low valuation of $5/barrel implies potential revenues of $1.3 trillion. It would be unlikely that 100 percent of reserves could be produced. Typical recovery rates are in the 30 to 40 percent range. Reserves figures from BP, *Statistical Review of World Energy 2015* (London: BP, 2015). In 2016, Saudi Aramco's valuation was variously estimated at between $780bn and $10 trillion. See Robin Mills, "Aramco IPO Talk Has Message for Saudi State Firms," *The National* (Abu Dhabi), January 10, 2016, http://www.thenational.ae/business/energy/aramco-ipo-talk-has-message-for-saudi-state-firms.

29. Using the formula in note 28, Kuwaiti reserves would be worth something like $500 billion. Concession terms from Yergin, *The Prize*, 297–98.

30. Steven Jay Epstein, "The Cartel That Never Was," *Atlantic*, March 1983, https://www.theatlantic.com/magazine/archive/1983/03/the-cartel-that-never-was/306495/.

31. Timothy Mitchell, *Carbon Democracy: Political Power in the Age of Oil* (Brooklyn: Verso, 2013).

32. Edith Penrose, George Joffe, and Paul Stevens, "Nationalisation of Foreign-Owned Property for a Public Purpose: An Economic Perspective on Appropriate Compensation," *Modern Law Review* 55, no. 3 (1992): 351–67.

33. Manzano and Monaldi, "The Political Economy of Oil Contract Renegotiation in Venezuela."

34. Yergin, *The Prize*, 434–35, 447.

35. Yergin, *The Prize*, 447–48.

36. Arthur Ross, "OPEC's Challenge to the West," *Washington Quarterly* 3, no. 1 (1980): 50–57.

3. THE BIG PAYBACK

1. Parra estimates the remuneration for "participation" paid by Abu Dhabi, Iran, Iraq, Kuwait, and Saudi Arabia at US 23 cents per barrel of oil produced and less than half a cent per barrel of reserves. Francisco Parra, *Oil Politics: A Modern History of Petroleum* (New York: I. B. Tauris, 2004), 155–59.

2. Valerie Marcel, *Oil Titans: National Oil Companies in the Middle East* (Washington, DC: Brookings, 2006).

3. Natural gas, or methane, is a far more powerful greenhouse gas than carbon dioxide. Historical emissions data from EDGAR ([EU] Emissions Database for Global Atmospheric Research), "Fossil CO_2 & GHG Emissions of All World Countries, 2017," http://edgar.jrc.ec.europa.eu/overview.php?v=CO2andGHG1970-2016.

4. Andy Flower, "LNG in Qatar," and Justin Dargin, "Qatar's Gas Revolution," both in *Natural Gas Markets in the Middle East and North Africa*, ed. Bassam Fattouh and Jonathan Stern (Oxford: Oxford Institute for Energy Studies, 2011).

5. Telegram from the Embassy in Saudi Arabia to the Department of State, Jidda, May 21, 1970, *Foreign Relations of the United States, 1969–1976*, vol. 24, *Middle East Region and Arabian Peninsula, 1969–1972*, Jordan, September 1970, https://history.state.gov/historicaldocuments/frus1969-76v24/d141.

6. Telegram from the Consulate General in Dhahran to the Department of State, Dhahran, August 31, 1969, *Foreign Relations of the United States, 1969–1976*, vol. 24, *Middle East Region and Arabian Peninsula, 1969–1972*, Jordan, September 1970, https://history.state.gov/historicaldocuments/frus1969-76v24/d128.

7. Telegram from the Embassy in Saudi Arabia to the Department of State, Jidda, May 21, 1970.

8. Bruce Riedel, *Kings and Presidents: Saudi Arabia and the United States Since FDR* (Washington, DC: Brookings, 2018), 50–54.

9. Edward R. F. Sheehan, "Sadat's War," *New York Times Magazine*, November 18, 1973, http://www.nytimes.com/1973/11/18/archives/sadats-war-sadats-war-canal-crossing.html.

10. In the West, the Yom Kippur War is typically misconstrued as a "war of survival" for Israel, which was, by then, the strongest regional power, with an advanced air force and a nuclear arsenal. Even Yergin's narrative succumbs to the fiction of an Israel facing destruction. Daniel Yergin, *The Prize: The Epic Quest for Oil, Money, and Power*, paperback ed. (New York: Free Press, 1991), 603–5. More credible histories document the limited aims and weakness of the Syrian and Egyptian armies. Arab leaders' war aims were calibrated to reclaim occupied territory and no more. Sadat was so circumspect about Egypt's chances versus the far superior Israeli Army that he told his generals they only needed to recapture "ten millimeters" of the Sinai and hold it long enough for the Americans to intervene and force the Israelis to negotiate. Patrick Seale, *Asad: The Struggle for the Middle East* (Berkeley: University of California Press, 1995), 194–200; Moshe Ma'oz, *Syria and Israel: From War to Peacemaking* (Oxford: Clarendon, 1995), 126–30; Craig Daigle, *The Limits of Detente: The United States, the*

Soviet Union, and the Arab-Israeli Conflict, 1969–1973 (New Haven, CT: Yale University Press, 2012), 285.

11. Arab oil production totaled 20.8m b/d in October 1973 and 15.8m b/d in December, the most severe point in the embargo. Yergin, *The Prize*, 614.

12. Yergin, *The Prize*, 590–94.

13. US Energy Information Administration, "Imported Crude Oil Prices, Monthly," Short-Term Energy Outlook, August 8, 2017, https://www.eia.gov/outlooks/steo/real prices/.

14. Yergin, *The Prize*, 647.

15. Telegram from the Embassy in Saudi Arabia to the Department of State, Jidda, May 21, 1970.

16. In 1988, the Saudi national oil company finally assumed the name it still holds: Saudi Aramco. Even then, Saudi Aramco retained many of the Western engineers and families in its compound in Dhahran. "Saudi Aramco by the Numbers," *Aramco World* 59, no. 3 (May/June 2008): 2–5, http://archive.aramcoworld.com/issue/200803/75 .years.saudi.aramco.by.the.numbers.htm.

17. IOC access to global reserves has continued to dwindle relative to that controlled by NOCs and other state-controlled entities. By 2005, IOCs had full access to just 7 percent of global reserves. PFC Energy, "Constrained Worldwide Oil & Gas Reserve Access," 2007, slide illustration, reprinted in Sajjad Jasimuddin and A. Maniruzzaman, "Resource Nationalism Specter Hovers Over the Oil Industry: The Transnational Corporate Strategy to Tackle Resource Nationalism Risks," *Journal of Applied Business Research* 32, no. 2 (March 1, 2016): 387–400, https://doi.org/10.19030 /jabr.v32i2.9584.

18. Exxon Public Affairs Department, "Exxon Background Series: Middle East Oil," 1976, https://www.gpo.gov/fdsys/pkg/CZIC-hd9576-n36-e8-1976/html/CZIC-hd9576 -n36-e8-1976.htm. See "Table 4: Cost and Profitability of Middle East Oil."

19. Exxon Public Affairs Department, "Exxon Background Series: Middle East Oil." Not all of the increase was attributable to higher prices. Higher output was also a factor.

20. Arthur Ross, "OPEC's Challenge to the West," *Washington Quarterly* 3, no. 1 (1980): 50.

21. Ross, "OPEC's Challenge to the West," 50.

22. Seymour M. Lipset, "Some Social Requisites of Democracy: Economic Development and Political Legitimacy," *American Political Science Review* 53, no. 1 (1959): 69–105; Karl Deutsch, "Social Mobilization and Political Development," *American Political Science Review* 55, no. 3 (September 1961): 493–514; Samuel P. Huntington, *Political Order in Changing Societies* (New Haven, CT: Yale University Press, 1968).

4. FROM ENERGY POVERTY TO ENERGY EXTREMISM

1. Chris Kutschera, "Oman: The Death of the Last Feudal Arab State," *Washington Post*, December 27, 1970, http://www.chris-kutschera.com/A/Oman%201970.htm.

2. Marc Valeri, *Oman: Politics and Society in the Qaboos State* (London: Hurst, 2009).

3. Figures from Oman's National Center for Statistics and Information and other sources cited on *Times of Oman* graphic published November 18, 2015. See https://twitter.com /CIL_Oman/status/667228402680791040.

4. Even the Quran—and orthodox Islam—had not penetrated some of Oman's isolated mountain reaches, where some villagers did not speak Arabic or know how to pray in Islamic fashion. By one account I have heard, religious practices in remote Dhofari communities included animist and other non-Islamic aspects into the 1970s.

5. That equates to two doctors and fewer than one hospital per 100,000 people. In 2015, Oman counted 67 hospitals and 217 doctors per 100,000 people; life expectancy reached 77 years.

6. Omanis used a tenth of a metric ton/person in 1971 and 7 metric tons/person in 2013. *IEA World Energy Balances*, 2015 ed.

7. Further discoveries came in 1963 and 1964, but since oilfields were so far from the coast, a 175-mile pipeline had to be built before any could be exported. The first export came in 1967. Omani oil production grew from 57,000 b/d in 1967 to reach 332,000 b/d by 1970, roughly a third of current Omani oil-production levels. Oman Ministry of Oil and Gas, "Brief History of the Oil and Gas Sector in Sultanate of Oman," n.d., http://www.mog.gov.om/Portals/1/pdf/oil/history-Oil-Gas-en.pdf. Production data from BP, *Statistical Review of World Energy 2015* (London: BP, 2015).

8. Fred Halliday, *Arabia Without Sultans* (London: Saqi, 1974), 275.

9. Valeri, *Oman*.

10. Halliday, *Arabia Without Sultans*, 373–75.

11. Kutschera, "Oman."

12. Jim Krane, *City of Gold: Dubai and the Dream of Capitalism* (New York: St. Martin's, 2009), 58–59.

13. Major cities in Saudi Arabia, Kuwait, Bahrain, and Qatar began receiving municipal power in the 1950s.

14. Christopher M. Davidson, *The United Arab Emirates: A Study in Survival* (Boulder, CO: Lynne Rienner, 2005).

15. Saudi Arabia also cancelled once-crucial fees on religious pilgrims and rescinded several other taxes. Kiren Aziz Chaudhry, *The Price of Wealth: Economies and Institutions in the Middle East* (Ithaca, NY: Cornell University Press, 1997), 143–44.

16. OECD and IEA, cited in United Nations Environment Program, "Reforming Energy Subsidies: Opportunities to Contribute to the Climate Change Agenda," white paper (Geneva: UNEP, 2008), 11.

17. Some hold that Saudi Arabia is a special case: that its low domestic energy prices do not constitute subsidies because spare production capacity allows it to set or influence global market prices. I acknowledge these arguments but, in the interest of simplicity, accept the IEA's characterization of Saudi underpricing as a subsidy. For a more nuanced argument, see Yousef Alyousef and Paul Stevens, "The Cost of Domestic Energy Prices to Saudi Arabia," *Energy Policy* 39 (2011): 6900–5.

18. According to the Little-Mirrlees Rule, allocative efficiency is achieved when the domestic price equals the real marginal opportunity cost, the best estimate of which is the world reference price. Ian M. D. Little and James A. Mirrlees, *Manual of Industrial Project Analysis in Developing Countries* (Paris: OECD, 1968); Dagobert L. Brito and Juan Rosellon, *Pricing Natural Gas in Mexico: An Application of the Little Mirrlees Rule—The Case of Quasi-Rents* (Berlin: German Institute for Economic Research [DIW], 2010).

19. Sufficient domestic refining capacity in the Gulf has always been a temporary phenomenon. Domestic refineries are periodically built to cope with rising fuel demand. Surpluses are exported until demand surpasses production and a new refinery is needed.

20. "Foundations: The Keystone," *Aramco World*, December 1982, http://www.saudia ramcoworld.com/issue/198206/foundations-the.keystone.htm.

21. EDGAR ([EU] Emissions Database for Global Atmospheric Research), "Fossil CO_2 & GHG Emissions of All World Countries, 2017," http://edgar.jrc.ec.europa.eu/over view.php?v=CO2andGHG1970-2016.

22. David Scott, Executive Director, Economic and Energy Affairs, Abu Dhabi Executive Affairs Authority, telephone interview by Jim Krane, 2010.

23. There is debate about whether electricity provision was an explicit quid pro quo for citizen political support or whether its subsidization owes itself to an unintentional failure to index tariffs to inflation.

24. Rents can be defined as profits left over after deducting the cost of exploration, production, transport, refining, and marketing and after a reasonable rate of return.

25. David Victor, "The Politics of Fossil Fuel Subsidies," Global Subsidies Initiative working paper, October 2009, 20.

26. Lisa Anderson, "Democracy in the Arab World: A Critique of the Political Culture Approach," in *Political Liberalization and Democratization in the Arab World*, ed. Rex Brynen, Bahgat Korany, and Paul Noble (Boulder, CO: Lynne Rienner, 1995), 1:77–92.

27. Early rentier literature includes Hossein Mahdavy, "The Patterns and Problems of Economic Development in Rentier States: The Case of Iran," in *Studies in the Economic History of the Middle East*, ed. M. A. Cook (London: Oxford University Press, 1970), 428–67; Giacomo Luciani, "Allocation vs. Production States: A Theoretical Framework," in *The Rentier State*, ed. Hazem Beblawi and Giacomo Luciani (New York: Croom Helm, 1987), 63–82; Hazem Beblawi, "The Rentier State in the Arab World," in *The Rentier State*, ed. Hazem Beblawi and Giacomo Luciani (New York: Croom Helm, 1987), 85–98.

28. Jill Crystal, *Oil and Politics in the Gulf: Rulers and Merchants in Kuwait and Qatar* (Cambridge: Cambridge University Press, 1990), 6–11.

29. F. Gregory Gause III, *Oil Monarchies: Domestic and Security Challenges in the Arab Gulf States* (New York: Council on Foreign Relations, 1994), 80; Davidson, *The United Arab Emirates*.

30. Crystal, *Oil and Politics in the Gulf*, 6–11; Davidson, *The United Arab Emirates*, 70–96.

31. Victor, "The Politics of Fossil Fuel Subsidies."

5. UNNATURALLY COOL

1. "World's Highest Substation from ABB Powers World's Tallest Building," ABB, January 7, 2010, http://www.abb.com/cawp/seitp202/ebfffeeed935ef0cc12576a200382295 .aspx.

2. Energy-poor Dubai has been an early adopter of public transport, which has expanded throughout the Gulf over the last decade.

3. BP, *Statistical Review of World Energy 2017* (London: BP, 2017), https://www.bp.com /content/dam/bp/en/corporate/pdf/energy-economics/statistical-review-2017/bp -statistical-review-of-world-energy-2017-full-report.pdf.

4. Eckart Woertz, "The Water-Energy-Food Nexus in MENA," *Energy Forum*, Oxford Institute for Energy Studies, no. 102 (2015).

5. International Energy Agency, "Betwixt Petro-Dollars and Subsidies: Surging Energy Consumption in the Mideast and North Africa States" (Paris, 2008).

6. BP, *Statistical Review of World Energy 2016* (London: BP, 2016) https://www.bp.com /content/dam/bp/pdf/energy-economics/statistical-review-2016/bp-statistical-review -of-world-energy-2016-full-report.pdf. Note that BP totals include crude oil and natural gas liquids (NGLs).

7. US Energy Information Administration, "Saudi Arabia Country Brief," September 10, 2014, http://www.eia.gov/beta/international/analysis.cfm?iso=SAU.

8. "Saudi Direct Crude Burning Set for Decrease," *Middle East Economic Survey* 59, nos. 51/52 (December 23, 2016).

9. Various sources put air-conditioning demand at between 70 and 80 percent of peak electricity demand or of total electricity demand in the various GCC states.

10. Figures on average size and electricity demand for Kuwaiti homes comes from data supplied by the Kuwait Ministry of Electricity and Water in October 2016.

11. World Energy Council, "Average Electricity Consumption per Electrified Household," Energy Efficiency Indicators, May 2016, https://www.wec-indicators.enerdata.eu /household-electricity-use.html.

12. 44 percent of Saudi power was derived from liquid fuel–based generation, as was 64 percent in Kuwait and 3 percent in Oman, where (as in Saudi Arabia) diesel generation provides electricity in areas beyond transmission grids: International Energy Agency, "World Energy Balances," statistics database (Paris, 2018).

13. Qatar began LNG exports in 1997 and started pipeline exports of gas to the UAE and Oman in 2006. The UAE and Oman export small amounts of LNG. The UAE's gas exports are outweighed by imports.

14. International Energy Agency, "Betwixt Petro-Dollars and Subsidies."

15. Per capita GDP growth is PPP and averages all six GCC growth rates since 1981 on an unweighted basis. International Monetary Fund (2012): World Economic Outlook (October 2012 ed.).

16. Kenneth B. Medlock III, "Energy Demand Theory," in *International Handbook on the Economics of Energy*, ed. Joanne Evans and Lester C. Hunt (Northampton, MA: Edward Elgar, 2011), 89–111.

17. Jim Krane, *City of Gold: Dubai and the Dream of Capitalism* (New York: St. Martin's, 2009), 89.

18. Hiba Nayif Khalil Harara, "Restructuring the Electricity Supply Industry in the Kingdom of Bahrain and Its Implications for a Unified GCC Structure," University of Hull, 2008, 183.

19. Khalil Harara, "Restructuring the Electricity Supply Industry," 184.

20. Electricity and Co-Generation Regulatory Authority, "2015 Annual Statistical Booklet for Electricity and Seawater Desalination Industries," statistical bulletin (Riyadh: ECRA, 2016), http://www.ecra.gov.sa/en-us/MediaCenter/DocLib2/Lists/SubCate gory_Library/Statistical%20Booklets%202015.pdf.

21. Electricity tariff and cost details are from the Kuwait Ministry of Electricity and Water, in data received and interviews conducted during visits in March 2012. Jaffar et al. put government costs of electricity provision at 16 US cents per kWh. The long-standing tariff of 0.7 cents covers about 4.4 percent of the cost. B. Jaffar, T. Oreszc-zyn, and R. Raslan, "A Framework to Evaluate the Energy Efficiency Potential of Kuwaiti Homes," *WIT Transactions on Ecology and the Environment* 186 (2014): 25–38, https://doi.org/10.2495/ESUS140031. Even so, Kuwait only manages to collect about half the revenues it is owed. International Business Publications, *Kuwait Energy Policy, Laws and Regulations Handbook*, vol. 1: *Strategic Information and Basic Laws* (Washington, DC: International Business Publications, 2015).

22. Although falling commodity prices toward the end of 2014 reduced the implied opportunity cost of low domestic prices. International Energy Agency, Fossil Fuel Subsidies Database, 2015 World Energy Outlook.

23. This theme is addressed in greater detail in Jim Krane, "Guzzling in the Gulf: The Monarchies Face a Threat from Within," *Foreign Affairs*, December 19, 2014, http://www.foreignaffairs.com/articles/142692/jim-krane/guzzling-in-the-gulf; and Jim Krane, "Stability Versus Sustainability: Energy Policy in the Gulf Monarchies," PhD diss., University of Cambridge, 2014, http://dx.doi.org/10.17863/CAM.5943.

24. Michael O'Hanlon, "How Much Does the United States Spend Protecting Persian Gulf Oil?" in *Energy Security: Economics, Politics, Strategies, and Implications* (Washington, DC: Brookings, 2010), 59–72.

25. The useful "oil for security" paradigm underestimates the strength and rationale underpinning the Washington-Riyadh friendship. Other shared factors include a long tradition of US-educated Saudi elites in key positions, a shared and deep Cold War aversion to the Soviet Union and Soviet atheism, and mutual hostility toward Iran and Syria (and Russia's backing of those regimes). See Rachel Bronson, "Understanding US-Saudi Relations," in *Saudi Arabia in the Balance*, ed. Paul Aarts and Gerd Non-neman (London: Hurst, 2006), 372–98.

26. Arizona average household electricity costs were $1,358 per year versus just $994 for Abu Dhabi nationals and $1,060 for expatriate residents in the emirate.

27. Academic estimates of price elasticity on various energy products in the Gulf range from zero to –0.46. Naief H. Al-Mutairi and M. Nagy Eltony, "Price and Income Elas-ticities of Energy Demand: Some Estimates for Kuwait Using Two Econometric

Models," *Journal of Energy and Development* 20, no. 2 (1995); M. Nagy Eltony and Naief H. Al-Mutairi, "Demand for Gasoline in Kuwait: An Empirical Analysis Using Cointegration Techniques," *Energy Economics* 17, no. 3 (1995): 249–53; Paresh Kumar Narayan and Russell Smyth, "A Panel Cointegration Analysis of the Demand for Oil in the Middle East," *Energy Policy* 35, no. 12 (2007): 6258–65; Tarek N. Atalla and Lester C. Hunt, "Modelling Residential Electricity Demand in the GCC Countries," *Energy Economics* 59 (2016): 149–58.

28. A price elasticity of –1 implies a one-to-one relationship between price and demand. Here, I use a modest but plausible estimate of –0.3, which implies a 1 to –0.3 relationship. This means that a one-point increase in price would produce a 0.3-point reduction in demand. This figure lies within the range covered in the literature and represents the lower of two estimates of price elasticity used by the IMF in a 2012 paper on Kuwait. The formula I use to calculate demand effects is nonlinear so that it can take into account large fluctuations in price. See Pedro Rodriguez, Joshua Charap, and Arthur Ribeiro da Silva, "Fuel Subsidies and Energy Consumption: A Cross-Country Analysis," Kuwait Selected Issues and Statistical Appendix, IMF Country Report (Washington, DC: International Monetary Fund, June 2012).

29. Fouquet argues that energy systems are particularly susceptible to strong and long-lived path dependence because of technological, infrastructural, institutional, and behavioral lock-ins. Roger Fouquet, "Path Dependence in Energy Systems and Economic Development," *Nature Energy* 1 (July 11, 2016): 16098.

30. Harold Hotelling, "The Economics of Exhaustible Resources," *Journal of Political Economy* 39, no. 2 (April 1931): 137–75.

6. WE HAVE A SERIOUS PROBLEM

1. Daniel Fineren, "Oman Oil Minister Slams Gulf Culture of Energy Subsidies," *Reuters*, November 10, 2013, http://www.reuters.com/article/2013/11/10/gulf-energy-subsidies-idUSL5N0IV07V20131110.

2. Hazem Beblawi and Giacomo Luciani, "Introduction," in *The Rentier State*, ed. Hazem Beblawi and Giacomo Luciani (London: Croom Helm, 1987), 16–17.

3. Jill Crystal, *Oil and Politics in the Gulf: Rulers and Merchants in Kuwait and Qatar* (Cambridge: Cambridge University Press, 1990), 191.

4. Samih K. Farsoun, "Class Structure and Social Change in the Arab World," in *Arab Society: Class, Gender, Power, and Development*, ed. Nicholas S. Hopkins and Saad E. Ibrahim (Cairo: American University of Cairo Press, 1997), 21.

5. Beblawi and Luciani, "Introduction," 16–17.

6. For a full review of rentier theory and its treatment of subsidy reform, particularly on energy, see Jim Krane, "Stability Versus Sustainability: Energy Policy in the Gulf Monarchies," PhD diss., University of Cambridge, 2014, http://dx.doi.org/10.17863/CAM.5943.

7. F. Gregory Gause III, *Oil Monarchies: Domestic and Security Challenges in the Arab Gulf States* (New York: Council on Foreign Relations, 1994), specifically mentions state payment of citizen utility bills in this formulation (82, 61).

8. Gause, *Oil Monarchies*, 147.

9. F. Gregory Gause III, "The Political Economy of National Security in the GCC States," in *The Persian Gulf at the Millennium*, ed. Gary Sick and Lawrence Potter (New York: St. Martin's, 1997), 80.

10. Michael Herb, *All in the Family: Absolutism, Revolution, and Democracy in Middle Eastern Monarchies* (Albany: SUNY Press, 1999), 241–42.

11. Kiren Aziz Chaudhry, *The Price of Wealth: Economies and Institutions in the Middle East* (Ithaca, NY: Cornell University Press, 1997), 149, 274–75.

12. Sean Foley, *The Arab Gulf States: Beyond Oil and Islam* (Boulder, CO: Lynne Rienner, 2010), 85.

13. Oliver Schlumberger, "Rents, Reform, and Authoritarianism in the Middle East," *Internationale Politik Und Gesellschaft* 2, no. 2006 (2006): 3.

14. Rolf Schwarz, "The Political Economy of State-Formation in the Arab Middle East: Rentier States, Economic Reform, and Democratization," *Review of International Political Economy* 15, no. 4 (2008): 607.

15. Steffen Hertog and Giacomo Luciani, "Energy and Sustainability Policies in the GCC," Kuwait Programme on Development, Governance, and Globalisation in the Gulf States, London School of Economics, 2009, 7, 40; emphasis added.

16. F. Gregory Gause III, "Saudi Arabia in the New Middle East," *Special Report No. 63 New York: Council on Foreign Relations*, 2011, 11–12. Gause also touches on distinctions between fiscal expenditures and on the implications of resource demand for the income side of the budget. See also F. Gregory Gause III, "Kings for All Seasons: How the Middle East's Monarchies Survived the Arab Spring," Brookings Doha Center Analysis Paper (Doha, 2013).

17. Gulf-based IOC executive, interview with author on condition of anonymity, November 15, 2011.

18. Mabro and Razavi argue that Mideast gas *exports* are also driven by subsidies, since low domestic prices incentivize firms to reap higher export returns, even when those gains are outweighed by the economic benefits of using gas domestically. See Robert Mabro, "Egypt's Oil and Gas: Some Crucial Issues," Distinguished Lecture series (Cairo: Egyptian Center for Economic Studies, 2006). See also Hossein Razavi, "Natural Gas Pricing in Countries of the Middle East and North Africa," *Energy Journal* 30, no. 3 (2009): 1–22.

19. Matthew Gray, "A Theory of 'Late Rentierism' in the Arab States of the Gulf," scholarly paper (Doha: Georgetown University Center for International and Regional Studies, 2011); Christopher M. Davidson, *The United Arab Emirates: A Study in Survival* (Boulder, CO: Lynne Rienner, 2005).

20. See note 27 in chapter 1 for a list of references on the "resource curse."

21. Jim Krane, "Reconsidering the Role of Energy in the Rentier State," International Association for Energy Economics annual conference, Bergen, Norway, June 21, 2016.

22. Glada Lahn, "Fuel, Food, and Utilities Price Reforms in the GCC: A Wake-up Call for Business," Chatham House, June 2016.

23. BP, *Statistical Review of World Energy 2015* (London: BP, 2015). Note that emissions from Oman and Bahrain are not included in the GCC total.

24. Flaring is particularly prevalent in Iraq. International Energy Agency, "World Energy Outlook 2015 Special Report on Energy and Climate Change," June 15, 2015, http://www.worldenergyoutlook.org/energyclimate/#d.en.143801.

25. Jeremy S. Pal and Elfatih A. B. Eltahir, "Future Temperature in Southwest Asia Projected to Exceed a Threshold for Human Adaptability," *Nature Climate Change* 6, no. 2 (February 2016): 197–200.

26. Jeff Masters, "Eastern Hemisphere's All-Time Temperature Record: Kuwait Fries in 54°C (129.2°F) Heat," Weather Underground Wunder Blog, July 22, 2016, https://www.wunderground.com/blog/JeffMasters/eastern-hemispheres-alltime-temperature-record-kuwait-frys-in-54c.

27. BP, *Statistical Review of World Energy 2017* (London: BP, 2017).

28. APICORP, "The Future of Coal in the MENA Power Mix" (Khobar, Saudi Arabia: Arab Petroleum Investments Corp., August 2017).

29. BP, *Statistical Review of World Energy 2017*.

30. This notion forms the basis for Jim Krane, "Beyond 12.5: The Implications of an Increase in Saudi Crude Oil Production Capacity," *Energy Policy* 110 (2017): 542–47.

31. Once prices are raised, other demand-side reforms, such as efficiency standards, can provide further reductions.

32. Paul Pierson, "The New Politics of the Welfare State," *World Politics* 48 (1996): 143–79.

33. David G. Victor, "The Politics of Fossil-Fuel Subsidies," working paper, Global Subsidies Initiative, International Institute of Sustainable Development, 2009.

34. Pierson, "The New Politics of the Welfare State"; Douglas R. Arnold, *The Logic of Congressional Action* (New Haven, CT: Yale University Press, 1992); Eric Patashnik, "After the Public Interest Prevails: The Political Sustainability of Policy Reform," *Governance* 16, no. 2 (2003): 203–34; Steffen Hertog, *Princes, Brokers, and Bureaucrats: Oil and the State in Saudi Arabia* (Ithaca, NY: Cornell University Press, 2010), 223–45.

35. International Monetary Fund, "Energy Subsidy Reform: Lessons and Implications" (Washington: IMF, 2013), https://www.imf.org/en/Publications/Policy-Papers/Issues/2016/12/31/Energy-Subsidy-Reform-Lessons-and-Implications-PP4741.

36. Lucas Davis, "Historic Opportunity to Reduce Global Fuel Subsidies," November 9, 2015, Energy Institute at Haas blog, https://energyathaas.wordpress.com/2015/11/09/historic-opportunity-to-reduce-global-fuel-subsidies/; Noel D. Uri and Roy Boyd, "An Evaluation of the Economic Effects of Higher Energy Prices in Mexico," *Energy Policy* 25 (1997): 205–15.

37. "Mexico Electricity Market Reforms Attempt to Reduce Costs and Develop New Capacity," *Today in Energy*, US Energy Information Administration, July 5, 2016, http://www.eia.gov/todayinenergy/detail.php?id=26932.

38. "Malaysia Scraps Fuel Subsidies as Najib Ends Decades-Old Policy," *Bloomberg*, November 21, 2014, http://www.bloomberg.com/news/articles/2014-11-21/malaysia-scraps-fuel-subsidies-as-najib-ends-decades-old-policy.

39. International Monetary Fund, "Energy Subsidy Reform: Lessons and Implications."

40. "Five Reasons Why Nigeria Ended Fuel Subsidies," *DW.com*, May 13, 2016, http://www.dw.com/en/five-reasons-why-nigeria-ended-fuel-subsidies/a-19255388.

7. IRAN AND DUBAI LEAD THE WAY

1. Hossein Mahdavy, "The Patterns and Problems of Economic Development in Rentier States: The Case of Iran," in *Studies in the Economic History of the Middle East*, ed. M. A. Cook (London: Oxford University Press, 1970), 428–67.
2. International Monetary Fund, "Energy Subsidy Reform: Lessons and Implications" (Washington: IMF, 2013), https://www.imf.org/en/Publications/Policy-Papers/Issues/2016/12/31/Energy-Subsidy-Reform-Lessons-and-Implications-PP4741.
3. Lin Noueihed, "Smuggling to Iran Rife in Dangerous Gulf Waters," *Reuters*, May 12, 2008.
4. Dominique Guillaume, Roman Zytek, and Mohammed Reza Farzin, "Iran: The Chronicles of Subsidy Reform" (Washington: International Monetary Fund, 2011), http://www.greenfiscalpolicy.org/wp-content/uploads/2013/08/Iran-The-Chronicles-of-the-Subsidy-Reform1.pdf.
5. Guillaume, Zytek, and Farzin, "Iran."
6. "The Implementation of Targeted Subsidies Starts Today with Public Participation," *Iran*, December 19, 2010.
7. "The Implementation of Targeted Subsidies Starts Today with Public Participation."
8. Guillaume, Zytek, and Farzin, "Iran."
9. Lester C. Thurow, "Cash Versus in-Kind Transfers," *American Economic Review* 64, no. 2 (1974): 190–95; Paul Segal, "Resource Rents, Redistribution, and Halving Global Poverty: The Resource Dividend," *World Development* 39, no. 4 (2011): 475–89.
10. Initial public support is documented in International Monetary Fund, "Energy Subsidy Reform"; Guillaume, Zytek, and Farzin, "Iran." See also Hamid Tabatabai, "The Basic Income Road to Reforming Iran's Price Subsidies," *Basic Income Studies* 6, no. 1 (2011): 1–24.
11. Paolo Verme, "Subsidy Reforms in the Middle East and North Africa Region: A Review," working paper (Washington: World Bank, July 2016), 11, https://papers.ssrn.com/sol3/papers.cfm?abstract_id=2812302.
12. "Second Phase of Subsidy Reform Plan to Await Budget Approval," *Middle East Economic Survey*, April 30, 2012, 17–18. See also "Petrol Rationing Saves Iran $38 Billion: Official," *Tehran Times*, December 31, 2011.
13. Najmeh Bozorgmehr, "Subsidy Dispute Adds to Iran's Woes," *Financial Times*, 2012; International Monetary Fund, "Energy Subsidy Reform."
14. International Monetary Fund, "Energy Subsidy Reform."
15. International Monetary Fund, "Islamic Republic of Iran: Selected Issues," Country Report (Washington: IMF, December 2015), 11, https://www.imf.org/external/pubs/ft/scr/2015/cr15350.pdf.
16. "Rouhani: Protests Are an Opportunity," *Tehran Times*, January 1, 2018, http://www.tehrantimes.com/news/419912/Rouhani-Protests-are-an-opportunity.
17. I discussed its details with an adviser in the Saudi Ministry of Petroleum and Minerals, October 17, 2012. The official displayed a thorough understanding of the Iranian reforms and their relevance for the kingdom.

18. Author interview with Saudi energy policy maker on condition of anonymity, Riyadh, October 16, 2012.

19. The UAE's constitution designates natural resources as the property of the emirate in which they are found.

20. Jim Krane, *City of Gold: Dubai and the Dream of Capitalism* (New York: St. Martin's, 2009), 49–50.

21. Priced under $2 per million BTUs.

22. In 2008, Dubai signed a fifteen-year LNG supply agreement with Shell and QatarGas and purchased a floating storage and regasification unit for Jebel Ali port that opened in 2010.

23. This material and much of this section is based on multiple interviews with Dubai government officials in the energy sector and municipal government who spoke on condition of anonymity, 2011–2013.

24. Nejib Zaafrani, CEO, Dubai Supreme Council of Energy, author interview, Dubai, April 14, 2012.

25. Nejib Zaafrani, CEO, Dubai Supreme Council of Energy, speech at the Dubai Global Energy Forum, April 18, 2011, Dubai, quoted by the author.

26. A Dubai government interviewee told me in 2012 that the government discussed the impending increases in a closed-door session with leaders of prominent families.

27. Author interviews with Dubai government officials in the energy sector and municipal government who spoke on condition of anonymity, 2011–2013.

28. Comment no. 31 in Zaher Bitar, "Dubai Residents Complain of Hikes in Water, Electricity Tariffs," *Gulf News*, October 19, 2011, http://gulfnews.com/news/gulf/uae/government/dubai-residents-complain-of-hikes-in-water-electricity-tariffs-1.903101.

29. Author telephone interview with UAE government official on condition of anonymity, October 29, 2013.

30. Author interview with member of UAE government on condition of anonymity, Dubai, April 8, 2012.

31. In discussing this point during a November 11, 2010, interview with David Scott, executive director, Economic and Energy Affairs Unit, Abu Dhabi Executive Affairs Authority, Scott noted that tribal sheikhs required others to participate in guarding water sources and it was thus more of a community task than simply a source of patronage.

32. Newspaper websites allowing reader comments on stories about the price increases included some purporting to be from citizens. Most lamented rising prices, an insufficient quota of free water, and the fact that prices were higher for citizens in Dubai than for those in other emirates. See, for example, http://www.emaratalyoum.com/business/local/2010-12-09-1.326917, http://www.alwasluae.com/vb/showthread.php?t=154768, and http://www.emaratalyoum.com/local-section/hotline/2011-10-04-1.427746.

33. The most vehement protests, clashes, and government crackdowns in Bahrain and to a lesser extent Oman took place between February and June 2011.

34. Author results from expert elicitation with UAE policy makers, March 2012. Fifteen of 25 respondents said the Arab Spring events made the government "less willing" to

raise utility rates; 21 of 26 respondents said the government was either "very sensitive" or "extremely sensitive" to citizen opinion on subsidies.

35. Author interview with member of UAE government on condition of anonymity, Dubai, April 8, 2012. Also detail from policy making focus group held at UAE Prime Minister's Office, March 5, 2012.

36. Dubai electricity sector official, interviewed by author on condition of anonymity, January 9, 2013. See also Zaher Bitar, "DEWA to Introduce Fuel Surcharge," *Gulf News*, July 14, 2011, http://gulfnews.com/business/general/dewa-to-introduce-fuel-surcharge -1.838387.

37. The Media Office for HH Sheikh Mohammed bin Rashid al-Maktoum, 2011. Note that some citizen families never received an increase at all. Some of these were headed by current or retired members of the security services or by important tribal or ruling family members who continued to receive free or discounted electricity thanks to favored relations with the ruling family.

38. Dubai Electricity and Water Authority, "DEWA Sukuk 2013 Limited," financial disclosure for investors (Dubai: DEWA, February 28, 2013), 81–82, 91.

39. The Dubai benefit reform came just three months prior to a petition for increased democratic representation that emerged in 2011. That petition, signed by 132 prominent Emiratis, circulated prior to the tariff hike. Several signers of that petition were jailed. Kristian Coates Ulrichsen, "The UAE: Holding Back the Tide," *OpenDemocracy*, August 5, 2012, http://www.opendemocracy.net/kristian-coates-ulrichsen/uae -holding-back-tide.

40. Author interview with Abdulkhaleq Abdulla, UAE political scientist, Dubai, January 31 2012.

41. Author interviews with energy policy officials in Dubai government, 2012 and 2013.

42. Hazem Beblawi and Giacomo Luciani, "Introduction," in *The Rentier State*, ed. Hazem Beblawi and Giacomo Luciani (London: Croom Helm, 1987), 16.

43. Material in this section is based on Jim Krane, "The Political Economy of Subsidy Reform in the Persian Gulf Monarchies," in *The Economics and Political Economy of Energy Subsidies*, ed. Jon Strand (Cambridge, MA: MIT Press, 2016), 191–222.

44. The 42 percent responded that subsidies represented "their share" of the national energy wealth.

45. Sixty-one of 76 respondents (80 percent) said "yes" to the question "Several academics have stated that subsidies in the GCC are perceived by nationals as rights of citizenship. Do you agree?"

46. Bruce Bueno de Mesquita et al., "Political Institutions, Policy Choice, and the Survival of Leaders," *British Journal of Political Science* 32 (2002): 559–90; Gordon Tullock, *Autocracy* (Hingham, MA: Kluwer, 1987), 122–23; Timur Kuran, "Sparks and Prairie Fires: A Theory of Unanticipated Political Revolution," *Public Choice* 61 (1989): 41–74; Ronald Wintrobe, "How to Understand, and Deal with Dictatorship: An Economist's View," *Economics of Governance* 18, no. 3 (2001): 35–58.

47. Wintrobe, "How to Understand, and Deal with Dictatorship"; Bueno de Mesquita et al., "Political Institutions, Policy Choice and the Survival of Leaders"; Bruce Bueno de Mesquita et al., *The Logic of Political Survival* (Cambridge, MA: MIT Press, 2003),

73–74; Brandon J. Kinne, "Decision Making in Autocratic Regimes: A Poliheuristic Perspective," *International Studies Perspectives* 6 (2005): 114–28.

48. UAE government official, interviewed by the author on condition of anonymity, April 8, 2012.

49. UAE government official, interviewed by the author on condition of anonymity, April 8, 2012.

50. Omer Ali and Ibrahim Elbadawi, "The Political Economy of Public Sector Employment in Resource Dependent Countries," Economic Research Forum working paper, 2012, http://erf.org.eg/publications/political-economy-public-sector-employment-resource-dependent-countries/.

8. SHIFTING GEARS IN SAUDI ARABIA

1. Giles Tremlett, "Marbella Feels Loss of Saudi King," *Guardian*, August 5, 2005, https://www.theguardian.com/world/2005/aug/06/saudiarabia.spain.

2. Electricity and Co-Generation Regulatory Authority, "2015 Annual Statistical Booklet for Electricity and Seawater Desalination Industries," statistical bulletin (Riyadh: ECRA, 2016), http://www.ecra.gov.sa/en-us/MediaCenter/DocLib2/Lists/SubCate gory_Library/Statistical%20Booklets%202015.pdf.

3. Majid al-Moneef, author interview, Riyadh, October 17, 2012.

4. Saudi energy official interviewed on condition of anonymity, October 19, 2012.

5. Author interview with Abdullah M. al-Shehri, governor of Electricity and Co-Generation Regulatory Authority of Saudi Arabia, Dhahran, October 21, 2012. ECRA had been forced by political outcry in 1999 to retract its previous attempt to raise rates for large residential consumers. A previous residential electricity tariff increase, imposed amid the oil bust in 1985, was retracted after just a few months by Saudi Arabia's King Fahd.

6. Electricity and Co-Generation Regulatory Authority, "2015 Annual Statistical Booklet for Electricity and Seawater Desalination Industries," 74.

7. Hifa al-Zahrani, "Only a Quarter of Buildings Thermally Insulated," *Arab News*, April 30, 2013, http://www.arabnews.com/news/449917?page=1; P. K. Abdul Ghafour, "KSA Power Consumption 3 Times World Average," *Arab News*, July 8, 2014, http://www.arabnews.com/news/598481.

8. Consumption thresholds vary by region, with higher levels of power allotted for hot and humid areas and lower levels for cooler, drier regions.

9. Electricity and Co-Generation Regulatory Authority, "2015 Annual Statistical Booklet for Electricity and Seawater Desalination Industries."

10. Muhammad bin Nayef attended Portland State University and Lewis and Clark College in Oregon during the 1970s and 1980s but did not earn a degree.

11. "The House of Saud: A View of the Modern Saudi Dynasty," *PBS Frontline*, 2005, https://www.pbs.org/wgbh/pages/frontline/shows/saud/tree/.

12. Nahlah Ayed, "Why Saudi Arabia Is the World's Top YouTube Nation," *CBC News*, April 1, 2013, http://www.cbc.ca/news/world/nahlah-ayed-why-saudi-arabia-is-the -world-s-top-youtube-nation-1.1359187.

13. See, for example, Simon Henderson, "Saudi King in Hospital: Succession Crisis Looms," *Washington Institute Policy Alert*, December 31, 2014; as well as his previous works "After King Fahd: Succession in Saudi Arabia," 1995, http://www .washingtoninstitute.org/policy-analysis/view/after-king-fahd-succession-in-saudi -arabia-2nd-ed; and "After King Abdullah: Succession in Saudi Arabia," 2009, http:// www.washingtoninstitute.org/policy-analysis/view/after-king-abdullah-succession -in-saudi-arabia. Also see Patrick Clawson and Simon Henderson, "Reducing Vulnerability to Middle East Energy Shocks," *Washington Institute for Near East Policy: Policy Focus* 49 (2005); and scenarios in Amy Myers Jaffe and Meghan L. O'Sullivan, "The Geopolitics of Natural Gas," July 2012, http://bakerinstitute.org/media/files/Research /d11add8e/EF-pub-HKSGeopoliticsOfNaturalGas-073012.pdf.

14. Freedom House reduced the kingdom's score by 3 points in 2018.

15. Samia Nakhoul and Nick Tattersall, "Saudi Source Gives More Detail on Crown Prince's Dismissal," *Reuters*, July 21, 2017, https://www.reuters.com/article/us-saudi -palace-mbn/saudi-source-gives-more-detail-on-crown-princes-dismissal-idUSKBN 1A62FF.

16. Abdul Ghafour, "KSA Power Consumption 3 Times World Average."

17. Abdul Ghafour, "KSA Power Consumption 3 Times World Average."

18. Mishal Al-Otaibi, "New Water and Electricity Tariff to Rationalize Consumption: Minister," *Saudi Gazette*, December 29, 2015, http://saudigazette.com.sa/saudi-arabia /new-water-and-electricity-tariff-to-rationalize-consumption-minister; Canada water figure from Statistics Canada, "Land and Freshwater Area, by Province and Territory," 2005, http://www.statcan.gc.ca/tables-tableaux/sum-som/l01/cst01/phys01 -eng.htm.

19. Thomas L. Friedman, "Letter from Saudi Arabia," *New York Times*, November 25, 2015; "Transcript: Interview with Muhammad Bin Salman," *Economist*, January 6, 2016, http://www.economist.com/saudi_interview.

20. Ibrahim al-Hatlani, "Gas Price Hike, Subsidy Cuts Shake up Saudis," *Al-Monitor*, January 25, 2016, https://www.al-monitor.com/pulse/originals/2016/01/saudi-arabia-oil -hike-cut-subsidies-taxes.html.

21. Simeon Kerr, "Riyadh Speeds Reforms Alongside Energy Price Rises," *Financial Times*, December 22, 2016, https://www.ft.com/content/ace7b490-c86b-11e6-9043 -7e34c07b46ef.

22. Prices increased from 12 halala (US$0.03) to 16 halala (US$0.04) per kWh for commercial users and to 18 halala ($0.05) per kWh for industrial users.

23. The first two tiers, covering up to 4,000 kWh per month, are untouched at 5 halala ($0.01) per kWh for below 2,000 kWhs and at 10 halala ($0.03) per kWh between 2,000 and 4,000 kWhs. But for consumption above 4,000 kWh, even residential customers have to pay more, with rates rising from 12 halala ($0.03) to 20 halala ($0.05) per kWh.

24. Saudi residential consumers received a new rising block tariff that reduced the amount of very inexpensive water from 50 to 15 cubic meters per month, with prices rising for each additional 15 cubic meters, to reach $1.50 per cubic meter beyond 50 meters. Glada Lahn, "Fuel, Food, and Utilities Price Reforms in the GCC: A Wake-up Call for Business," research paper (London: Chatham House, June 2016), 16.

25. "Saudi Arabia's Water Minister Sacked After Complaints Over Tariffs," *The National*, April 24, 2016, http://www.thenational.ae/world/middle-east/saudi-arabias-water -minister-sacked-after-complaints-over-tariffs.

26. Vivian Nereim, "Saudi Arabia Begins Payouts to Buffer Belt-Tightening Blow," *Bloomberg*, December 21, 2017, https://www.bloomberg.com/news/articles/2017-12 -21/saudi-arabia-begins-payouts-to-buffer-belt-tightening-blow.

27. On January 1, 2018, the price of Saudi 91 octane gasoline rose 83 percent from US$0.76 to $1.40 per gallon (US$0.20 to $0.37 per liter; SAR 0.75 to 1.37), and 95 octane rose 127 percent, from US$0.91 to $2.04 per gallon (US$0.24 to $0.54 per liter; SAR 0.90 to 2.04/liter). Rashid Hassan, "Hike in Gasoline Prices Across KSA Will Help in Govt Plan for Efficient Energy Use: Experts," *Arab News*, January 2, 2018, http://www .arabnews.com/node/1217656/saudi-arabia.

28. Message posted on Twitter, January 1, 2016, under the name Ali al-Ali (@alialali26). Translated from Arabic.

29. Essam al-Zamel, "Removal of Subsidies on Gasoline, Diesel, and Electricity Prices. Is it in the Interest of the Citizen and the Economy?" Video commentary, YouTube, January 3, 2016, https://www.youtube.com/watch?v=osqSugDwyxA.

30. Ben Hubbard, "Saudi Arabia Detains Critics as New Crown Prince Consolidates Power," *New York Times*, September 14, 2017, https://www.nytimes.com/2017/09/14 /world/middleeast/saudi-arabia-clerics.html; "Rights Groups Slam Saudi Arrests of Religious Figures," *Al-Jazeera*, September 15, 2017, https://www.aljazeera.com /news/2017/09/rights-groups-slam-saudi-arrests-religious-figures-170915153115745 .html.

31. See, for example, Kate Dourian, "Saudi Arabia Warns Domestic Oil Use Growing at 'Frightening Level,'" *Platts*, November 26, 2012, http://www.platts.com/RSSFeed DetailedNews/RSSFeed/Oil/7284877; Summer Said, "Saudi Arabia Minister Warns Against Energy Waste," *Dow Jones Newswires*, November 27, 2012; Summer Said, "Saudi Arabia Among World's Least Energy-Efficient Nations—Naimi," *Wall Street Journal*, November 25, 2012, http://online.wsj.com/article/BT-CO-20121125-700692 .html. Note that Ahmed al-Khateeb, the CEO of a Riyadh investment bank, called for the elimination of all energy subsidies for all but the poor: "Al-Khateeb: Energy Subsidies Need Review," *Arab News*, February 13, 2013, http://www.arabnews.com/al -khateeb-energy-subsidies-need-review.

32. This simple illustrative exercise takes no notice of depletion, population growth, changes in technology, plateauing of demand for structural reasons, or any of the myriad factors that affect oil demand and production.

33. "SEC Set for Split by Year-end," *Middle East Economic Survey* 59, no. 36 (September 9, 2016): 7.

34. Electricity and Cogeneration Regulatory Authority (ECRA) data and statistics, 2017, http://www.ecra.gov.sa/en-us/DataAndStatistics/NationalRecord/HistoricalData/Pages/Home.aspx.

35. "JODI Oil World Database," Joint Organizations Data Initiative, 2018; see also "Saudi February 2018 Official Oil Data," *MEES* 60, no. 16 (April 20, 2018).

36. Ali al-Naimi, *Out of the Desert: My Journey from Nomadic Bedouin to the Heart of Global Oil* (London: Portfolio Penguin, 2016).

37. BP, *Statistical Review of World Energy 2018* (London: BP, 2018), https://www.bp.com/en/global/corporate/energy-economics/statistical-review-of-world-energy.html.

38. "Kingdom of Saudi Arabia's Oil Production Witnesses Increasing Demand," *Saudi Press Agency*, August 8, 2016, http://www.spa.gov.sa/1526974.

39. Saudi Aramco executive, Dhahran. Interviewed by the author, January 28, 2016, on condition of anonymity.

40. Suhasini Ramisetty-Mikler and Abdulkarim Almakadma, "Attitudes and Behaviors Towards Risky Driving Among Adolescents in Saudi Arabia," *International Journal of Pediatrics and Adolescent Medicine* 3, no. 2 (2016): 55–63, https://doi.org/https://doi.org/10.1016/j.ijpam.2016.03.003.

41. Interviews on condition of anonymity, Dhahran, January 27, 2016.

42. Interviews on condition of anonymity, Dhahran and Riyadh, February 2018.

9. THE POLITICS OF REFORM

1. The detail about the Kuwait mosque bombing comes from various news reports, including Ahmed Hagagy, "Islamic State Suicide Bomber Kills 27, Wounds 227 in Kuwait Mosque," *Reuters*, June 26, 2015, http://www.reuters.com/article/us-kuwait-blast-idUSKBN0P618L20150626.

2. A compendium can be found on Wikipedia: https://en.wikipedia.org/wiki/Terrorism_in_Kuwait.

3. IMF World Economic Outlook, October 2015. Updated figures provided in Justin Gengler and Laurent A. Lambert, "Renegotiating the Ruling Bargain: Selling Fiscal Reform in the GCC," *Middle East Journal* 70, no. 2 (2016): 322.

4. Paul Pierson, "The New Politics of the Welfare State," *World Politics* 48 (1996): 143–79.

5. Jim Krane, "Political Enablers of Energy Subsidy Reform in Middle Eastern Oil Exporters," *Nature Energy* (April 2018), https://doi.org/10.1038/s41560-018-0113-4.

6. BMI Research, "Kuwait Power Report Q4 2016," executive summary, http://store.bmiresearch.com/kuwait-power-report.html.

7. International Business Publications, *Kuwait Energy Policy, Laws and Regulations Handbook*, vol. 1: *Strategic Information and Basic Laws*, 43.

8. For more on Kuwaiti populism, see Steffen Hertog, "Defying the Resource Curse: Explaining Successful State-Owned Enterprises in Rentier States," *World Politics* 62, no. 2 (April 2010): 261–301.

9. "Kuwait Cuts Diesel Fuel Prices After Political Pressure," *Reuters*, January 28, 2015.

10. Habib Toumi, "Kuwait Joins GCC Countries in Raising Fuel Prices," *Gulf News*, August 31, 2016.

11. "Kuwait Water, Electricity Prices up by 500 Percent," KUNA Kuwait News Agency, *Khaleej Times*, August 23, 2017, https://www.khaleejtimes.com/region/kuwait/kuwait -water-electricity-prices-up-by-500-per-cent.

12. Santhosh V. Perumal, "Moody's Says Qatar Could Hike Electricity Tariff," *Gulf Times*, March 22, 2016, http://www.gulf-times.com/story/485600/Moody-s-says-Qatar-could -hike-electricity-tariff.

13. "Qatar's Kahramaa Hikes Water, Electricity Tariffs," *NRICAFE*, October 14, 2015, http://nricafe.com/2015/10/qatars-kahramaa-hikes-water-electricity-tariffs/.

14. Qatar Ministry of Development Planning and Statistics, 2017.

15. International Energy Agency, "Electricity Information and Natural Gas Information," http://wds.iea.org/

16. Qatari nationals' access to free electricity is not *quite* unlimited. A Qatari household receives unlimited free electricity in its primary residence. If the family has another home, perhaps a weekend retreat, it is technically required to pay for electricity at the secondary residence. However, that limitation does not hold for Qatari men who have multiple wives ensconced in separate households, each of which is eligible for free electricity. Author discussion with Qatari executives at leadership forum, October 8, 2015, Baker Institute for Public Policy, Houston.

17. Government official in Qatar electricity sector, one of two cointerviewed by author on condition of anonymity, Doha, April 4, 2012.

18. In 2005, Oman consumed 9,517 gigawatt-hours. In 2015, it consumed 28,912 GWh. IEA Electricity Data, 2017.

19. Author interview with John Cunneen, executive director, Authority for Electricity Regulation, Oman, Muscat, November 15, 2011.

20. Author interviews, Oman. See also James Worrall, "Oman: The 'Forgotten' Corner of the Arab Spring," *Middle East Policy* 19, no. 3 (2012): 98–115; Abdulkhaleq Abdulla, "Repercussions of the Arab Spring on GCC States" (Doha: Arab Center for Research and Policy Studies, 2012), http://aihr-resourcescenter.org/administrator/upload/docu ments/aka.pdf. For a broader explanation of scholarly surprise at the Arab uprisings, see F. Gregory Gause III, "Why Middle East Studies Missed the Arab Spring: The Myth of Authoritarian Stability," *Foreign Affairs* 90, no. 4 (August 2011): 81–90.

21. Protest demands included increased government jobs, marriage subsidies, and increased freedoms of expression and of the press. Protesters demanded an end to government corruption while expressing support for Sultan Qaboos. Worrall's article "Oman" provides a useful cataloging of events throughout the Omani uprising. See also Thomas Fuller, "Rallies in Oman Steer Clear of Criticism of Its Leader," *New York Times*, March 1, 2011, http://www.nytimes.com/2011/03/02/world/middleeast /02oman.html.

22. From $0.007 to $0.009 (3 to 3.5 Omani baiza) per gallon. "Oman's Public Authority for Electricity and Water Announces Hike in Water Tariffs," *Times of Oman*, March 15, 2016, http://timesofoman.com/article/79520/Oman/Government/Oman-announces -hike-in-water-tariffs.

23. "Oman Plans 7–8% Cut in Electricity Subsidies," *Reuters*, March 3, 2016, http://www .khaleejtimes.com/region/oman-plans-7-8-cut-in-electricity-subsidies.

24. Marc Valeri, "Simmering Unrest and Succession Challenges in Oman" (Washington: Carnegie Endowment for International Peace, 2015), https://carnegieendowment.org /2015/01/28/simmering-unrest-and-succession-challenges-in-oman-pub-58843.

25. Author interview with Zaid al-Siyabi, director-general for oil and gas exploration and production, Oman Ministry of Oil and Gas, Muscat, November 13, 2011.

26. "New Tariff for Water & Electricity," *Hello Bahrain*, January 15, 2016, http://hellobah rain.com/news/new-tariff-water-electricity.

27. "Bahrain Natural Gas Prices for Industry Rise 25 Cents per mmBtu—Agency," *Reuters*, January 30, 2015, http://af.reuters.com/article/energyOilNews/idAFL6N0V 91BW20150130.

28. Kenneth Katzman, "Bahrain: Reform, Security, and U.S. Policy," US government report (Washington: Congressional Research Service, September 29, 2017).

29. Abu Dhabi Distribution Co., "Water & Electricity Tariffs 2017," utility rate sheet (Abu Dhabi: Abu Dhabi Distribution Co., 2017), https://www.addc.ae/en-US/residential /Documents/02-English.pdf.

30. Sharjah Electricity and Water Authority (SEWA) raised electricity and water rates for industrial and commercial users in 2014 but left residential rates unchanged: "No Power Shortage in Sharjah: Sewa Chief," *Emirates 24/7*, March 29, 2016, http://www .emirates247.com/business/no-power-shortage-in-sharjah-sewa-chief-2016-03-29-1 .625584. See also "Fewa Bills Increase by 5 Fils per kw/h," *Gulf News*, December 15, 2014, http://gulfnews.com/news/uae/environment/fewa-bills-increase-by-5-fills-per -kw-h-1.1427257.

31. Author interviews with Nick Carter, director general, Regulation and Supervision Bureau–Abu Dhabi, Abu Dhabi, November 9, 2010; and David Scott, executive director, Economic and Energy Affairs Unit, Abu Dhabi Executive Affairs Authority, November 11, 2010.

32. Author interview with David Scott, executive director, Economic and Energy Affairs Unit, Abu Dhabi Executive Affairs Authority, November 11, 2010.

33. Jim Krane and Elsie Hung, "Energy Subsidy Reform in the Persian Gulf: The End of the Big Oil Giveaway," Baker Institute for Public Policy, Rice University, April 28, 2016, http://www.bakerinstitute.org/media/files/research_document/0e7a6eb7/BI-Brief -042816-CES_GulfSubsidy.pdf; Jean-Francois Seznec, "Saudi Energy Changes: The End of the Rentier State" (Washington: Atlantic Council, March 2016), http://www .atlanticcouncil.org/images/publications/Saudi_Energy_Changes_web_0323.pdf; Sultan al-Qassemi, "The Gulf's New Social Contract" (Middle East Institute, February 8, 2016), http://www.mei.edu/content/article/gulfs-new-social-contract; Gengler and Lambert, "Renegotiating the Ruling Bargain."

34. Oliver Schlumberger, "Rents, Reform, and Authoritarianism in the Middle East," in *Dead Ends of Transition*, ed. Michael Dauderstadt and Arne Schildberg (Frankfurt: Campus Verlag, 2006), 100–113; Rolf Schwarz, "The Political Economy of State-Formation in the Arab Middle East: Rentier States, Economic Reform, and Democratization," *Review of International Political Economy* 15, no. 4 (2008); also Steffen Hertog, "Oil Prices:

Eventually the Gulf States Will Run out of Power," Middle East Center Blog, London School of Economics, January 5, 2015, http://blogs.lse.ac.uk/mec/2015/01/07/oil-prices -eventually-the-gulf-states-will-run-out-of-power.

35. Some reformers had minimal fiscal buffers in 2015, including Bahrain, Oman, and Egypt. Saudi currency reserves were high but dwindled at an alarming rate.

36. Sheikh Mohammed bin Zayed has assumed control of most UAE governance functions during the long convalescence of his elder half-brother Khalifa, age sixty-eight. At the time of writing, Sheikh Khalifa retained official status as head of state.

37. Peter Kovessy and Shabina S. Khatri, "Qatar Emir: Government Can No Longer 'Provide for Everything,'" *Doha News*, November 3, 2015, http://dohanews.co/qatar-emir -government-can-no-longer-provide-for-everything.

38. Rana Rahimpour, "Iran Protests Pose an Unpredictable Challenge for Authorities," *BBC News*, January 2, 2018, http://www.bbc.com/news/world-middle-east-42541171.

39. Saleh al-Shaibany, "Oman Caps Fuel Price After Protests," *The National*, February 8, 2017, https://www.thenational.ae/world/oman-caps-fuel-price-after-protests-1.77195.

40. "Arab Gulf States: Attempts to Silence 140 Characters," Human Rights Watch press release, November 1, 2016, https://www.hrw.org/news/2016/11/01/arab-gulf-states -attempts-silence-140-characters.

41. Lindsay Benstead, "Why Some Arabs Don't Want Democracy," Monkey Cage blog, *Washington Post*, September 30, 2014, https://www.washingtonpost.com/news/mon key-cage/wp/2014/09/30/why-some-arabs-dont-want-democracy.

42. Gengler and Lambert, "Renegotiating the Ruling Bargain," 327.

43. Al-Qassemi, "The Gulf's New Social Contract."

44. Jim Krane, "The Political Economy of Subsidy Reform in the Persian Gulf Monarchies," in *The Economics and Political Economy of Energy Subsidies*, ed. Jon Strand (Cambridge, MA: MIT Press, 2016), 191–222.

45. Hazem Beblawi and Giacomo Luciani, "Introduction," in *The Rentier State*, ed. Hazem Beblawi and Giacomo Luciani (London: Croom Helm, 1987), 16–17.

46. F. Gregory Gause III, "The Political Economy of National Security in the GCC States," in *The Persian Gulf at the Millennium*, ed. Gary Sick and Lawrence Potter (New York: St. Martin's, 1997), 80.

47. F. Gregory Gause III, *Oil Monarchies: Domestic and Security Challenges in the Arab Gulf States* (New York: Council on Foreign Relations, 1994), 147.

48. Partha S. Dasgupta, "The Environment as a Commodity," *Oxford Review of Economic Policy* 6, no. 1 (1990): 51–67.

CONCLUSION: THE CLIMATE HEDGE

1. Jim Krane, "Beyond 12.5: The Implications of an Increase in Saudi Crude Oil Production Capacity," *Energy Policy* 110 (2017): 542–47. See also Bill Spindle and Summer Said, "Saudi Aramco Likely to Step up Production," *Wall Street Journal*, May 10, 2016, http://www.wsj.com/articles/aramco-aiming-to-double-gas-production-in-10 -years-1462864819.

2. Jim Krane, "A Refined Approach: Saudi Arabia Moves Beyond Crude," *Energy Policy* 82 (2015): 99–104.

3. For more on Saudi-US ties, see Rachel Bronson, "Understanding US-Saudi Relations," in *Saudi Arabia in the Balance*, ed. Paul Aarts and Gerd Nonneman (London: Hurst, 2006), 372–98; F. Gregory Gause III, "Saudi Arabia in the New Middle East," Special Report 63 (New York: Council on Foreign Relations, 2011).

4. Jeffrey Goldberg, "The Obama Doctrine," *Atlantic*, April 2016, https://www.theatlantic .com/magazine/archive/2016/04/the-obama-doctrine/471525/.

5. US Energy Information Administration, "U.S. Field Production of Crude Oil," https:// www.eia.gov/dnav/pet/hist/LeafHandler.ashx?n=PET&s=MCRFPUS2&f=A.

6. Krane, "A Refined Approach."

7. Wael Mahdi, "Aramco Mulls Indian Refinery in Plan to Boost Asia Footprint," *Bloomberg*, March 9, 2016, https://www.bloomberg.com/news/articles/2016-03-08/aramco -mulls-indian-refinery-in-drive-to-increase-asia-footprint.

8. Jim Krane, "Climate Change and Fossil Fuel: An Examination of Risks for the Energy Industry and Producer States," *MRS Energy & Sustainability* 4 (2017), https://doi.org /https://doi.org/10.1557/mre.2017.3.

9. This material is based on an author discussion with a former Saudi Aramco official on condition of anonymity, March 24, 2016. For a similar depiction of Saudi depletion strategy, see John V. Mitchell and Paul Stevens, *Ending Dependence: Hard Choices for Oil-Exporting States* (London: Chatham House, 2008), 12.

10. See Joseph A. Kenny, "Saudi Aramco still aiming for 12 million barrel production capacity by June 2009," diplomatic cable, 2009, US Department of State, Dhahran, via WikiLeaks. Also see Mitchell and Stevens, *Ending Dependence*.

11. "Saudi King Says Keeping Some Oil Finds for Future," *Reuters*, April 13, 2008, http: //uk.reuters.com/article/saudi-oil-idUKL139687720080413.

12. See Kenny, diplomatic cable; James B. Smith, "Reinvigorating an energy dialogue with Saudi Arabia a key step to a stronger strategic partnership," diplomatic cable, October 22, 2009, US Department of State, Riyadh, via WikiLeaks.

13. Naimi said in March 2016 that the world would not be able to stop extracting fossil fuels in the next fifty years. Grant Smith, "Saudi Arabia's Oil Chief Prepares for a World After Fossil Fuels," *Bloomberg*, March 17, 2016, http://www.bloomberg.com /news/articles/2016-03-17/saudi-arabia-s-oil-chief-prepares-for-a-world-after-fossil -fuels.

14. Peter Waldman, "Saudi Arabia's Plan to Extend the Age of Oil," *Bloomberg*, April 12, 2015, http://www.bloomberg.com/news/articles/2015-04-12/saudi-arabia-s-plan-to -extend-the-age-of-oil.

15. Smith was reporting his conversation with then deputy oil minister Prince Abdulaziz bin Salman al-Saud. James B. Smith, "What concerns Saudi Arabia about the future of energy and climate change," diplomatic cable, US Department of State, Riyadh, via WikiLeaks, https://wikileaks.org/plusd/cables/10RIYADH213_a.html.

16. Mohammad S. Masnadi, Hassan M. El-Houjeiri, Dominik Schunack, et al., "Well-to-Refinery Emissions and Net-Energy Analysis of China's Crude-Oil Supply," *Nature Energy* 3, no. 3 (2018): 220.

17. Krane, "Beyond 12.5"; Jim Krane, "Saudi Arabia's Oil Strategy in a Time of Glut," *Foreign Affairs*, May 24, 2016, https://www.foreignaffairs.com/articles/saudi-arabia /2016-05-24/saudi-arabias-oil-strategy-time-glut.

18. Thijs Van de Graaf and Aviel Verbruggen, "Saving OPEC: How Oil Producers Can Counteract the Global Decline in Demand," *Foreign Affairs*, December 22, 2014, https: //www.foreignaffairs.com/articles/persian-gulf/2014-12-22/saving-opec.

19. Hans-Werner Sinn, "Public Policies Against Global Warming: A Supply Side Approach," *International Tax and Public Finance* 15, no. 4 (2008): 360–94; Hans-Werner Sinn, *The Green Paradox: A Supply-Side Approach to Global Warming* (Cambridge, MA: MIT Press, 2012).

20. Cheap oil encourages a path-dependent route to energy-intense development by reducing urban density. Cities that sprawl into suburbs require more energy. Commutes lengthen, bigger homes require more fuel to heat and cool, and private cars are mandatory. Higher levels of demand, encouraged by low prices, become locked in—even when prices rise again.

21. Jason Hill, Liaila Tajibaeva, and Stephen Polasky, "Climate Consequences of Low-Carbon Fuels: The United States Renewable Fuel Standard," *Energy Policy* 97, suppl. C (2016): 351–53, https://doi.org/https://doi.org/10.1016/j.enpol.2016.07.035.

22. C. McGlade and P. Ekins, "The Geographical Distribution of Fossil Fuels Unused When Limiting Global Warming to 2 [deg] C," *Nature* 517, no. 7533 (2015): 187–90.

INDEX